The Pilgrim's Guide
to The Sacred Earth

The Pilgrim's Guide
to The Sacred Earth

Sherrill Miller
Photo tips by Courtney Milne

Voyageur Press

Printed and bound in Canada
91 92 93 94 95 5 4 3 2 1

Library of Congress Cataloging-in-Publication
Data available

Published in the United States by
Voyageur Press, Inc.
P.O. Box 338, 123 North Second Street
Stillwater, MN 55082 U.S.A.
From Minnesota 612-430-2210
Toll-free 800-888-9653

Voyageur Press books are also available at discounts for quantities for educational, fundraising, premium, or sales-promotion use. For details contact the marketing department. Please write or call for our free catalog of natural history publications.

Contents

Acknowledgements

Special thanks to my dear friends Sarah Bowman, Sharron Milstein, Enda Bardell, Liesje Ryerson, Dorothy Barkley, Thérèse Durdin, Leslie Borleske, and Joanne Roberts who supported me to follow my heart—and Courtney Milne—around the world. To our mothers, Dorothy Miller and Grace Milne, who kept us connected with home; to faithful friends Adele Curtis, Tana Dineen, Loreen Wilsdon, Lori Labatt, Lori Sopher, and my family, Lorraine and Bill Richey and Dennis Miller and Evelyne Pytka and their collectively wonderful kids, who kept the support letters flowing. Thank you for the home away from home provided by the Mulder family in London, Zulie Nakhooda in India, the Karanassopolous family in Greece, and Kim Gotlieb in Australia. To Jim Berenholtz who gave continuous support, information, and enthusiasm to our project, and to Nora Russell, a wonderful editor and researcher for the project; to Tilley Endurables for outfitting us with expedition clothing, and to Bob Gibbs of Air Canada for assisting us with travel.

A special mention to all those supportive people along the way whose fascination with our pilgrimage kept us going, and to the friends at home—Sherry and Glen Christianson and family, Sherry Morris, Patricia Joudry, Cathy Lacey, Lee Christie, and Denny Carr—who continued to keep the flame burning and the excitement alive throughout the task of putting this together.

But most of all to Courtney Milne, whose vision never wavered, and whose awe with the world continues to inspire us to carry this to completion.

Introduction

"Want to go around the world with me?" Who could resist such an invitation to travel the globe and see some of the most exotic landscapes in the world—the sacred places, which from antiquity to the present have inspired human beings in their search for the eternal, a search that transcends all cultural boundaries.

This is the story of our journey. We started with a list of The Twelve Sacred Places of the Earth, which had come via Cuba and was given to Courtney in Toronto—a mysterious-looking document by Robert Coon called "Revelations From the Melchisadek Priesthood." The journey so far has covered all seven continents and more than 140 sacred sites. While researching these sites, I discovered that the bookstores had little to offer me, perhaps half a dozen books with the word "sacred" in the title. Now there are hundreds of titles to choose from.

What has happened in the few years since we began our quest? There seems to be a worldwide awakening linked to the ecological movement—the comprehension that we have only one earth to share, and that we must change our attitudes and our lifestyles lest we destroy ourselves. We are all searching for meaning in the world around us; perhaps one route to finding it is to live our lives in a more spiritual way, to care for each other and for the land that nourishes us. One thing we learned on our journey is that the common denominator of all cultures is their mythology—the stories that explain their creation and give credence to their lives. These are the root of the spiritual beliefs that shape our view of the world and guide our actions on a daily basis.

We are all on a pilgrimage. Ours is just more tangible and perhaps more romantic sounding to most people. Sometimes it *is* exotic, and we feel very privileged to be able to go to unusual and beautiful places. Other times it's just hard work, learning to negotiate in unfamiliar cultures and spending long hours photographing, frequently before dawn and after dusk, and often in inclement weather. We began to understand how those early pilgrims must have felt, treading arduous pathways, abandoning the comforts of home for the ascetic experience, wandering in strange lands in search of spiritual or moral benefit that would bring them peace in this world, or perhaps in the next.

The pilgrimage is still a common feature of many countries in the East, where the devoted feel duty bound to honor holy places, seek atonement, or hope to gain merit or healing. Many of these places are natural sites—a holy mountain, sacred spring, hallowed grotto, or a particular landscape feature imbued with mythological associations. They may be marked with a temple, church, or perhaps a stone cairn to direct the faithful. In the West we have tended to seek inspiration within a church rather than in nature. We seem to have lost that communion with the natural world that so strongly guided our forefathers, who saw symbols of the divine all around them. The growth of so-called New Age ideas is a reflection of that history; they are not really new, but very old, based on esoteric philosophies and mystical beliefs that view all of humankind and nature as divine creation. According to these beliefs, we are all enlivened with the same spirit. The earth is alive, breathes the same air we do, is nourished by the same waters, and has nerve centers where her energy is particularly strong and can be felt if we are in tune with them. These are the sacred places, the places set aside by humanity as special, where we can feel particularly close to the spirit of creation. These are places where our spirit is awakened, where the land acts as a catalyst that moves us emotionally, spiritually, and physically, through a doorway that transforms our consciousness.

It is obvious from our quest that most ancient cultures relied on spiritual techniques to guide them, using intuitive, psychic, and emotional practices to understand the world around them. Their world was imbued with spirits of all kinds, giving them what they felt was a means of protecting the land and the cosmos, and providing them with a feeling of some degree of control over nature. Today we turn to scientific technology for that control, mistakenly believing that this will provide for all our economic needs, and failing to see that our ecology *is* our economy, and that our survival depends on how we interact with the land. The first step is to connect emotionally with the world around us, to understand how it fosters the spirit as well as providing bounty for the body.

Recently there has been an immense proliferation of interest in the spiritual world, suggesting a deep and often unmet human need for peace and love, and a search for meaning in our daily lives. Perhaps this is an unconscious yearning for that "Paradise" that is promised in so many cultural myths and religious stories, another manifestation of that inner peace so beautifully expressed by His Holiness, The Dalai Lama, in his foreword to Courtney Milne's book, *The Sacred Earth*. Perhaps the areas we set aside as sacred are the best places to feel that inspiration—to literally breathe in the world around us, to feel that sense of awe, to connect with the earth that nourishes us, and let our whole body smile at the wonder of it all.

How to Use this Book

This book is both a personal journey and a resource manual. So many people have asked us about these sacred places: where are they, why are they there, how do I get there, what can I expect to find, what problems did you have travelling, can I take a tour? We gleaned a great deal of valuable information during our travels that we did not find in other books, and felt other people would find it useful. In addition, our personal experiences never failed to amuse and enthrall our listeners; somehow Courtney has a knack of being in the right place at the right time!

I am not attempting to be comprehensive, and have avoided repeating basic information that can be found in primary travel guides or from a good travel agent. I have tried to concentrate on local conditions that we observed or experienced, and how to deal with them or avoid them. The **Travel Tips** at the beginning of each section give basic locations and how to get there, while the **Local Resources** give specific recommendations of services we used and details that will make your experience a little easier. A few countries needed longer explanations and suggestions, for example, travel in India. The information about the sacred places is interwoven with some history, mythology, and cultural themes that help to explain their meaningfulness, along with our personal comments and suggestions. Courtney Milne's **Photo Tips** will be of particular interest to photographers and will also provide additional information about the sites and his personal experiences there. The **Appendix** will further assist photographers to plan for their special travel needs. The **Bibliography** includes travel handbooks that we found useful, and references and suggested readings on mythology, mysticism, religious doctrine, history, New Age philosophy, geomancy, nature philosophy, and ecology.

On one level this book contains a certain amount of repetition, but that is because the sacred can be experienced in the world around us, and this common theme runs through all the cultures we experienced. It will arise again and again, whether you actually travel to these places, or experience them from your armchair reading this book as a companion guide to the photographs in Courtney Milne's book, *The Sacred Earth*, or in subsequent volumes of The Sacred Earth Collection.

We are all searching for experiences that will give meaning to our lives. Canadian song maker Graeme Card repeats this theme again in his "Hymn to Wakantanka": . . . "I've come to dream, and think of quiet. I don't believe it's everywhere . . . I have no love for the cursed machinery . . . I have no love for the urban scenery . . . I only long for the places I belong to on this earth . . . like the sanctuary plains, where the quiet still remains, on the belly of the land."

We hope that these books will help each of you to feel the spirit of the earth and find your own sacred places—your own Shambhala.

We would ask you to please mention our names when you use any of the services cited in this book. We would also welcome any comments or suggestions you may have about other sacred places you would like to see included in subsequent volumes of The Sacred Earth Collection.

We will be touring with our multimedia slide presentation, "The Sacred Earth Show," across Canada and the United States and to selected international locations. If you are interested in reserving this show for your special group meeting or conference, please contact us at:

Earth Vision
Box 88, R.R. 2, Saskatoon
Saskatchewan, Canada S7K 3J5

About the Author

Sherrill Miller was born in Vancouver, British Columbia. With a degree in both nursing and science, she worked for a number of years as a psychiatric nurse clinician in Vancouver. Following that she took up a career in real estate and is now the public relations and business manager for Courtney Milne Photography and the Sacred Earth Project in Saskatoon, Saskatchewan.

Sherrill and her husband, photographer Courtney Milne, recently spent a year travelling in search of the sacred places of the earth. The results of that journey can be seen in Courtney's stunning volume of photographs, *The Sacred Earth*, and in this comprehensive companion guidebook.

The photograph above shows Sherrill and Courtney on a ferryboat on the way to Iona, a wind-swept island off the coast of Scotland, which marks the arrival point of Celtic Christianity in the country.

Sherrill and Courtney live on an acreage outside Saskatoon. This is Sherrill's first book.

Scotland

IONA

November 12 ... Wild and windswept with sou'westers, the light on this island has an other-worldly clarity as it beams on jagged rock and produces rainbows over the frantic sea. The wind does not murmur here—it howls through ill-fitted windows and penetrates ancient stone walls to leave a chill and dampness hanging over the ancient monastic cells.

Iona is one of two holy islands in old Britain, and is the birthplace of Celtic Christianity on the west coast of Scotland. It has been a pilgrimage destination since the sixth-century arrival of Columba, as well as being a sacred burial spot for Scottish kings and nobles.

Travel Tips

The west coast of Scotland is easily accessible by air, train, or car via Glasgow. We took the train from London, and then a further three hours from Glasgow to the port city of Oban, the jumping-off point to Iona. A forty-five minute car ferry ride to the island of Mull, and a one-and-a-quarter-hour bus trip across Mull in pouring rain brought us to the five-minute Iona crossing on a bargelike ferry that slides into the shallow bays only in good weather. Travel and accommodation information can be had from the Scottish Tourist Board offices in all major towns; their Glasgow office is open Monday to Saturday at 14 South St. Andrews Street, Edinburgh EH2 ZAZ; Tel: (301) 332–2433, and their London office is open Monday to Friday at 19 Cockspur St., London, England SW1 5BL; Tel: (01) 930–8661. All car ferries are heavily booked in summer. Reservations can be made through Caledonian McBrayne, The Ferry Terminal, Gourock, Scotland PA19 1QP; Tel: (0475) 34531; Telex: 77913. Be sure to inquire about rail passes and multiple-trip ferry tickets, which can save an enormous amount of money. Tickets can be bought in Oban at the ferry office adjacent to the train station. Local buses are available throughout the Scottish mainland and the islands but service may be infrequent. A car is not necessary on Iona, but is handy if you want to wander around Mull, and to get to the Outer Hebrides, so we rented one at Hazelbank Motors, Stevenson Street, Oban, Argyll; Tel: (0631) 66476.

Local Resources

In Oban we stayed up the hill at the SandVilla Guest House, which had good food (but small towels!); write Breadalban Street, Oban, Argyll, Scotland PA34; Tel: (0631) 62803. The large Lancaster Hotel, originally an eighteenth-century manor house, is more deluxe, near the colorful harbor on The Esplanade, Oban, Argyll, Scotland PA34 5AD; Tel: (0631) 62587.

Iona is a tiny island, 1 mile (1.6 km) across and 3 miles (5 km) long, with basically two main streets; one runs south along the east coast sea front, and the other branches north and west to the abbey, the hub of the island. Arriving without reservations, and finding all the hotels and B&Bs closed, we were rescued by a fellow traveller who took us to "Duncraig" where we were provided with a private room and wonderful home-cooked meals in a steamy old-fashioned kitchen. This home of Christian fellowship is operated by a group of American trustees, and can be reserved through 15 Morningside Road, Edinburgh EH10 4DP; Tel: (031) 447–9383, or call Duncraig at (06817) 202. The abbey also offers some accommodation, meals, and work-exchange programs; write The Abbey, Iona, Argyll, Scotland PA76; Tel: (068) 17404.

The Island

The main site on **Iona** is the abbey complex, but the landscape itself is wonderful to immerse oneself in, whether it be climbing the 328-foot (101 meter) Dun Hill to the sea-forever view, or tramping through pastures to the caves on the east coast or Columba's Bay in the south. The latter is well worth the trek—as wild and wonderful now as it must have been nearly fifteen hundred years ago when the fiery Irish Celtic monk landed his small coracle on the rocky beach. Having left Ireland after clashing with his church superiors, when Columba realized he could still see Ireland, he continued up the island to establish his church away from "the dreaded sight." For six centuries Christianity spread through Britain from this small haven renowned for its library, where the tradition of illumination of manuscripts was refined; it is thought that the famous Book of Kells was partly completed here. All was not tranquil, however, as the community was often under attack from Viking invasions and from the influence of the Church of Rome, which led to its decline. The Benedictines eventually took over Iona, and the last Celtic monks left early in the thirteenth century.

The abbey is square and somewhat foreboding in its starkness. But this solidity is balanced by the delicately ornate carvings of Scottish birds and flowers around the cloister walls, by the elegant statue of creation in the courtyard, and by the lilting Scottish voices with their warm welcome and gentle regard for all creation as Columba practised. The small chapel seems to resonate if you are lucky enough to be there during a traditional hymn service. And the Ionic cross with its stone circle and avenues incorporating the four directions is a constant reminder of strength and grace. The Wild Goose, the emblem of the Iona Community, is the Celtic symbol of the Holy Spirit.

Iona is not a genteel island. Terrain is rough and mostly soggy or rocky. You will be very glad of sturdy shoes in the summer, and waterproof boots in the winter. A warm jacket goes a long way in the winds that constantly assail its shores. But the air is bracing, the aura is magical, and the simplicity of life is appealing. Iona has been called a "thin" island, meaning there is not much difference here between land and spirit.

CALLANISH

November 19 ... This remote place is wild and barren, rolling hills strewn with coppery heather tinged with the faint leftover bloom of summer purple, with the occasional group of long-horned, red, shaggy Highland cattle posing against the lime green moss tucked between craggy rocks. The pungent smokiness of peat fires permeates the mists swirling in the persistent dampness, making us yearn for a roaring fireplace to toast our frozen toes.

The forty-eight standing stones at Callanish are one of the best-preserved and awesome megalithic monuments of prehistoric Britain. Their remote location in a small village in the Outer Hebrides off Scotland's northwest coast adds to their aura of intrigue, along with the sense of pilgrimage experienced to get there.

Travel Tips

Glasgow, Scotland, is easily reached by air, train, or car. From our base at the west coast harbor town of Oban, we visited the monastic island of Iona, then rented a car to drive up the west coast and onward to the northernmost tip of the Isle of Skye, where a car ferry services the major islands of the Outer Hebrides group. From the town of Tarbert on Harris (joined by a peninsula, but still called the Isle of Lewis), Callanish is a 40-mile (64 km) drive on a good road. Alternatively, the Harris east coast port of Stornaway is accessed by air from Inverness or Glasgow, or by ferry from Ullapool on the mainland. (See travel tips under Iona.) A good map of Harris and Lewis is useful to find the many ruins and historical sites strewn around back roads.

Local Resources

The Isle of Skye is considered one of the most beautiful islands on earth, and well worth the time to explore the Cuillan Mountains in the southwest, quaint fishing villages like Portree and Broadford, and twelfth-century Dunvegan Castle and its environs. We loved the 1648 inn near Dunvegan: contact the Stein Inn, Waternish, Isle of Skye; Tel: (047083) 208; the Ben Lee, Bosville Terrace, Portree, Isle of Skye; Tel: (0478) 2664, was beautifully located on a hill overlooking the busy fishing harbor; the Broadford Hotel, Kyleakin, Isle of Skye; Tel: (04712) 204/5 is close to one of the ferry terminals connecting Skye with the mainland. In Tarbert, on the island of Harris, the Harris Hotel, Isle of Harris, Scotland; Tel: (0859) 2154 offers old world hospitality with a fabulous dining room.

In the forty-house community of Callanish, tourist services are limited, even in the summer season. When we arrived unannounced in November, the one hotel was closed, and a list of B&Bs from the Scottish Tourist Board in Glasgow yielded only one that would take us in the next day (Mrs McLeod, The Cairns, 32 Callanish, Isle of Lewis). The first night we had to rely on the hospitality of Margaret Ponting, the transplanted English woman who has spent the last twenty years studying the stone circles. She provides guided tours and also runs a small shop of artifacts and knitted goods where her own published information about the stones can be obtained. The closest alternative accommodation would be a B&B near Achmore, 7 miles (11 km) on the highway south, or 16 miles (26 km) to Stornaway. A small shop has basic provisions and the only restaurant is in the hotel 5 miles (8 km) away on the road to the north (A858), which was only open for pub-style lunches. Our B&B provided dinner on request.

These islands are cold and damp in the winter, although the locals insisted the sun shines in the summer and there is good swimming at the golden sand beaches down the west coast. Bring warm clothes, long underwear, wool socks, and Wellingtons (rubber boots that can be purchased in larger mainland towns) to stomp over the peat-soggy moors. Even during the day we took refuge in our bed heated with an electric blanket, as houses are not centrally heated and portable electric heaters seem to be at a premium.

Locals are generally laconic and sometimes seem suspicious. Although they appreciate the economic boost of tourism, they seem to take the stones for granted and have little to say to contemporary pilgrims who inquire about the spiritual nature of the place. Myth is still alive here, as is a strict community code based on Scottish Presbyterian principles. You will not see children playing or laundry hanging on a Sunday in Callanish, and we were uncertain if our photographing on Sunday was frowned upon, although nothing was said.

The Stones

Callanish is not just one stone circle, but a cluster of nineteen sites within a 2-mile (3 km) radius, the largest and most complete known as Callanish 1, located within the village on a ridge above Loch Roag, walking distance from our B&B. In daylight the stones are impressive in size—12 to 15 feet (4 to 5 m) high—contour, arrangement, and their position overlooking the valley. At night they become ominous, feeling like Ku-Klux-Klan-shrouded humans moving behind us. Approaching the circle via the 270-foot-long (81 m) avenue of guardian stones feels like an ancient ritual; the central chambered mound in the form of a flattened Celtic cross is thought to have been a burial place.

Dating from as early as 3400 BC, Callanish is generally accepted to be an astronomical calendar associated with the moon. The most profound marker is the 18.6-year cycle of maximum lunar declination displayed as the moon, viewed from the end of the avenue, is seen through the center of the stone circle, nestled in a notch in a distant hill. What a spectacle of excitement this must have engendered as the silver moon spirit played peek-a-boo behind the stones, and probably once in the average person's lifetime it reappeared at the sacred spot, focusing the power of that heavenly body on all gathered to witness the miraculous event. One can almost hear the joy of the festive celebration.

The other Callanish circles suggest that a complex of lunar observatories was integrated here into the landscape, allowing priestly astronomers, after generations of systematic observations, to calculate seasonal variations for planting and reaping, and to predict the dreaded lunar eclipses which caused so much fear as the night darkened seemingly forever. It is not known if this was a temple of worship (suggested by the sacred circle shape and evidence of burials), or a place of ritual to ensure the harmony of cosmic forces and the earth. Some authorities suggest the stones act like cosmic needles, conducting electromagnetic energy from deep within the earth to the surface where the geomantically tuned pilgrim will receive the vibrations collected within the stone circle. Whatever the explanation, the power and spirit of the place remain today, leaving a legacy for us to capture that spiritual energy and seek to integrate this type of resonance into our own daily lives.

England

STONEHENGE

August 18 ... From a distance we could see a rather insignificant-looking clump of stones lying like a child's toy casually cast aside. Then, driving up the final hill from the highway, the grandeur of the past became apparent as the familiar stolid-looking circle topped with tablelike stones took shape, nestled among hundreds of cream-colored sheep dotting the green slopes.

Stonehenge, one of the most visited and photographed monuments in Britain, is still an enigma. Used by succeeding generations of prehistoric peoples for a variety of rituals, it is generally conceded that Stonehenge is a solar calendar, with its major alignment being sunrise at the summer solstice.

Travel Tips

From London's Heathrow airport, it is a two-hour drive (on the left-hand side of the road!) through the pastoral English countryside to the town of Amesbury, Wiltshire, and a further 4 miles (6 km) to this famous monument. Train service links from London to Swindon, 9 miles (14 km) north of Avebury, and local buses are available, but a car gives much more flexibility to see the many important relics of the Salisbury Plain and the surrounding quaint market towns. Excellent regional maps show all the historical monuments, and are well worth the investment as British back roads can be very convoluted. There are a multitude of guided tours around southern England; check with the British Tourist Office, 12 Regent Street, London SW1 Y4PQ; Tel: (01) 730–3400 (Monday to Saturday). Many North American tour groups now specialize in sacred sites involving the Celtic and Arthurian legends of southwest England. Check with your local travel agent.

Local Resources

Amesbury has several hotels and B&Bs, ranging from budget to luxury. A list is available through the British Tourist Office, or drop into the local tourist bureau on the High Street when you arrive, but reservations are advised in the summer season. Car rentals are available from Avis, Trident House, Station Road, Hayes, Middlesex UB3 4DJ. For information about permission to take photographs at Stonehenge write to English Heritage, Historic Buildings and Monuments Commission, 25 Saville Row, London W1X 2BT; Tel: (01) 734–6010; Fax: (01) 634–1799.

The Stones

Possibly the most-studied stone circle in the world, **Stonehenge** is still impressive despite being overrun by tourism. The large car park, souvenir shop, and concession are strictly controlled by British Heritage. The monument is fenced from the road as well as roped off within 50 feet (15 m) of view, so it is now impossible to walk among the stones as one could twenty years ago. There are continuing problems with various cult groups; in the early eighties the stones were desecrated with spray paint, and while we were there, threats were made about a human or animal sacrifice during the full moon. The June 21 summer solstice regularly attracts thousands, so entry is completely restricted for that period. Despite heavy security, night guards regularly catch fence jumpers and escort them out, sometimes with the help of local police.

Despite all the hassle, the stones have not lost their ambience. This site was in use for more than a thousand years before the earliest of these stones were set more than four thousand years ago, which predates the Egyptian pyramids. Many stones weigh up to 50 tons each; the inner circle bluestones are known to have come from more than 130 miles (209 km) away in Wales. The 35-ton heelstone, set outside of the circle on the northeast, aligns with the familiar sunrise of the summer solstice. Volumes have been written and will continue to be written by succeeding generations of scholars trying to explain this phenomenon as a ritual meeting place, a tribute to the gods, a sacred burial ground, and a cosmic temple for astronomer priests to focus the light of heavenly bodies for a variety of ceremonies—perhaps a symbol of the universe, and one of many ancient examples of using the sacred circle as a tool to attune with the natural world.

This ongoing fascination with Stonehenge indicates a resonance with the past that may still have some deep meaning for contemporary humanity. The ancient world view was based on a cosmology that recognized the powerful influence of spiritual forces upon the fate of humankind. Their world was designed to understand and focus those spiritual energies to balance their everyday lives. One wonders what wisdom we might glean from this Bronze Age legacy.

Photo Tips   *Stonehenge Mist*

Stonehenge is one of the most carefully guarded and thoroughly patrolled sites in the world. Unless special permission is granted, one is not allowed inside the chain-link fence that cordons off the entire monument and the surrounding lawn. It is almost impossible to spend a quiet time in meditation here because the asphalt walkway is inundated with thousands of visitors daily. And unfortunately, the site is also quite close to the intersection of two highways, providing a continuous reminder of the intrusion of the twentieth century.

Photographers can get permission to enter Stonehenge after hours, particularly if you are involved in a project and have credentials to prove it. The fees are extraordinarily high, but do allow one to photograph at sunset, at night, and at dawn, but not during the normal hours of public viewing.

Stonehenge with mist at sunrise, Amesbury, England, August 1989/ Sacred Earth, *p. 20*

I spent several nights at Stonehenge, concentrating on images that for me had a feeling of timelessness. I carefully avoided showing the fence, the highway, the traffic, or people in their contemporary dress. I purposely visited at the time of the full moon and also paid attention to the alignments of the stones with the rising sun. I tried long exposure times holding the shutter open on "B" and experimented with lighting the stones with flash, and also "painting" them with flashlight. Electronic flash gives the stonework a cool, bright, daylight appearance, while the incandescent flashlight bathes the stones in a warm rich glow. My favorite visual effect happened only briefly one morning as the sun shone brightly on the mists that clung to the stones. The best angle, shown here, was to photograph outside the circle, pointing in the direction of the sun, though hiding it behind one of the monoliths. A dozen quick exposures, and the mist had vanished in the warmth of the increasing daylight.

AVEBURY

August 21 . . . Avebury should be experienced at dawn, walking through dew-kissed meadows among the sheep and cows scratching themselves against the four-thousand-year-old standing stones. The only sound is the occasional sheep bell tinkling against the background rustle of grass being chewed, as the sky turns into a faint pink backdrop for the mists rising off the moors.

Avebury is renowned as the largest of the nine hundred megalithic stone rings in Britain. The contemporary village has grown between and around the ancient stones which seem now to wander over the moors as do the grazing animals.

Travel Tips

Avebury is 16 miles (26 km) from the A40; go north on A345, bypassing Woodhenge, to Marlborough, then west on the A4 past Silbury Hill and the West Kennet Long Barrow, and take a short jog north on the A345 to the large car park. A tourist information center is available as well as many charming shops and a wonderful natural food restaurant called The Stones, found within the gardens of the twelfth-century church and Elizabethan manor house—a delightful place for afternoon tea.

Local Resources

Several small hotels and charming B&Bs grace the main street. We stayed at a sixteenth-century pink manor house owned by Heather Peak-Garland, a lifelong resident of Avebury; write St. Andrew's Cottage, High Street, Avebury, Marlborough, Wilts SN8 1RF; Tel: (06723) 247, but please cancel if you cannot honor your reservation. We could have stayed a month, waking to the sound of birds and a delicious country breakfast in the Victorian dining room.

The Stone Circle

This site covers 28 acres (11.3 ha), originally containing one hundred stones, forming two inner circles dated to 2600 BC, and a large outer circle with two avenues like the body of a serpent passing through—a traditional alchemical symbol. Now only twenty-seven stones remain, largely due to early Christian dismantling of this pagan ritual site, and to locals who may have broken the stones to use for building materials. Archaeological remains indicate fertility rites took place here, both human and animal as well as crop ceremonies, and modern scientific instrumentation shows a concentration of natural earth energies associated with ley lines, electromagnetic forces, and ground water. The adjacent ancient trade route known as "The Ridgeway" is evidence of an area highly utilized by ancient peoples as early as 2600 to 1600 BC, predating the time of Druidic priests.

Nearby Silbury Hill, 1,350 feet (411 m) high with a base of 5 acres (2 ha), is the largest man-made mound in Europe, forty-five hundred years old and still a mystery, although it is presumed to be a Great Goddess effigy with a nearby spring coming from the River Kennet (Cunnit). The pre-3000 BC West Kennet Long Barrow is the largest chambered tomb in Britain. The predominance of so many prehistoric sites in this area suggests **Avebury** was a center of religious ritual, probably a political center, and possibly a market center. Its decline is thought to have occurred around 2100 BC.

The charm of Avebury is its gentle atmosphere, where one can freely stroll the path of the stones, dodging cars as you cross the highway several times, and wandering over pastures. It feels like a large-scale scavenger hunt where the treasure is very visible: you can touch it, talk to the sheep and cows pasturing nearby, and wonder at the immensity of it all.

GLASTONBURY

August 23 . . . Here is the ancient site of Avalon, isle of the blessed dead and gateway to the spirit realm, where the veil to the Celtic Other World is very thin, and always at the edge of awareness. Mythology feels very much alive here as the sacred landscape reveals its hidden mysteries.

Glastonbury has long been a place of pilgrimage to honor Britain's first Christian church purportedly founded by Joseph of Arimathea. Many Christian monuments stand on Celtic and earlier Stone Age sites of pagan ritual and powerful earth energies, which are an attraction for contemporary mystics.

Travel Tips

Glastonbury is a one-and-a-half-hour drive on the motorway from Amesbury (see Stonehenge section). We chose the slightly longer route winding through old market towns and the more charming back roads of the Salisbury Plain, with a picnic by a canal on the River Avon at Milksham. Glastonbury is also a market town, its narrow roads clogged with tourist traffic exploring the abbey in the town center.

Local Resources

The Tourist Information Centre (open April to mid-October) off Northland Street, at 1 Marchants Buildings, Northland Street, Glastonbury, Somerset, England BA6 9JJ; Tel: (0458) 32954 offers long lists of hotel and B&B accommodation. The GAIA center off High Street has information on accommodation with holistic resources, natural foods, massage, and counselling. We enjoyed a New Age counselling session from Sue Barnet, 8 King Street, Glastonbury, Somerset, England BA6 9JY; Tel: (0458) 31970, who also offers reiki and other healing therapies. Glastonbury is a center for many Christian groups as well as people of diverse mystical traditions, including Robert Coon, whose writing about global sacred places prompted our pilgrimage.

Glastonbury Sites

Glastonbury is a crossroads of history, legend, myth, and ancient and modern science. A meeting ground of traditional and alternative thinking, a variety of spiritual groups share the landscape and ancient monuments to celebrate their holy festivals.

The abbey is a focal point in the town center. It is said to be where the old wattle church was built by Joseph of Arimathea, who, according to some legends, brought the body of Jesus with him to England, and marked the site on nearby Weary-All Hill. Here, say the legends, he planted his staff which took root to become the famous thorn tree, now marked by a stone, but whose descendents still blossom annually on the anniversary of Christ's birth. The old church, rededicated in 166 AD, became the first Christian Abbey and a powerful priestly center, confirmed by the Domesday Book which considered Glastonbury too sacred to be subject to secular control or taxation. Ireland's St. Patrick died here and his shrine was visited by St. Brigit and other priests and scholars from throughout Christendom. The abbey was destroyed by fire in 1184 and rebuilt by the Benedictine order.

Legend also holds that Joseph brought with him the Holy Grail, the cup Jesus drank from at the Last Supper. This sacred vessel is symbolic of life itself, and in many traditions it stands for the quest for eternal life. Many think the Grail still lies hidden in Chalice Hill or in the adjacent **Chalice Well** which is fed by the iron-tainted waters of Blood Spring, with its unceasing flow of 25,000 gallons per day at a constant temperature of 52°F (11°C). The **Chalice Well Garden**, managed by a Christian charity trust, also has pre-Christian roots; as it is oriented to the east and the summer solstice sunrise—the time of celebration in many old cultures—it is possibly a site of Celtic Druid priestly worship associated with the sun and water. In the mid-eighteenth century this magical place was declared to have miraculous healing powers and was inundated with pilgrims. Today it still feels like a haven of renewal, a few steps from the busy roadside into a timeless past, nourished by flowing water, colorful flowers, and bountiful fruit trees in the shadow of the Tor.

The 520-foot-high (158 m) **Tor** abounds in mystery and legend: is it a magic mountain, a Grail castle, an entrance to the Other World, a center of Druidic initiation, an Arthurian hill fort, a magnetic power point, a crossroads of ley lines, a fertility ritual center in honor of the earth goddess, or a landing place for flying saucers? Tradition suggests it was a processional sacred way that followed a third-millenium BC spiral maze pattern on its hillside to an open sun temple crowned with standing stones. This was subsequently replaced by the twelfth-century Christian church named after St. Michael, who was known to subdue the powers of Satan and the underworld. An earthquake later left only the upright tower, ironically a pagan symbol. This is one of several shrines to St. Michael, many of which are located on ancient ley lines stretching from Cornwall to Glastonbury; others can be seen in Europe, (see section on European Lowlands) the most famous being Mont-St.-Michel in France. The oldest connections are to the Great Goddess Cult of the fifth millenium BC which honored the cosmic mother who produced the balance and harmony of the natural world. She was often celebrated on hills with spiral patterns, the sacred symbol of the equally ancient coiled serpent or dragon that represented the natural energy of earth and sky.

The legendary **Avalon** was glorified by third-century AD Celtic worshippers who lived near the Tor, where natural energies met with the supernatural. This misty isle of Avalon was a symbol of earthly paradise, honored by Roman and Anglo Saxon alike. It was prominent in the legends of King Arthur, with his knights of salvation and his Shangri-La of Camelot, fostering the hope of a saviour King and the quest for the Holy Grail. Two ancient coffins found in the ruins of the Abbey fire were said to contain the relics of Arthur and Gwenhwyfer, whose traditional burial place was Avalon. Avalon also embodied an earlier myth of awakening the earth goddess, and it continued in the imagination of later scholars such as the nineteenth-century British visionary poet, William Blake.

Glastonbury and its Tor are obviously powerful symbols from many points of view. Whatever your belief system, it is a place of high energy, linking the misty English earth with the open sky, seemingly far away from the bustling town and nearer to those ancient and ever-present spiritual forces. Perhaps it is true, as a young child was overheard to say, that the Tor does have an elevator to God.

Photo Tips   *Glastonbury Tor*

One of my favorite lenses is my 1400–4200mm zoom. Actually a spotting scope with a camera adaptor, it is relatively small, lightweight, and easy to pack in a suitcase. And though the range of focal length is unbelievable, the price is surprisingly little, partly because the quality of the optics is not superior. Because the effective aperture is small, ranging from f16 to f90, as you zoom in, the scene in the viewfinder is appreciably dark; the lens is best for photographing the rising or setting sun, juxtaposed with silhouetted shapes on the horizon. In order to depict the objects on the landscape as small in relation to the sun, it is necessary to photograph them from an appreciable distance away. Here, recording St. Michael's Tower with the man and sheep, I stood over half a mile (about 1 km) away, making this image at about the 3000mm mark on the zoom.

Silhouette of St. Michael's Tower and sun, Glastonbury, England, August 1989/ Sacred Earth, p. 237

I did a series of exposures as I followed the sun down, beginning with my 80–200mm zoom, then my 300mm lens, 500mm lens, and finally the spotting scope. Here too I zoomed in as the sun continued to descend, making tighter compositions as the sun dropped behind the tower. I am pleased with the results, not only because of the strong graphic effect of the image, but also because, like the surrealism of Glastonbury, this image too has an unworldly quality.

A few more notes about technique. The lens can be mounted on a tripod with the camera coupled to the end of the lens. Because the sun can be extremely bright, even looking through the small lens opening I squint to compose and try to avoid looking directly at the sun itself. Secondly, I set my exposure on automatic, as it is extremely difficult to see the meter readout in the viewfinder when pointing right at the sun. And lastly, take caution. I only recommend pointing this lens at the sun when it has already lost its daylight brilliance and has taken on its red, orange, or golden coloration. Then is the magic hour to transport your audience with images that reach out to the mysteries of the Other World.

Photo Tips   *Chalice Well Garden*

I had a great deal of difficulty photographing here because I was confined to visiting during their regular hours. This unfortunately coincided with a high sun, which was bright every day, and though it was wonderful to feel the warmth in the garden, it was frustrating to deal with the harsh shadows and uneven tones. I concentrated most of my time on the well and the holy waters that tumbled over the rocks throughout the garden. But my greatest joy came from receiving and working with a goblet from Robert Coon, the man whose writing had inspired my global pilgrimage. I placed the cup in several locations along the stream in an attempt to find it a ray of sunlight while photographing the tumbling water and rocks in the shade. During several attempts, the light and shadow gave a mottled effect to the landscape which I found distracting and displeasing. I had more success by moving in quite close and including less of the surroundings yet still depicting the stream, as the cup sparkled in the sunlight as well as seeming to emit a radiant glow from within.

Goblet and waterfall, Chalice Well Gardens, Glastonbury, England, August 1989/ Sacred Earth, *p. 238*

The Chalice Well Garden was one of the few locations where I attempted to introduce a replica in order to depict the predominant story—here being the search for the Holy Grail. My usual inclination is to seek out expressions in the landscape that hint at the theme or mood of the relevant mythology, but I couldn't resist working with the golden tones of the goblet, and the notion that symbolically the fulfillment of the Holy Grail does come to those who seek it. When photographing places associated with a specific story, explore the possibilities for an explicit depiction, but also look carefully and sensitively at the qualities of the landscape that gave rise to the mythology. Then choose, not from the head, but from the heart.

Egypt

GIZA

December 1 . . . After battling the incredible noise, dust, and vehicle fumes on the drive across Cairo, suddenly, around the last corner, the famous shapes appear, washing over one's psyche like a cleansing stream. Finally we are here, and the wonder—the simplicity—of those three pyramidal shapes sends a shiver up my spine.

The Pyramids of Giza, one of the seven wonders of the world, have been a destination for pilgrims from time immemorial. Whether they are monuments to an ego, or places of initiation to higher spiritual realms, their splendor remains despite their edges crumbling under the watchful eye of the Sphinx for the past forty-five hundred years.

Travel Tips

Cairo is serviced by air from London and all major continental centers. Although we were warned about limited currency and camera equipment restrictions, our entry at 10:00 PM was incredibly easy, with the primary concern being registration of video equipment. Tourist information at the airport will assist in finding budget or luxury hotels. Taxi service is efficient, but be prepared for a harrowing ride through erratic and noisy traffic, day or night. A short stay in Cairo is a must for most tourists to see the impressive relic-crowded (and crowded!) Cairo Museum, the old market place, and the ancient monuments of Islam, but we were glad to leave central Cairo for the less-jangled feeling of Giza, 10 miles (16 km) west at the edge of the Western

Desert. The taxi trip is about forty minutes; be sure to establish the price first.

Travel agents and tours abound in Cairo and can be arranged as you step off the plane. Do believe the tour books—it *is* easier to take a guided tour, but it is not impossible to do it on your own, even if the tour agencies tell you the hotels will all be full. If you don't want a tour, be adamant—but use their services to help you book flights with Egypt Air (our phone calls were useless) or train or boat tickets to Luxor. We liked Mena Tours, El Nasr Building, El-Nil Street, PO Box 46, Giza, Egypt; Tel: 730403/730420; Fax: 728825. Air and train costs to Luxor are almost the same, and we heard that the overnight train is very comfortable. Alternately, look for package tours offered through your travel agent at home; many of these will include a Nile cruise on a luxury boat to Luxor and Aswan, as well as a ride on a single-masted felucca, which has plied these waters for centuries. Many tours will include additional trips through the Sinai, Jordan, and Israel, which should not be missed.

Local Resources

There are only two major hotels near the pyramids, although a third was to open in 1990. The Mena House, Oberoi, Sharia el-Ahram, Giza; Tel: 853789; Telex: 92316 OB UN is well established, luxurious, and walking distance up the hill to the pyramids. We preferred the less expensive Delta Pyramid Hotel, five minutes away by taxi; it is modern, with excellent food (although no alcohol as it is a Moslem hotel) and service, and a sincere willingness to help the visitor. Every window has a spectacular view of the distant pyramids. Write Delta Pyramid Hotel, King Faisal Road, PO Box 45, Giza, Egypt; Tel: (20–2) 859935; Fax: (20–2) 853616.

The Pyramids

Despite years of study, the mystery of the pyramids still challenges archaeologists. Is a pyramid simply a tomb from which the pharaoh, the earthly embodiment of God, could symbolically ascend to the heavens and eternal life? Or does the orientation and proportion of the pyramids portray the sacred geometry and ritual practice that facilitated initiation into the ancient mystical understanding of the universe? Whatever the purpose, the initial wonder one feels does not diminish. In fact it probably increased as we again and again gazed at them in awe from the hotel window, their symmetry so perfect that they could have been painted on the curtain. The awe increased as the famous shapes, so long known in the imagination, became tangible as we walked in the hot sun with dust in our eyes and nostrils, and examined the craggy rock faces. Long gone is the patina that inspired the Egyptian name for the great pyramid, Ta Khut, meaning The Light; the original sheen must have reflected the dazzling desert sun, the symbol of the all powerful god Amun Ra.

At every step out of the hotel, someone wanted us to buy: a taxi, camel, horse, or donkey ride; a guide to the top of the pyramid (illegal to climb); an "original" papyrus; exotic perfume and jewelry. Unfortunately it is difficult to smile and be friendly as this is interpreted as an invitation, and the pleading looks start anew. The cumulative irritation of it all is overwhelming—until one glances at the enigmatic Sphinx who has lived through it all, and learns to flow with it. This 60-foot (20 m) statue, another work of sacred art, is a symbol of the sun, considered the eye of

Amun Ra; his head stands for intelligence and consciousness, and his lion body is power and strength. His toes alone are large enough to make one shudder!

Don't let the hassle of the street stop you from negotiating the unique experience of a camel ride; we chose an all day trip to Abusir and other nearby pyramids, starting from our camel driver's home deep in the back alleys of a tenement complex near the Sphinx. Our perch between the humps allowed us a birds-eye view of the bustle of early morning through a curtain of colorful laundry draped from walls around the hovels where extended families shared one room and cooked over an open fire as our camels daintily negotiated past kids, cats, dogs, goats, and chickens sharing the narrow passageways. Our journey took us past cultivated fields to a small village at the edge of the desert where we stopped for tea—a great relief to our already sore bottoms that jostled with every step of the rolling gait, massaging us from side to side on the hard saddle—but the relief was gained only after clutching onto the saddle pom as the camel folded his knees and lurched forward, threatening to tip us over his head, but finally allowing a descent from the side.

One does get into the rhythm and adventure of it all, but the major bruising of our posteriors and resultant difficulty walking made us glad we had not been tempted by the exotic-sounding five day journey to a desert oasis! Despite the complaints, we would not have missed this unique form of transportation and the brief taste of a desert experience.

The other exotic experience in Giza is the internal climb of the **Great Pyramid** to the **King's Chamber**, which is also not for everyone. It was closed for restoration when we were there, but we were able to get special permission for our photography. We scrambled, alone, up more than two hundred stair rungs in a narrow, almost vertical passageway, and then crawled through the boxlike horizontal 15-foot (5 m) trough leading to the chamber. I can't imagine doing this with people crowding from above and below, and trying to pass on the way down, in this narrow shaft with poor ventilation and lighting. Don't go if you have any degree of claustrophobia. The reward at the end is a completely bare, rough stone room with a corbelled roof, and one fluorescent light box illuminating an empty stone sarcophagus. One needs great imagination here—there is no splendorous decor or artifacts like the tombs in the Valley of the Kings. The acoustics are incredibly resonant, but I fear that a crowd of tourists would diminish the strange aura that does exist here. We did feel it—a tingly light-headedness, renewed physical and emotional energy, and a strange and gentle contentment which supported the mystical idea that the King's Chamber was a place of initiation, where high levels of psychic energy were utilized in rituals of spiritual transcendence. Whatever the energy here, all of Courtney's electronic equipment failed to work, but came to life again outside of the pyramid.

Photo Tips   *The Sphinx*

Egypt proved to present a unique set of photographic challenges because much of the archaeological remains are quite colorless in daylight. The Sphinx, pyramids, temples, and monuments portray little more than the gray tones of their granite slabs, hardly evoking the glories of their colorful past. Thus, for most of the monuments that were lit artificially, I chose to photograph at night. The Sphinx, the pyramids at Giza, and the temples of Luxor and Karnak all have at least some

Sphinx and night sky, Giza, Egypt, December 1988/ Sacred Earth, *p. 4*

floodlighting. As well, there are magnificent sound and light shows offered in several languages at the Temple of Karnak and in front of the Sphinx.

If you want to do a thorough job of any one location, go to the show several times. The lighting changes quickly and dramatically. Some parts of the show are missed simply for changing film. Using a tripod for five- and ten-second exposures is essential, as flash photography at these shows is not possible because practically all the distances are beyond flash range. For this photograph of the Sphinx, I arranged to pay a guide to take me to the "forbidden area" at the base of the Sphinx, where we were out of sight of the other spectators but positioned for a dramatic angle as the monument changed color. I had paid five dollars for the privilege of photographing close up, but once in position, the price soared to one hundred dollars. I held my ground, both physically and in my bargaining, and took a second person with me for moral support!

I was assured warm rich colors by recording the Sphinx bathed in incandescent floodlights, using daylight film, and refraining from the use of color-correction filters. A ten-second exposure on the Sphinx gave time enough to record the stars glimmering with appreciable brightness. I first went to the English version of the light show in order to get background information, then photographed during the German and Japanese versions. Because I couldn't understand a word of the narrative, there were no distractions, and I was free to concentrate on the aesthetic aspects of the show, while enjoying the inspiration of the music.

THEBES

December 10 . . . At Karnak, we walked through the temples at night, guided by the seductive words of the sound and light show . . ."try to hear the whispered response of the ever-present God . . . you will travel no further because you are at the beginning of time, crossing the threshold which was forbidden to common mortals, up stairways leading to the ramparts of heaven . . . this is the wonder that was Thebes."

The modern city of Luxor is the gateway to two of the most famous sacred places in ancient Egypt: the temples of Luxor and Karnak, the largest place of worship in the ancient world, in this, the oldest of the great archaic civilizations.

Travel Tips

Air service from Cairo to Luxor is frequent, as are luxury or budget trains and buses. (See notes in Giza section.)

Local Resources

Luxor is a constant hub of activity; the waterfront series of piers docks everything from the most luxurious Nile ship to the single-masted felucca, and the adjacent main street is lined with hotels ranging from deluxe five-star to budget. Our taxi driver took us to the budget Horus Hotel on Sharia el-Mahatta Street, and we also stayed at the nearby moderately priced Savoy on Shari El Nil in Luxor; Tel: 2200 2518; Telex: 92160 WINTER UN. We took advantage of the amenities of the luxury Sheraton and the Winter Palace Hotel.

The dawn breaks and the day begins with the first of five daily prayer calls by the muezzin, his chant over the inevitable loudspeaker competing with the backyard roosters. This is followed by the horns of cars, trucks, and bicycles, and the clippety-clop of horse-drawn carriages amidst the shouts of pedestrians, all of whom compete for the two-lane road. It is impossible to oversleep in Egypt! But who would want to for there is so much to see and do that we didn't want to miss any of it—and an early start helps to beat some of the tourist buses, as well as the heat. The old market place behind the main street is a good place to start to experience exotic spices and foodstuffs, as well as the smells of old Egypt, although while walking here we were constantly accosted to buy goods. We were equally irritated at most of the tourist sites by guides and local children trying to outwit each other (and us) by claiming baksheesh (tips) for pointing out details we had already seen, or didn't want to see. It sometimes felt like a game of tag, with a price tag attached. We tried to keep our cool by ignoring them, joining a passing tour group, or finding a hidden corner to contemplate the marvels on our own.

Boats, trains, and buses continue south from Luxor to the temples at Edfu and Aswan; a local taxi can also be hired at a reasonable price (if you bargain) from the roundabout on Shari Maabad el Karnak, the street down from the Luxor museum. Tours of everything (some very expensive) can be arranged through the larger hotels. There is no photography allowed in any of the tombs in the valley of the Kings or Queens. It is wise to carry a cotton scarf (to moisten against the dust and heat) and a canteen of water, although bottled pop is available many places. We also carried fruit and snacks to avoid relying on local food outside of Thebes, but there is a restaurant in the Habu Hotel, beside Medinet Habu, the mortuary temple of Rameses III. *Always* carry toilet paper, as facilities may be limited or nonexistent, and you never know when you may react to the local food.

A highlight for us was an overnight felucca ride down the Nile. Despite the dirty water, it was fascinating and relaxing to float past women washing dishes and clothing, children annointing each other with water, and water buffalo and burros going about their various duties upstream. We chanced the local food from the market; it was delicious, and Courtney survived his stomachache. Feluccas, which can be hired for a few hours or a few days, travel all the way to Aswan and are a good way to escape the tourist hype on shore.

The Ancient Glories of Thebes

The elegant **Temple of Luxor** is on the main street, less than a five-minute walk from the hotels. Some authorities believe the design of this temple incorporates the ancient Egyptian philosophy of the laws of creation and humanity's spiritual development. The architecture is an unusual geometric design shaped like a human body; scholar Schwaller de Lubicz and other esoteric writers believe this temple emits powerful vibrations, especially in the area of the solar plexus. We felt the spirit of the place, perhaps enhanced by the ideas about this initiatory temple.

The four-thousand-year-old **Temple of Karnak**, a fifteen-minute horse carriage ride from town, stretches over 5 acres (2 ha) of buildings surrounding the sacred lake of priestly purification dedicated to the sun god, Amun. The predominant symbol of Karnak is the lotus, the emblem of Upper Egypt, signifying fertility and resurrection. The lotus also signifies newly created earth, renewed each year around Luxor by the annual Nile floods (before the Aswan Dam was built) which brought fresh earth to till and precious water to irrigate this dry land. Like the lotus stretching its pure white petals above the muddy waters, Karnak stands as the universe created out of the primeval swamp. The monumental hypostyle hall is the most glorious remnant of this concept, its huge ornately carved pillars seeming to reach to the sky, dwarfing the mere mortal staring upward. Stylizations of the lotus, as well as the Lower Egypt emblem of the papyrus and an array of birds and animals from Egyptian mythology, decorate all the temples and obelisks of Karnak which was worked on for twenty centuries by a succession of pharaohs trying to ensure their immortality. The splendor of this world-in-miniature is even more evocative during the nightly sound and light show. Wear comfortable shoes, as the show starts from the entrance gate and visitors are guided from there (to the accompaniment of processional music) through the floodlit ruins to the finale of the show, a point overlooking the sacred lake. The contemporary pilgrim can then experience these pillars of time silhouetted under the bright stars much as they would have been at the time of the pharaohs who created this "citadel of god."

The west bank of the Nile is reserved for the tombs of ancient Egypt, perhaps because it is closer to the sun god's exit into the underworld. The immensity of this grand mausoleum reinforces the pervasive Egyptian theme of the quest for immortality and the promise of an afterlife if the soul was properly protected in its journey through eternity. The building style of the earlier pyramids was apparently abandoned because of vandalism, with the newer ones cut into the rock and dug deep into the earth. Some may be so well hidden they will never be found—the most recent find of the tomb of Tutankhamun was only accidentally discovered after years of searching. The **Valley of the Kings** is best seen in the morning before the heat settles onto the sandy treeless desert. Many tours are available, or you can rent a taxi or bicycle (hot work!) and take the ferry across the Nile, but first decide which places you want to see because tickets must be bought from a kiosk near the western dock. The **Colossi of Memnon** still form the gateway to the valley, the two 60-foot (20 m) replicas of Amenhotep III guarding the famous oracle of the past. Queues to the tombs may be long if you arrive after the first onslaught of tour buses, but there is lots to see, and some of the lesser-known tombs are very beautiful. All the tombs incorporate art from the vast array of funerary books, including the famous Book of the Dead. A repetitive theme is the transformation of the soul after death in the region of the Duat, described as a spirit state rather than a place. The texts follow the progress of the solar principal (the pharaoh-king) through the night, as he floats in his solar barque along the celestial river, encouraged by the deities in the stages of transformation. These teachings, inscribed in colorful and incredibly detailed hieroglyphics, were apparently directed at the living observer, a reminder that the process of transforming the flesh into spirit is the responsibility of earthly dwellers. It seems a monumental task.

It is worth the climb to see Amenhotep's tomb with its fine detail against a yellow background. The tomb of the adolescent Tutankhamun is always crowded even though it is empty of its fabulous treasures, which can be seen in the Cairo Museum. At the time of Seti I, art had reached a great pinnacle and this is reflected in the colorful paintings and reliefs that completely cover the wall space of his tomb.

The mortuary temples in other parts of the valley have a very different impact. The Ramesseum is a strong reflection of the arrogant and prolific style of Rameses II. Here one still sees Ozymandias' "vast and trunkless legs of stone" which inspired the romantic poetry of Shelley. The Rameses III temple at Medinet Habu offers hieroglyphics incised as deep as 8 inches (20 cm). The Valley of the Queens is mostly bypassed because the tomb of Nefertari, Rameses' favorite wife, is still closed, but the **Temple of Hatshepsut** at Deir el Baharis is an impressive monument to this queen known as "the Most Splendid of All." Considered by some to be an architectural masterpiece in its integration into the natural rock, this mortuary temple sits on ground sacred to the goddess Hathor. It is a strong-looking structure, perhaps fitting to the only Egyptian queen who dared to declare herself pharaoh, and wore a false beard to maintain her position. The temple is rather stark but it seemed a fitting site for the sumptuous 1988 performance of Verdi's opera *Aida*, which commemorated the 175th anniversary of the illustrious composer's birth, as well as the ever-present glory of ancient Egypt.

Photo Tips   *The Nile*

The Nile beckons you to bring an 80–200mm f2.8 lens. Because you will be photographing from the water, and probably from a small boat called a felucca, you will want to zoom out to a 200mm focal length to catch the action along the shore. The long focal length and unsteady boat will make it necessary to expose at shutter speeds of 1/500 sec and 1/1000 sec. An f2.8 lens allows enough light at its largest aperture to expose ISO 50 or ISO 100 film at these rapid shutter speeds. Keep in mind that when you photograph at f2.8 the depth of field is extremely shallow; thus it is critical that your focus be extremely accurate.

The color and exitement found on its banks makes the Nile a most enjoyable river to travel on. To see contemporary Egyptian families in their colorful robes is to step back into time, and because you will be travelling on a small sailboat, you can direct your captain to locations of your choice, like closer to the bank, for the most evocative images.

A longer trip on the river—an overnight jaunt might even bring an invitation to stay in a neighboring village—may present the opportunity to photograph at each end of the day as well as to sample rural life in Egypt. I greatly enjoyed the spontaneity of the people, particularly when I could sail away from the hustle and bustle of the tourist-oriented city of Luxor. If you stay overnight on a felucca trip, remember to take a tripod for those low-light moody reflections on the sacred Nile, and be sure to get up early to catch the first rays of sun as the daily activity starts anew.

*West bank of the Nile River near Luxor, Egypt, December 1988/*Sacred Earth, *p. 80*

THE SINAI

December 15 . . . This barren flat land of the west coast is so uninviting as we pass by military installations and garbage dumps, with the occasional cluster of open houses amidst clumps of gray-green vegetation. Finally the bus climbs through rolling sandy hills with gold-colored shale falling from hoodoo formations, and into the ridge of mountains cradling the monastery of St. Catherine.

The desert is, for many, a spiritual wasteland. But it is here that Moses was instructed at the burning bush to return to Egypt and lead the children of Israel to the Promised Land, and it is here he later received the Ten Commandments. For the ancient Egyptians, Hathor was the patron goddess of this area rich in gold, copper, and turquoise, and it was also the sacred spot where the goddess Isis crossed in search of her husband, the god Osiris.

Travel Tips

Other than a guided tour, the only way to get here is by bus (cheap) or by private car and driver (expensive). Buses are comfortable and air-conditioned, although be aware that the newer Renault models have videos blaring constantly with the Egyptian equivalent of American soap operas. Buses leave at 7:00 AM and 10:30 AM daily from the Sinai Terminal near Abbassya Square off Saleh Salem Street. They make several convenience stops on this six-hour trip from Cairo, but toilets can be very dirty and the only sanitary-looking food choice is yogurt and packaged biscuits.

Local Resources

The bus delivers you to the small village center and a local taxi will take you to the nearby hotel called St. Catherine's Tourist Village. (Write MISR Sinai Tourist Co., St. Catherine's, Sinai, Egypt.) However, many people prefer to stay at the monastery, which can be reserved in advance in Cairo through Mr. Antoine at 18 Midan El Daher, Cairo, Egypt; Tel: 828513 (between 1:00 and 4:00 PM only). It is wise to reserve ahead; although it is very inexpensive and rustic, many tour groups come here. This is also the person to contact for permission to photograph inside the monastery. This experience is for the more adventurous traveller; mattresses, sheets, and towels are thin, as are the walls against the cold, but the water is hot with a primitive shower. There is a communal kitchen where you can cook in between tour groups (bring your own food), or you can walk twenty minutes to the Tourist Village restaurant and pay U.S. dollar prices, or to the few simple inexpensive cafes in the village.

From St. Catherine's, local daily buses return to Cairo, or go to the south and west at 1:30 PM or 2:30 PM where the beaches and scuba diving of Sharm el Shiekh and Dahab at the tip of the Sinai Peninsula are reported to be spectacular. We chose to go west and north to Nuweiba, another beach resort, and the terminus for the gulf ferry which delivered us to Aqaba, Jordan, the gateway to the wadis and the ancient Rose Red City of Petra.

St. Catherine's Monastery and the Mountain

St. Catherine's is a serene place, as though time has stilled, with black-robed Greek Orthodox monks tilling the garden, picking black olives, and toiling over the olive press. There is little sound except the birds and church bells, with tourist voices floating above the sound of vespers. Guests are invited to observe some of the rituals in this sixth-century Church of the Transfiguration, its heavy wooden door reflecting brightly colored stained glass and its hundreds of different brass lamps hanging from the ceiling while a multitude of ikons and religious paintings crowd the walls. Long-bearded monks in heavy robes hurry in from their courtyard cells, remove their shoes, and raise melodic voices in chant as the votive bells chime and the heavy aroma of incense wafts over all. The services are very long and may be tiring if you are standing, although it is possible to leave before the end.

The small **Chapel of the Burning Bush** was built in 342 AD by Empress Helena, mother of Constantine the Great. The church was added later and named after St. Catherine who was tortured by the Romans and beheaded in 307 AD for her adherence to Christianity. Several nearby mosques mark the first spot where Islam was celebrated by the Bedouin tribes in Egypt.

The highlight of a visit to St. Catherine's is the predawn climb of **Mount Sinai** to greet the sun, the symbol of the rebirth of a new day. It is said that one monk carved the more than two thousand steps to the top, in penance for an undisclosed deed. He must be thanked, as the way is long and the air bitterly cold at the 4:00 AM starting time from the monastery. Even the fittest legs seem to scream on this two-hour jaunt, and an extra blanket is most welcome at the top. The view can be misty and disappointing to some, but the effort of this pilgrimage is just reward, and the scenic views on the way down can be breathtaking.

Photo Tips   *Door, Chapel of the Burning Bush*

Plan to stay at St. Catherine's Monastery when you visit Mt. Sinai. You will be allowed to photograph around the grounds of the monastery, but need special permission to photograph inside the old buildings (see address under Local Resources). Even when I was granted approval (which took two days before the right authority was available), I was limited to three photographs of the interior of the church, and none within the chapel—a sparse amount indeed for someone who enjoys shooting a variety of angles and views! Then upon arrival, I discovered that the building is almost always crowded with visitors, making a tripod setup extremely awkward, and that I was not able to enter the interior except during these visiting hours.

The door shown here was the only entrance to the hallway of the chapel and thus in constant use. I would no sooner focus and compose before the door would again swing open to receive a bevy of pilgrims who would then block my view and crowd my tripod out of position. St. Catherine taught me much patience that day before I was finally able to make an exposure of the old door. She also taught me the art of counting creatively. I interpreted three "photographs" as meaning three "locations" within the monastery buildings, each requiring a number of exposures to assure the best result. It was for the good of St. Catherine, I reasoned. After all, I did want to portray her monastery in the best possible light and that meant ample time, careful observation, the utmost in sensitivity, and enough preliminary exposures to assure three superb images, worthy of the monastery's ancient beauty.

My best advice is to arrive at the door when it first opens and pray fervently that the tour buses get delayed! The light on the old door is cast from a stained-glass window nearby, and remains somewhat constant throughout the day. Though we organized our photography permit on arrival in Cairo (with the help of the Canadian embassy), it would pay to write ahead for permission to photograph, explaining your purpose for doing so.

*Door, Chapel of the
Burning Bush, St.
Catherine's Monastery,
Mount Sinai, Egypt,
December 1988/* Sacred
Earth, *p. 222*

Jordan

PETRA

*December 20 . . . The natural array of color in the sandstone carved by wind,
rain, and man is unsurpassed in visual elegance. Pink, red, blue, cream, white,
and ochre swirl together in unimaginable formations of landscapes within
the landscape.*

Described by an early traveller as "half as old as time," an erroneous but colorful statement, this marvel of preclassical times is another rich study in ancient Hebrew, Christian, and Moslem history. Petra, the naturally fortressed red sandstone city in the middle of the Jordanian desert, was a sacred burial ground of the Nabateans in the fifth century BC, later becoming a thriving city with temples and tombs carved out of the living rock to welcome desert caravaners and their luxury trade goods.

Travel Tips

Petra is a three-hour drive south of Amman, the capital of Jordan, and less than two hours from Aqaba, the sea port on the Gulf of Aqaba (Eilat) where the twice-daily local ferry from the Sinai port of Nuweiba carries few tourists among the many itinerant Egyptian workers who are normally bound for Iran and Iraq. Consequently, loading and unloading can take hours—our 3:00 PM scheduled departure melted into 6:00 PM as thousands of workers disembarked on foot, carrying bags and bundles half the size of a car, all of which needed to be searched (presumably for weapons and other contraband). Ticket purchase and immigration was not difficult for us, apart from being a little convoluted with the negotiation in very few words of English, and behind a queue of truck drivers that seemed endless.

Amidst loaded trucks and huge buses, our heavy luggage seemed miniscule as we were finally herded on, and invited by two Egyptian diplomats to join them in the ferry's first-class lounge; we were the only non-Middle Eastern travellers and the three-hour journey seemed to pass quickly over a good dinner. Our friends also helped to expedite our arrival in Aqaba, but we were again delayed as papers and camera equipment were thoroughly examined. At 11:00 PM we were given tea as all the customs inspectors gathered round to be sociable, proudly and pointedly telling us of their extended families when we admitted we had no children! Finally, we pleaded fatigue through pantomime and a young immigration official drove us to a hotel because the taxis had stopped for the night.

Local Resources

Aqaba is an under-appreciated holiday destination that offers sandy beaches, good scuba diving, tennis, desert excursions, wonderful weather, and beach-front resort-style hotels. Money can be exchanged for Jordanian dinars in most hotels. The Holiday Inn on Kings Boulevard is well located, with good service and a private beach; reserve through PO Box 215, Aqaba, Jordan; Tel: 31–2426; Telex: 62263 HOLDIN JO; Fax: 313424. From here, we hired a private taxi and driver to take us to Wadi Rum and to Petra, although the JETT (Jordan tours and transport company) is planning an extension of their service to Amman that would include a stop at Petra. The Petra Forum Hotel offers excellent friendly service, good food, pool, fitness center, spacious lounge and patio, and views over the valley from rooms which cascade down the hill. Reserve through Box 30, Wadi Mousa, Jordan; Tel: (03) 83246/7 or in Amman at 634200; Telex: 64001 FORTEL JO. Guides to Petra can be found just outside the hotel, as well as horses to rent, and the occasional carriage which will fit through the narrow Siq.

The Jordanian people are friendly and speak more English than their Egyptian counterparts. The country is small, people receive more education, and western dress is more apparent. Food includes a delicious array of traditional Middle Eastern cuisine.

The Rose Red City of Antiquity

Petra was home to the ancient Nabateans, a nomadic Arab tribe known as early as the eighth century BC. They moved from southern Arabia and settled in this area by the sixth century BC, driving out the Edomite tribes identified in the Old Testament of the Bible, and entrenching themselves in the natural fortress formed by the high limestone ridges cradling the valley known as Wadi Arabah. Two lower parallel ridges of exotic Nubian sandstone formed a natural basin for water, the most important commodity in the desert. It is only at this point down the length of the Rift Valley that a corkscrewlike opening appears in the rock—this is Petra. This vital geography provided the life blood of the ancient world, and probably the route for Moses to lead the Israelites on their exodus from Egypt to the Promised Land. This same spot became the crossroads for two major trade routes to supply the rich Mediterranean markets at Gaza, and the Egyptian markets via Aqaba. A continuous supply of goods flowed from the Arabian gulf port of Kuwait in the east and via Mecca in the south, and from Damascus, the northern end of the Silk Road trade in spices, silk, gauze, and damask from the Orient. Precious gold, copper, and iron from Solomon's mines in the south also found its way into the slave trade markets in Gaza. These routes flourished, protected by the Nabateans for more than four hundred years, until they gradually declined after the occupation by the Roman emperor Trojan in 106 AD.

Nature and human ingenuity worked together here as the Nabateans built channels and cisterns to irrigate their land and provide fresh water for thirsty caravaners struggling into this oasis after days spent crossing the deserts. The tradesmen must have been delighted to finally penetrate the Siq, the .75-mile (1.2 km) narrow corridor of rock that opens onto the glory of the ornately carved Pharaoh's Treasury, and the 25-square-mile radius (65 km²) that was Petra. One can still make the long climb to the Monastery (the Ad Deir), the unfinished Nabatean tomb with a view of Wadi Arabah, the Dead Sea, and the Jordan River. The High Place on the 4,920-foot (1,500 m) Jabal Madbah harbors the most completely preserved cultic altar and sacrificial complex from the prebiblical Edomite period; this is approached from the Sacred Temenos gate, via a processional way lined with temples, tombs, obelisks, altars, fountains, and forts. The Nabatean pantheon had two principal gods. Dusares, the male god, was represented by a squared block of stone which served not only as the sacred image of the deity, but also as his abode and altar. Evidence indicates blood sacrifice occurred here, animal and perhaps human, symbolic of a mystical union with the god. Other ceremonies probably included goddess rituals to Al Uzza, often portrayed in her manifestation as a lion, and thought to have received the sacrifice of boys and girls in her role as the Morning Star. The deification of Nabatean kings is most likely the reason for so many carved tombs.

Many other monuments at Petra display the glory of humanity's art combined with nature; a good example is the fluted and reeded columns of the red, mauve, and silver-gray sandstone in the Triclinium, the place of funeral feasts probably dating from the Roman period. Kasr el Bint shows the elaborate decor of the architectural plasterwork of the Nabateans, much of which is now destroyed by time and the blackening of the caves by the campfires of the nomadic Bedouins who have used many caves in Petra as dwellings. It is only in the last ten years that the government of Jordan has succeeded in relocating these nomadic groups in nearby planned towns.

At Beida, a nearby smaller Nabatean settlement dating from 7000 BC, the distinctive black Bedouin tents and flocks of sheep can be seen scattered around the valley. The Bedouin are also found in **Wadi Rum**, the valley to the east; the contemporary Hashemite Kingdom of Jordan emerged from the World War II battles fought here. The 4000 BC Edomite community of Tawilan overlooks the town of **Wadi Mousa** (Moses' Valley), where the Spring of Moses, said to have sprung from the earth where Moses struck his staff, can be found. In the distance the summit of Jebel Horun (Mount Hor) marks the tomb of Aaron, brother of Moses.

Petra started to decline in the second century AD when the Romans controlled the trade routes via Palmyra to the north. Damascus and Baghdad then thrived, and while Petra remained a caravan stop until the early sixteenth century, it disappeared for three hundred years until it was rediscovered in 1812. Today it is a deserted but elegant remnant of antiquity, a pink oasis in a brown desert, one of the most exotic and mysterious sites we have visited.

Photo Tips   *Petra*

Petra is a photographer's paradise. Everywhere you turn there are colors, textures, and forms beckoning to be photographed; allowing enough time is the key. Because so many of the best shapes and colors are found in the caves carved out of the cliff, a tripod and long shutter speeds are necessary for these locations of subdued light. I found that the simplest way to proceed was to set my lens for the desired

The Pharaoh's Treasury, Petra, Jordan, December 1988/ Sacred Earth, *p. 47*

exposure and depth of field, place my camera on automatic exposure mode, and let the built-in meter determine the required shutter time. With ISO 50 or ISO 64 film, the exposures at f22 would often require durations of one or two minutes. If I wanted to repeat another exposure in the same light I would time the automatic exposure, then place the shutter speed knob on "T." For each subsequent exposure I would lock in the shutter with my cable release for the same duration as that established by the automatic exposure time. By resorting to the "T" setting, you are not relying on your camera battery, thus adding significantly to its life if you are doing a lot of long exposures. Because of the way many color films react to long shutter speeds (longer than one second), there is a tendency for the film to receive less exposure (and thus appear darker) than the meter would indicate. The longer the exposure, the more pronounced is this effect. Consequently you may want to make your exposures longer using a rule of thumb such as this:

Meter Calls for:	You Expose at:
1 sec	1 sec
3 sec	4 sec
5 sec	7 sec
10 sec	15 sec
30 sec	50 sec
1 min	2 min
15 min	1 hour

Different films require different treatment so experiment by trying several shutter times and noting the one you prefer. Because I often prefer my exposures on the dark side anyway (to maximize color saturation), I will sometimes refrain from adding the extra time and thus achieve the desired underexposed effect.

Israel

JERUSALEM

December 24 ... Christmas was ushered in with a candlelight service in a sixth-century Byzantine church on Mount Nebo in Jordan, overlooking the Judean Hills of the Promised Land. There was no star to follow to Bethlehem this year—the heavens had opened with the worst rain storm in twenty years pounding on the tin roof of the church, and the wind howled and tried to blow us down to the Jordan Valley. There was also no road open to Bethlehem—our visas were delayed, so the Allenby Bridge to the West Bank was closed to us.

Jerusalem, one of the holiest cities in the world, is the home and crossroads for three major religions: Judaism, Christianity, and Islam. The city is steeped in religious history, the skyline dominated by domes and steeples, and its back streets laden with religious momentos.

Travel Tips

See section on Galilee for access from the west. From Jordan, the procedure is complex but not difficult. The issue is to avoid having an Israeli stamp on your passport, which would prohibit future access to any Arab country. The Ministry of the Interior in Jordan therefore issues separate permits as travel documents, which are then stamped by both countries. Do not allow Israeli authorities to stamp your passport or list camera equipment as they wanted to do in ours. The application in Amman requires two passport pictures and two days minimum to process. We found out too late that a good travel agent could have expedited it (ask at one of the large hotels), including picking up the permits from the ministry which is closed Fridays, the Moslem holy day; the Allenby Bridge, the crossover point to the west bank, is closed at 1:00 PM daily and all day Saturday, the Jewish Shabat. U.S. and British consulates are closed Sunday.

A comfortable thirty-passenger bus leaves Amman for the Allenby Bridge at 7:00 AM and will pick up at major hotels if booked ahead. You cannot cross the bridge by taxi or bus. A one-hour ride through the Jordan Valley brought us to the official green buildings where we de-bused with our luggage and gave up our passports and permits for perusal by the Jordanians. We then took another bus across the short bridge to be met by Israeli officials. Each passenger was individually questioned and searched, entry forms were completed, all luggage was scanned and thoroughly searched, and cameras were checked for bombs by the owner taking a picture of the ceiling. No knives are allowed if the blade is more than 5 inches (13 cm) long, so our decorative Bedouin souvenir was confiscated.

Local Resources

We changed money at the border, shared a taxi for the thirty-minute ride into Jerusalem, and stayed at several hotels on the Mount of Olives. The Grand Palace Hotel, managed by Palestinian Christians, is close to the Damascus Gate, moderately priced, and has balconies overlooking the old city; PO Box 19143, Jerusalem; Tel: 271–126. If you want western-style luxury, the Intercontinental Hotel—7 Arches has a superb view; PO Box 19585, Jerusalem 91190; Tel: 282551; Fax: 285384. All hotels bill in U.S. dollars and add a healthy VAT (Value Added Tax); we were not given the option of paying in sheckels which was unfortunate as the exchange rate varied by more than twenty points when we were there.

There is good local bus service around Jerusalem as well as a multitude of tours, but we found it easiest to rent a car for our excursions. Rentals are busy so it is wise to reserve through Avis, 12 Hamasger Street, Tel Aviv, Israel 67774; Tel: (03) 384242; Telex: 341372; Fax: (03) 371169. Beware of one-way streets and many street names in Hebrew; it is easy to get lost and go in circles, although driving is not difficult. Taxi service was sometimes sporadic due to the Intifada (protest), and both Israeli and Palestinian drivers were often reluctant to enter each other's areas. The Tourist Information Center near the Jaffa Gate provides a wealth of help. The YMCA at PO Box 294, 26 King David Street, Jerusalem, Israel 91002; Tel: (02) 227111; Telex: 25247 YMCAW in the new town (across from the illustrious King David Hotel) offers excellent accommodation and sports facilities, as well as two informative multimedia shows on Israel and the Holy Land. Especially in the old city, we were frequently hustled off the street and urged to buy, as the economy is marginal and dollars are in demand. The black market is active and obvious, with good rates and seemingly little risk (although not recommended).

The Sacred Environs

Old **Jerusalem** is surrounded by sixteenth-century walls penetrated by eight gates. The ancient walkways are convoluted and poorly marked so a good map is useful. The city is divided into quarters, with much of the area taken up with religious structures and the many shops that keep this place a beehive of activity.

The glory of the old city is its buildings. The shining gold **Dome of the Rock** mosque with its mosaic ceiling and gorgeous inlaid pillars was built around the huge rock from which Mohammed is said to have made his nocturnal visit to heaven. This rock is second only to Mecca and Medina as a Moslem shrine and is also claimed by Christians and Jews as the site of Armageddon, the final struggle before the Second Coming. The nearby **El Aqsa** mosque, with its plain white arches, is afire with light streaming through the multicolored stained-glass windows which adorn every wall and echo the seemingly endless variegated patterns of Persian rugs covering every inch of floor. These two buildings on **Mount Moriah** (or the Temple Mount or Zion, the Hebrew symbol of piety and devotion) in the southwest quarter are on the site considered to be the traditional place where Abraham prepared to sacrifice his son, Isaac, and where Solomon's Temple and Herod's second temple were destroyed, leaving only the western wall intact. Also known as the **Wailing Wall**, the **Western Wall** is the most sacred place of Judaism, and is always attended by people in prayer. The historical vying for this site still fuels the fire between Jewish and Moslem factions.

The **Church of the Holy Sepulchre** is one of the most sacred Christian sites in the old city, the reconstructed, twelfth-century crusader basilica situated on the site of an early Roman temple to Venus. Located at the culmination of the Via Dolorosa (Way of Sorrows), this traditional site of the crucifixion and resurrection of Christ is marked by this massive church that exudes a powerful feeling, its ornate decor, holy relics, and strong scent of incense accompanied by the constant murmur of prayers, song, and tour guides. The queue to enter the tomb lit by perpetual candlelight is often long, as pilgrims wait to honor the place where tradition says Christ's body was laid to rest after the crucifixion. At that time this site would have been outside the city walls and is thought to have included Calvary.

Outside the old city, the **Garden Tomb** is one of the most rejuvenating havens we found on our whole journey. One block up Nablus Street from the bus depot on Sultan Suleiman Street, this private garden is tucked away from one of the busiest areas of town. The gentle caretakers and tranquil garden make it feel like a true resting place. Thought by some Christian Protestant groups to be the tomb of Joseph of Arimathea where Jesus was laid to rest, it is preserved as a Christian center, a place of reflection and quiet meditation.

More than any religious structure, the **Garden of Gethsemane**, another peaceful haven, fostered for us the sense of tragedy and martyrdom that marks so much of the religious history of this city. Doctrines aside, this garden has an ancient feeling; the tortuous faces created in the bark of its elderly gnarled and blackened olive trees somehow express the agony of Christ more than any other symbol. The adjacent Church of All Nations is a study in simplicity and beauty, built over the Rock of Agony where Christ was said to have prayed before his arrest. Above the garden gates, we continued to walk up the hill to another garden created by donations from the American Jewish community. Spacious and welcoming, this is one of few areas around Jerusalem that has a feeling of openness and of nature, with views over the ancient walled city. Continuing up the road to the summit of the Mount of Olives, we came to the Church of the Ascension.

The **Mount of Olives** hardly looks like a mountain, being more of a hill and now covered with buildings and ancient cemeteries. We were told that the cemeteries are frequently raided and desecrated, adding to the sorrow we felt in this area. The view from the lookout in front of the Intercontinental Hotel is spectacular at sunset, as attested by the busloads of holy men and tourists who are also given the opportunity for a camel ride by the local hucksters.

Bethlehem, a half-hour bus ride from Jerusalem, is a crowded hill-top village, with no sign of shepherds tending flocks although a traditional Shepherd's Field is designated nearby. Manger Square was almost deserted on the day after Christmas, with tour buses conspicuously absent. Traditional Christmas Eve services had been cancelled due to political upheaval, and soldiers were still much in evidence in the streets. Shared by three Christian denominations (Roman Catholic, Greek Orthodox, and Armenian Orthodox), the **Church of the Nativity** was still crowded on December 26, especially at the underground Grotto of the Nativity where pilgrims prayed over the plastic doll set behind an iron grate. The service we attended in another grotto chapel was a warm and compassionate experience led by South American, Spanish-speaking pilgrims who exchanged peace greetings with us.

The **Dead Sea** is an hour's drive southeast. This is the lowest body of fresh water in the world, lying 1,299 feet (396 m) below the Mediterranean. Famous for its healing spas such as Ein Gedi, it is a prime tourist destination in the summer. Further south is **Masada**, the site of the mass suicide of 960 Jews in 73 AD, in their last stand against the Romans.

Returning to Jerusalem, we are reminded that this name means Foundation of Shalem, later interpreted as Shalom, the Hebrew word for peace; hence it is now called the City of Peace. It is, however, thought to have been an ancient cult center even older than that described in nineteenth-century BC texts. The Ark of the Covenant, the symbol of Judaism, was placed here by King David in the tenth century BC when he conquered the Jebusites and established Jerusalem (Mount Moriah) as the Hebrew spiritual capital and messianic city. For Christians it is the spiritual symbol of the Kingdom of Heaven. For Moslems it is the symbolic "furthest mosque" from Mecca. It seems that Jerusalem has been under seige almost since the beginning of time, but still rises up like the eternal sea, a haven of spiritual timelessness. With this wealth of spiritual energy, one would hope that someday it really will become a city of peace.

Photo Tips   *Garden of Gethsemane*

A photograph that is a good likeness is a bonus, but an image that symbolizes the meaning a place holds for you can be a treasure. That's how I felt when I saw the results of my photography in the Garden of Gethsemane. I waited for a rainy day to photograph, to reflect the somber mood of that sorrowful day when Christ gave himself up to the Roman soldiers. The olive trees took on a sinister appearance, and I searched for those shapes that best characterized the theme. I underexposed each frame by one to one-and-a-half exposure settings in order to darken the tones and increase the somber mood. Then when I found a single leaf, lush and green against the threatening shapes of the bark, I felt that here I had found the ideal expression.

Learning the significance of historical sites and the stories that have brought them to prominence can give direction to our photographic quest for meaningful pictures.

*Detail of bark, olive tree, dieffenbachia leaf in foreground, Garden of Gethsemane, Jerusalem, Israel, January 1989/*Sacred Earth, *p. 228*

GALILEE

January 10 . . . past fertile valleys carved into lush fields of geometrically patterned groves of orange, lemon, and grapefruit in crisscrossed grids over gently rolling knolls, interspersed with thick clusters of low-growing palms

draped with bright blue plastic bags enveloping their bounty of unripe fruit.
Then look upward to see rock-strewn arid hills and appreciate the toil and
love poured into this land.

Northern Israel is a place of historical miracles of biblical times placed against the backdrop of five thousand years of culture. The map reads like the Hebrew scriptures and Christian gospels, every turn in the road imbued with sacred history.

Travel Tips

Tel Aviv and Jerusalem are the entry points for international flights from Europe and North America served by El Al (the official Israeli airline), Canadian Airlines, Lufthansa, KLM, British Airways, Pan Am, Swissair, and TWA. El Al does not fly on the Sabbath (sunset Friday to sunset Saturday) which of course will vary in different time zones. Security is stringent: check-in time is two hours ahead; expect thorough bag searches and in-depth questioning about who packed your bags and when, and whether you are carrying packages for anyone else (don't!). You will also be asked to prove that your camera is not a bomb by taking a picture of the ceiling. In these days of airline terrorism, such safeguards gave us an assurance not felt on any other international flight. Departure check-ins may be gone through in Haifa the night before; your bags are then transported under guard to Tel Aviv airport.

Getting around Israel is relatively easy on local buses or tours, or by private car. We rented a car for maximum flexibility while touring around Galilee. Roads are well maintained but buy a good map; although tourist attractions are marked with orange signs in Hebrew and English, other signs are primarily in Hebrew and do not give much warning for turnoffs.

Food and accommodation are generally expensive. Breakfast is often included: creamy yogurt, cheeses, eggs, breads, vegetables such as cucumbers, tomatoes, green and red peppers, olives, and often pickled fish. There are few restaurants on the road, so pack a lunch from the local market or rely on hotels in major centers.

Safety

Soldiers and evidence of war are everywhere, in the form of monuments to the fallen, and a landscape of ever-present barbed wire atop fences or rolled like tumbleweed. It is wise to obey signs such as "No Photography" or "Danger—Mines." One does become accustomed to these sights which evoked for us more of a feeling of security than terror. Under normal circumstances, it is safer to travel in Israel than in many large North American cities! Avoid areas of local skirmishes, which are clearly reported in daily news. It is unfortunate that press reports of the situation in Israel have kept many tourists from enjoying this country's splendor and genuine hospitality. The aftermath of the Gulf War (1991) may modify these comments.

Local Resources

We made Tiberias our center, and stayed at two delightful places: the Gilad Hotel, a quaint budget-style family-run hotel (with excellent breakfasts) nestled in a grove of trees at the south end of town across from the lake, and within easy walking distance to all tourist attractions. The adjacent Lakeview Chinese Restaurant is an added bonus, providing some of the best Chinese food we have ever enjoyed. Write Anne and Dov Tirosh, RH Hagalil 4, Tiberias, Israel 14200; Tel: (06) 720007; Telex: (06) 6715 (Att: Gilad). For luxury, the Laromme Hotel clings to the hillside like a white jewel, every room with fabulous views of the Sea of Galilee. It has a health club, which includes pools and tennis courts, topped off by excellent service and a great restaurant. Write Echad Ha-Am Street, Tiberias, Israel 1422; Tel: (06) 791888; Fax: (06) 722898. Car rental is available from Avis with multiple locations; reserve through 12 Hamasger Street, Tel Aviv, Israel 67774; Tel: (03) 384242; Telex: 341372; Fax: (03) 371169.

Sacred Galilee and the Golan Heights

The intersection of ancient cultural and religious history permeates this land known as the Levant, Canaan, and Palestine. Tiberias, one of four Jewish holy cities (including Jerusalem, Safed, and Hebron), was a center of cultural and spiritual activity, evidenced by the tombs of renowned religious scholars such as Maimonides and Rabbi Meir, the Illuminator. Now it is a major resort for water sports with luxurious beachside hotels and excellent restaurants featuring St. Peter's fish, indigenous to the Sea of Galilee which is really a large lake called Kinneret. A little more than a mile (2 km) south of Tiberias are the hottest mineral springs in Israel. Legend has it that they were created in 18 AD by King Solomon summoning devils to descend into the earth to heat the water, which subsequently healed ills from far and wide. Solomon wisely deafened the devils so they would not hear of his death and would continue to heat the water; today the medical clinic and health sanatorium are famous among the spas of Europe.

North of Tiberias are many Christian sites including Migdal, the home of Mary Magdalen; Tabgha, where Jesus miraculously fed the crowd with five loaves of bread and two fishes; and **Capernaum**, the site of Jesus' three-year ministry where He preached in the synagogue and performed many miracles. The exceptional stonework of the ruins of Capernaum is bathed with golden light and cascades of brilliantly colored bougainvillea harboring songbirds. Continuing around the lake, one sees vistas of reeds full of birds, several bathing areas with camping and amusement parks, and some of the oldest kibbutzim in Israel. Round the southern tip is Hammat Gader, another Old Testament site, now a large multipooled modern hot springs combined with an alligator farm! This road cuts through the southern slopes of the Golan Heights, overlooking the Yarmuk River, a tributary of the Jordan, with views of old Gilead (in present-day Jordan), evoking memories of the ancient Baths of Elijah. Nearby is a pilgrim baptism site at Kibbutz Kinneret in place of the original site of the baptism of Jesus by John the Baptist, near Jericho, currently inaccessible on the frontier between Israel and Jordan.

The mountains and valleys of northern Israel echo with ancient and modern history. Leaving the Sea of Galilee, the road going north near Capernaum leads to the Mount of Beatitudes where Jesus preached the Sermon on the Mount. Nearby Rosh Pinna on Mount Canaan was the first modern Jewish settlement in Galilee in 1882. Turning west, a short drive leads to the mountaintop retreat of **Safed** (Zefat), a center of rabbinical learning as early as the first century AD. One of Judaism's holiest cities, Safed was the heart of Kabbalistic (mystical) studies and Hebrew learning, resulting in the printing of the first Hebrew book in 1563. Now an orthodox religious center and artistic colony, Safed is the highest town in Israel, 2,790 feet (850 m) above the Jordan Valley; the quality of light here is truly pristine, giving a sense of the divine as the mists drape the surrounding mountains and lowlands.

Continuing north on the main road brings one to Tel Hazor, a major archaeological site dating to 3000 BC. Further on is the Huleh (Hula) Valley Nature Reserve, a former swamp that has been reclaimed by rigorous draining and planting of eucalyptus since 1948. It is now a haven for many exotic species of birds and animals, and one of the most fertile valleys in Israel. North and east of Quiryat Shemona is **Tel Dan**, the five-thousand-year-old site of the ancient city of Leshem. It is here that Jeroboam, King of Israel, erected one of his many altars in worship of the golden calf. Now a nature reserve, it is known as the Garden of Eden, a magical place of deep dark forests of gnarled serpentine growth penetrated by gurgling blind springs and babbling brooks melding into rushing torrents. Arab legends say Mohammed stopped here with his disciples to drink the refreshing waters; their staffs sprung roots, making this a sanctuary to the Moslems.

Nearby is **Banias** (the Arabic mispronounciation of Paneas), the ancient pagan center of cult worship to Pan, Greek god of the forests, shepherds, and wild places. In the first century BC this site became a temple to Augustus Caesar, built by Herod and later dedicated to Caesarea Phillipi. This heartland of paganism was chosen by the disciple Peter to declare his faith to Jesus; later it became a crusader town, and also a Moslem shrine to the prophet Elijah. Here, deep within the cave of Pan, one can almost hear his sprightly music as the cool water from **Mount Hermon** emerges to form pools and waterfalls, finally coalescing with two other tributaries to become the holy Jordan River, flowing south into the Sea of Galilee and the Dead Sea.

Continuing east past the crusader castle of Nimrod is the Arab Druse village of Magdal Shams, on the side of Mount Hermon where people still retain Syrian citizenship. Considered by some to be the Mount of Transfiguration and place of miracles by Jesus, Mount Hermon is popular today as a ski resort.

Finally, turning south, the eucalyptus-lined roads of the lower Golan Heights wend through prehistoric areas around Gamla, past dolmens (burial markers) and stone circles thought to have been used for cosmic rituals reminiscent of Stonehenge. On return to Tiberias, one cannot help feeling that the impact of Galilee as sacred earth is strengthened by the diversity and historical longevity of all its spiritual places.

Photo Tips   *Spring of Pan*

A day spent in a secluded glade affords not only the ambience of a sheltered and sacred place, but also a chance to enjoy and observe the changing light throughout the day. Staying put and becoming aware of subtlety is the best prerequisite to good photography. Here at the edge of the Spring of Pan, the leaves draped on the water's surface were motionless, giving me an opportunity for longer shutter speeds of 1/4 sec and 1/2 sec. The small lens opening (f22) and a focusing distance of about 3 feet (1 m) gave maximum depth of field, allowing foreground leaves and distant scenery to achieve maximum sharpness. Wide-angle lenses (here I used a 20mm) are wonderful for effecting a great depth of field, but to produce the ultimate feeling

*Spring of Pan, Banias, Israel, January 1989/*Sacred Earth, *p. 67*

of perspective, it is important (as I did here) to place the camera close to the foreground objects, making them appear relatively large. The size distortion then gives the appearance of a great depth, inviting the viewer into the realism of the setting.

As with almost all long exposures, the tripod becomes a necessity to keep the camera perfectly still during the exposure. By removing the center post from the tripod I was able to place the camera at a relatively low height, thus getting closer to the foreground leaves. As water absorbs about one f-stop of light, the reflected light from the surface is one exposure setting darker than the landscape being reflected. A scene in the shade, therefore, is actually about the same brightness as a reflection of sunlit material, making a good overall exposure relatively easy to accomplish. By remaining at the spring until sunset, the entire low land was covered in shadow while the colorful distant cliff face, receiving the last warm rays of direct sunlight, gave the Spring of Pan its radiant glow.

HAIFA

January 16 . . . We could feel the sense of protection and renewal these gardens must have provided for Baha'u'llah. The joy and peace engendered by the closeness to this part of divine creation molded by human hands felt like a spiritual renaissance. Even the pouring rain was welcome as it saturated the eucalyptus bark, and produced van Gogh-like color and pattern for Courtney to photograph as we huddled together under the huge umbrella I held.

Haifa is the seat of the Baha'i World Centre. In the middle of a busy seaport and industrial city, the gleaming white Universal House of Justice towers above lush gardens and stately pines on the side of Mount Carmel, offering a haven for Baha'i pilgrims who come worldwide to honor their prophet at the adjacent Shrine of the Bab.

Travel Tips

Haifa is a two-hour drive north of Tel Aviv, on a good road past the Michael Maa'gan Nature Reserve and kibbutz, and Caesarea, the site of Herod's 20 BC Roman city, which became a thirteenth-century crusader stronghold at the edge of the Mediterranean. We drove from Tiberias via Nazareth, the city inhabited since the second millenium BC and the site of the annunciation to Mary of the birth of her son Jesus, and where He grew to manhood. It is now a bustling Arab city that attracts Christian pilgrims from afar.

Local Resources

In Haifa we stayed on Mount Carmel. The Dan Panorama, at 107 Hanassi Ave., Haifa, Israel 34641; Tel: (04) 352–222; Telex: 471195; Fax: (04) 352235 offers efficient service, pool, and health club in an elegant setting. The nearby Nof Hotel, 101 Hanassi Ave., PO Box 6422, Haifa, Israel; Tel: (04) 88731 has spectacular views, and was recently renovated with spacious rooms and an outdoor pool. Both are close to shopping, cafes, restaurants, and a post office. We loved the Ristorante Italiano, family operated with home-style food, at 121 Hanassi Blvd, Carmel Center, Haifa; Tel: 381336. The Baha'i gardens and International Center have various opening times and access for tourists; for information contact the Baha'i Office of Public Information, PO Box 155, Haifa, Israel 31001; Tel: 520043.

The Baha'i Gardens

The Baha'i statement on nature declares "its essence is the embodiment of the creator . . . the grandeur and diversity of the natural world are the purposeful reflection of the majesty and bounty of God . . . therefore nature is to be respected and protected, as a divine trust for which we are answerable." And, it seems that everything the Baha'is touch becomes fertile. Because Israel is so small there are few green spaces created for enjoyment rather than food production. The Baha'i Gardens on Mount Carmel are like an oasis, a jewel of serenity amidst crowded buildings and noisy streets; the abundance of colorful flowers and winding paths is a haven for the two hundred thousand annual visitors.

An hour north of Haifa is the four-thousand-year-old Canaanite and Phoenician port city of Acre (Akka) which became the capital of the crusader kingdom after the fall of Jerusalem, and where the Baha'i founder, Baha'u'llah, was imprisoned for two years after his exile from Persia. The nearby gardens at Misre (Mazra'a) and Ridvan offer the same serenity that Baha'u'llah might have felt when he meditated there more than one hundred years ago.

But the Baha'i Gardens at Bahji are even more spectacular. Called the "Place of Delight," the focal point is the simple shrine with Baha'u'llah's tomb, filled with 15-foot (5 m) ferns and the sweet scent of roses and jasmine as the golden glow of candles flickers over the ornate Persian rugs. Nearby is the mansion where he spent his last days in 1892, now a sacred museum open only to Baha'i pilgrims. This planned garden is like a mini-Versailles but feels like another Garden of Eden, with fruit-laden trees, tall evergreens, and an array of flowers, the colors of which include the complete artist's palette. A small inner courtyard and pilgrims' house welcomes those who come from all corners of the earth to honor their founder.

Photo Tips   *The Baha'i Gardens*

It is a popular belief that the best time to photograph is on a bright sunny day. In reality, direct midday sunlight is often harsh, causing overly bright highlights and distracting black shadows that do not depict the joyous feelings of being out in the sunshine. An overcast or rainy day, however, provides rich saturated colors and even tones devoid of shadows, allowing color film to easily and effectively record the range of tones. Often, I will wait until the heaviest rains abate, then head out with tripod and umbrella.

*Baha'i Gardens at Bahji, near Akka, Israel, January 1989/*Sacred Earth, *p. 158*

Here, in the Baha'i Gardens at Bahji, a gentle rain blessed the grounds with an even light; I made many exposures of the gardens that day, but my favorite was this orange tree on the lawn outside the tomb of Baha'u'llah. For me the single orange fallen from its branch symbolized the death of the leader, yet, like Baha'u'llah, the lone small fruit seemed to influence all around it, and the orange color contrasted with the green of the garden made the setting appear all the more lush and nourishing.

Keep in mind that the next rainy or somber day can provide a garden of opportunities. Point your camera down, avoid the colorless sky, and immerse yourself in a magical world of nature's finest artistry.

Continental Europe

GREECE

January 15 . . . The halcyon days of an early spring smiled down on us, giving us renewed vigor to explore some of the secrets of the classical world. A visual feast awaited, from the spectacular sunset and rise of the full moon over Sounion, to the mist-shrouded oracle at Delphi, the dramatic pinnacles of Meteora, and the delicate palette of geometric landscapes reflected in the Spring of Daphne at the foot of sacred Mount Olympus.

The sacred sites of Greece offer a wealth of experience to the spiritual traveller, awakening echoes of the pantheon of gods that has influenced and penetrated western mythology more than any other legacy of the classical world.

Travel Tips

Athens is served by major airlines from North America, Europe, and Asia, as well as rail and bus services from all parts of the continent, and ferries from Italy, Yugoslavia, France, Israel, and Egypt. Travel within Greece is relatively easy by air, with extensive bus and rail lines providing routes highly travelled by locals and tourists alike. The Greek National Tourist Organization has many offices abroad and throughout Greece. Their head office is at 2 Amerikas Street, Athens; Tel: (01) 3223111; Telex: 5832. Car travel is popular and was our choice to provide the flexibility we required; reserve through Avis, 46 Queen Amalia Avenue, Athens, Greece 10558; Tel: (32) 3224951; Telex: 21–5568 AVIS GR. Roads are generally good but *many* signs are in the Greek alphabet, so carry a good map and learn the symbols for your destination! There is a plethora of tours available to all major sites including the islands of the Aegean. Write CHAT Tours, 4 Stadiou Street, Athens; Tel: 3230827.

Local Resources

Many hotels in smaller places were closed in the winter (November to March). In Delphi, a prime tourist site with lots of hotels, guest houses, and restaurants, the hilltop Amalia Hotel was open and comfortable, with a nice view. Write Amalia Hotel Delphi, Delphi, Greece 33054; Tel: (0265) 82101; or contact central reservations in Athens, Tel: (32) 37301; Telex: 215161 AMAL GR. Kalambaka offered several small hotels as well as camping (closed for the winter); the monasteries were open although hours varied and there was a dress code. Generally, visiting hours are 8:00 AM to 12:00 noon and 3:00 to 6:00 PM (winter hours are 9:00 AM to 1:00 PM and 3:00 to 5:00 PM; closed on Tuesday and Wednesday). The Grand Meteora, the largest and loftiest, is closed on Wednesday. The Barlaam and the Ayia Triadha are most popular to visit. The beach resort areas along the northern highway past Mount Olympus, with their views of the Aegean Sea, and the villages specializing in mountain climbing also had a variety of accommodation and restaurants. For climbing information, write the Hellenic Federation of Mountaineering Clubs, Karageargi Servias 7, Athens 126; Tel: 3234555. Salonika is a large modern city with a pleasant boardwalk by the sea, many hotels and tourist attractions, and an acclaimed archaeological museum. This is the northern departure point for rail service to Yugoslavia and central Europe and eastward to the monastic community of Mount Athos, an exclusively male enclave on an isthmus with twenty monasteries. Visiting permits should be requested well in advance and are obtained through the Ministry of Foreign Affairs, Directorate of Churches, No. 2 Zalokosta Street, Athens; Tel: 3626894. Outside of Athens, Delphi, and Salonika, English may be minimal but the average traveller's needs will be met with a bit of pantomime and pidgin-Greek.

A permit is needed to do photography outside regular visiting hours at Sounion and Delphi. We contacted our embassy in Athens who helped to facilitate this through the Archeological Institute. It is wise to start this process before arriving in Athens.

Sacred Sites

The **Parthenon**, probably the most visited place in Greece, is the ultimate classical monument. The fourth in a series of temples built on this site, it had been the abode of early kings, which was left to the gods in the sixth century BC, and then rebuilt by Pericles a century later, in 438 BC. This became the home of the goddess Athena, who had been worshipped for ten centuries as the goddess of war and the personification of wisdom. The Parthenon is the tallest building on the highest point of the Acropolis, and although the wooden roof is long gone, the white marble that still stands is testimony to its former glory. The ravages of time, earthquakes, and contemporary air pollution have led authorities to rope off the area, allowing it to be viewed only from a distance. No longer can one lean against the mighty pillars and watch the sunset, although this is still a popular site to honor the sun god's passage into night.

Forty-three miles (70 km) to the south, at **Sounion**, stands another magnificent temple, built in 444 BC and dedicated to the mighty god of the sea, Poseidon. Poseidon's temple, sitting 200 feet (60 m) above the sea, was a dazzling white beacon to sailors braving the rough waters caused by Poseidon's storms. The ancient Greeks also called him "earth shaker," attributing the frequent earthquakes of the area to the mighty god ruling from his golden palace in the depths. Perhaps he is to be blamed for the fourteenth-century BC violent quake centered around the island of Thera (Santorini) that claimed most of the Minoan treasures of Knossos on the island of Crete. Today, Poseidon is honored with a continuous stream of tour buses, especially on Sunday, and for the time-honored spectacular sunset on this southernmost point of the Grecian peninsula. Neither the sunsets nor the tourists stay long, but if you come early or linger past the magic moment, you may feel the power of this sacred place, and your breath may be inspired like Lord Byron's "mutual murmurs with the waves."

In the hinterland of central Greece lies the celebrated home of the sun god Apollo and the most famous oracle of the ancient world. This is **Delphi**, the legendary center of the world, proven by two eagles which, when released by Zeus from opposite ends of the earth, met here at the point marked by the omphalos, or navel stone, a replica of which can be seen in the nearby archaeological museum. But the sacred ground of Delphi was an even earlier place of cult worship, known as Pytho, originally dedicated to the earth goddess Gaia (also called Gè). Apollo, however, banished by Zeus from Mount Olympus, claimed Delphi by killing Python, the serpent who guarded Gaia's oracle, and setting up his own Pythia, a priestess. His oracle influenced the decisions of many Athenian city-states and powerful people who came from afar to purify themselves at the Castalian Spring before the rituals began. The Pythia sat on a three-legged stool over a vent in the earth, inhaling intoxicating vapors which would put her in a trance of prophecy; her babblings were then interpreted by a priest. The Delphic oracle flourished as a political tool until the second century BC when the Romans took over, and was finally abolished by Theodosius in 385 AD.

The ruins of Delphi are separated above and below by the modern road to the village. The Sacred Way winds up the hill, past largely unidentifiable temple ruins, including the Sanctuary of Earth or Ge-Themis, to the Temenos, the Sanctuary of Apollo, thought to contain the underground chamber of the Adyton or inner shrine where the oracular chasm opened. Continuing uphill, the fourth-century BC amphitheater is evident, and nearby is the Fountain of Kassotis which fed the spring the Pythia drank from before prophesying. At the top is the seven-thousand-seat stadium, the rows of rough stone seats peeking through overgrown grass. From here a splendid view of the three restored pillars of the **Temple of Athena** can be seen far below the highway, overlooking the sacred plain stretching to Itea on the Gulf of Corinth. We could imagine the hordes of ancient worshippers rushing up from the port through the muted sea of green olive trees, eager to hear their future.

January is a good time to experience Delphi, uninterrupted by the endless flow of summer tour buses; the birds and sheep bells (and unfortunately the ever-present trucks gearing up and down the hill) are the only major disruptions to the altered state of a modern pilgrim. We enjoyed climbing the back streets high up the hillside where children played amidst colorful laundry and the last blooms of summer flowers. The view is spectacular, and the true feeling of Greece is found here, away from the tourist shops, watching the light behind sacred Mount Parnassos fade into the golden waters of the Gulf of Corinth.

Driving north over the high mountain passes glistening with olive trees and evergreens covered with a light dusting of snow, we passed through small villages best known for their resistance efforts during World War II. Then to Kalambaka, nestled at the base of the precipitous rocks suddenly thrusting up like exclamation marks from the flat Thessalonian plain, some so sheer they could have been sliced with a cleaver. Copper-colored leaves on dark gnarled shapes soften the harsh lines of the pointed rocks, atop which the monasteries of **Meteora** are perched like toy houses. At night they are reminiscent of the ghostlike shapes of Callanish in Scotland. The only sound is the wind carrying the tinkling of sheep bells through the crisscross grids of dried grapevines covering the valley floor. Obviously people respect the sign at the entrance of this sacred valley: "DO NOT SHOUT—Respect the Unequalled Character of the Place."

The earliest monastic community, dating from 1336 AD, also became a haven for refugees from later Turkish invasions. Original access to these perched monasteries was by a series of rope ladders which could be retracted, or by a net drawn up with a rope and windlass. These methods were largely replaced by steps cut in the 1920s, and by secure bridges, although the ropes are still sometimes used to bring up goods. The few nuns and priests who now live here were present the day we visited, completing the monastic service still ordained by the Orthodox Church, and opening the monasteries for the public to view the frescoes and gilded ikons still predominant in spiritual rituals.

The drive across the eastern Thessalonian plain is rather uninteresting, past power poles, small industrial towns, and spent cotton fields offering only white puff balls to the fences and roadsides. But suddenly, north of Larissa, the miragelike pyramidal shape of **Mount Olympus** rises from the Macedonian countryside. Unfortunately for us, continuously hazy weather obliterated any future view of this dramatic mountain residence of the gods. We had to be content with driving up to the snow line and negotiating our way past charming villages like Litokhoron, the principle center for climbing the massif, as we made our way alongside rugged fields on narrow roads claimed by herds of goats. These bearded fellows reminded us of Zeus and his powerful retinue of gods who engendered the same respect then, as now, in refusing us passage to the snowy peak. The Greek Alpine Club will provide guides and keys for their refuge huts for the climbing season in July and August; this is considered an arduous two-day climb. Traversing the high summits is only recommended for experienced mountaineers.

We chose to linger at the **Spring of Daphne**, and savor the palette of autumnal colors in the leaves floating downstream. The Vale of Tempe was the center of Apollo worship and home to the story of the tragic love of Apollo for Daphne, remembered in the legend of Cupid. Angered by Apollo, Cupid shot him with a golden arrow of love, while Daphne received a leaden arrow which repelled love. Even the mighty Apollo could not overcome Cupid's work and entice this forest nymph, who finally beseeched her father to destroy her beauty—the only way to allay Apollo's pursuit— which he did by turning her into a laurel tree. Daphne, the Greek word for laurel, has immortalized the unrequited love of one of the greatest gods of ancient Greece.

There are many other remnants of the worship of the old gods nearby. Dion is the site of a temple to Zeus which incorporates a sanctuary to Demeter and to Isis, as well as an altar to Aphrodite. Continuing on the northern road following the Aegean Sea, we arrived in the modern city of **Salonika**, the biblical town of Thessalonika, where St. Paul preached in 50 AD, and whose monuments illustrate ten centuries of Byzantine influence. Eastward is the peninsula containing the monasteries of Mount Athos which can only be visited with a special permit, and only by men. It seems that the goddesses prevailed only in ancient Greece!

Photo Tips   *The Parthenon*

The poor old Parthenon is being continuously repaired and restored. After circling the edifice I realized that there was only one angle that portrayed the Parthenon devoid of cranes, scaffolding, and ropes. Unfortunately the exact location needed was beyond the barrier that cordoned off the building from the thousands of daily tourists, each wanting a tangible brush with antiquity. Furthermore, two sentries, one at each end, stood guard as a warning to would-be trespassers.

If I got the picture, I mused, I would have to be extremely fast! I decided to wait an hour until the sun was lower and the light warmer. When the time was right I coupled a wide-angle lens to the camera, preset my focus, depth of field, and exposure, then boldly stepped over the barrier and took several steps forward. As I crouched, it was hard to ignore the piercing blast of a whistle that signalled my transgression. Click. I advanced the shutter and made a second exposure as I felt a strong hand land on my shoulder. There was no denying it. I had sinned! I quickly apologized and left without ceremony, my coveted frames safely secured in my camera. Only after I had completed my hasty exit did I offer a quick prayer of thanks to Athena, patron goddess of the Parthenon, and a prayer asking forgiveness for shooting without using a tripod.

*Detail of the Parthenon on the Acropolis, Athens, Greece, January 1989/*Sacred Earth, *p. 40*

I don't recommend defying local rules when you travel, but if you do, do it right! Make sure you have enough unexposed film in your camera, the right lens for the job, and as many controls preset as possible.

Photo Tips   *Delphi at Night*

When I have the opportunity, I like to photograph sacred places at night; the darkness, the stars, the moon, and the solitude all help to enhance the mystique and mystery of a place. On a rare occasion I have the opportunity to simultaneously photograph and just sit and commune with the spirit of the place by setting my camera for an hour-long exposure, then relaxing while the lens does the recording for me.

Temple of Athena and moon, Delphi, Greece, January 1989/ Sacred Earth, *p. 43*

When I was at Delphi, a full moon set in the western sky while I was photographing the Temple of Athena at dawn. This is the ideal time to photograph the moon juxtaposed with an appropriate foreground, in this case, the Temple of Athena. The tones of the columns reflecting the morning light are only a shade darker than the western sky, and the brightness of the moon, muted by a thin layer of mist, only slightly greater than the tone of the sky. Only one day each month, one or two mornings after the actual date of the full moon is this special condition possible, the thin morning haze providing the ideal tonality of the moon. The moon is behaving itself, I murmur, as I expose normally for the sky tones, confident that the detail and color will record well on the temple columns and the moon itself will appear as a tiny accent to the composition. Following and acting on the cycles of the moon is the most fundamental technique to assure your presence at this most sacred cosmic ceremony.

THE ALPS

February 5 . . . From the air, the Alps evoke an image of chaos and terror, their jagged peaks looking more terrifying than pristine, a reminder of the belief that they harbor demons. Overcoming this horror, one can then see them as symbols of perfection and places of inspiration, the closest places on earth that one can attempt to contact the divine creation in the heavens above.

The Alps have been seen as home of many gods, both demonic and benevolent. Whatever your perspective, they are places of high physical and emotional energy, invoking awe and inspiration, and a feeling of oneness with the world.

Travel Tips and Local Resources

The Alps stretch across Europe from southern France to northern Yugoslavia via Switzerland, Italy, Liechtenstein, Germany, and Austria. Some peaks are accessible only to experienced climbers, while others attract many recreational tourists. See your travel agent for information about individual countries.

In the lowlands of France, all the sacred sites are accessible by car or local transportation from Paris. All areas have excellent hotels and pensions, including some delightful chateaus offering old world hospitality. Everything in France is expensive; camping is a popular cheaper alternative and many sites rent cabins or caravans, have hot water, cooking facilities, and restaurants. The Automobile Association publishes an excellent handbook on camping in Europe, or write the French Tourist Office, 178 Picadilly, London, WIVOAL England; Tel: (01) 491-7622.

The prehistoric caves at Les Eyzies are controlled; the original cave of Lascaux is officially closed to the public except for five visitors per day. For reservations write Direction des Antiquités, Préhistoriques D'Aquitaine, 6 Bis, Cours de Gourge, 33074 Bordeaux Cédex, France; Tel: 56-44-82-73. A section of the original cave has been recreated nearby and called Lascaux II; this facsimile is of excellent quality and there are many other sites to see, although it should be noted that photography is not allowed in any of the caves.

The prehistoric caves of Altamira are located near Santander on the north coast of Spain. Permission to view can be requested from Centro de Investigacion de Altamira, 39330 Santillana del Mar, Cantabria, Spain.

The Maltese islands are a popular holiday spot especially for the British. Scheduled and charter flights are available from many European airports. Several ferries operate from Marseilles (France), and from Livorno and Reggio de Calabria (Italy).

From the High Places to the European Lowlands

Mountain reverence is long standing and is found in all cultures of the world. Contemporary use of mountains as recreational places is a recent phenomenon, as most mountain ranges are represented in local mythology as the home of the gods, imbued with spirits that invoke terror and awe and command honor and obeisance. In the first century BC, the **Alps** were home to the preRoman Celtic god of the sky; a temple attributed to him was found on the summit of Great Saint Bernard Pass on France's 15,781-foot (4,810 m) Mont Blanc, where this Celtic benevolent spirit was transformed by the later Christians into a manifestation of

Satan. Exorcism was considered necessary, and Mont Blanc was subsequently known as Mont Maudit, "The Accursed Mountain," until the eighteenth century when outsiders renamed it Mont Blanc, "The White Mountain," in recognition of its pristine snows and inner light symbolic of a sublime sense of the infinite (Bernbaum, 1990, p. 124). Many other pagan monuments were similarly destroyed by Christians who replaced early sites with churches; the twelfth-century chapel to the Virgin Mary, our Lady of the Snows, on 11,685-foot (3,562 m) Roche Melon is still the site of an annual pilgrimage which is often cancelled because of bad weather on the summit. In the thirteenth century, the Alps and Pyrenees were considered haunts of witches, and spirits of the dead were said to wander there, a belief still popular in some Swiss villages today. Until the late sixteenth century, climbing Lausanne's Mount Pilatus was forbidden (and punished) for fear of disturbing the ghost of the evil spirit of Pontius Pilate whose body was believed to have been deposited in the pond near the summit, after being rejected elsewhere. Until the late eighteenth century, mountains were also thought to be the lairs of dragons, which were listed in an extensive Swiss catalogue. The Matterhorn was also avoided as spirits like the devil were said to reside at the summit and throw down rocks to keep people away.

By the late eighteenth century, the world view of the Romantic writers and poets finally overcame the earlier attitude of mountains as symbols of chaos and blights on the landscape. Mountains were subsequently recognized as manifestations of divinity; the sport of alpinism grew out of this change of attitude and facilitated many adventurers to seek a spiritual experience in the high places.

The Alps and other European mountains are popular today with both the secular and spiritual seeker. Mont Blanc is still considered one of the climbing world's greatest challenges, as is the north face of the Eiger, "The Ogre," that never fails to stir up terror in those seeking its summit. For the pilgrim, Greece's Mount Athos, the home of a strict Byzantine monastic community, is only open to male visitors. In contrast, Ireland's Croagh Patrick welcomes hundreds of pilgrims, and while Spain's Montserrat hosts an annual pilgrimage to the Virgin Mary, it also echoes with the legend of the Holy Grail—as does Britain's Glastonbury Tor. In Poland, a million pilgrims gather every July for the nine-day walk to the Shining Mountain of Our Lady of Czestochowa, the Black Madonna, who is regarded as the Queen and national symbol of the country.

Tourism and mountaineering bring a variety of pilgrims to the Alps, perhaps under the guise of adventure or sport, but often with an underlying hope of touching the mystery and power of the mountains. Climbers sometimes speak of mystical experiences as they exert themselves to their utmost physical, mental, and emotional capacity to overcome gravity (and perhaps the spirits?). It has been said that the real benefit of the sacred is only perceived when effort is involved—hence the need to step over sills into Chinese temples. (Does a cable car negate this benefit?) But perhaps it is mostly an effort of the mind that is necessary to step onto the temple of the mountain, open to the awe as well as the terror of the height, both of which must be faced and balanced in order to perceive the presence of the divine light.

Some of the natural grandeur of the Alps is echoed in the grottoes found in the lowlands of Europe. The most famous of these is **Lascaux**, where the life and spirit of Paleolithic man is recorded in paintings dated to at least seventeen thousand years ago. These prehistoric artists made use of the natural curvatures in the underground rock to tell the story of their world in some of the most incredible art known in the world today. The many decorated caves around Les Eyzies, near Perigord in the southwestern French province of Bordeaux, mark this as the birthplace of art as an expression of an earth-centered religion. Exquisitely colored and detailed paintings deep in the earth are thought to be places of ritual rather than living spaces. The many animal paintings are evocative of magical practices, and a preponderance of female figures suggests a goddess-oriented culture practising fertility rites. Similar multicolored frescoes are found in many caves in this area and in the caves of **Altamira** in northern Spain.

From this center of prehistory, it is only a few giant steps forward in time to the many Neolithic and early Bronze Age megalithic sites of Europe. One of the most impressive and extensive is **Carnac** on the coast of Brittany, considered to be one of the oldest continuously inhabited sites in the world. This area is essentially littered with five-thousand-year-old megaliths, the most notable being the Le Menec alignment which is part of three multiple rows stretching over 3,280 feet (1,100 m) and pointing to the east. Dolmens and earthmounds also abound; the highly decorated passage grave on the island of Gavrinis is rivalled only by a similar structure at Newgrange in Ireland.

Another step forward in time brings us to the eighth-century structure of **Mont-St.-Michel** on the northern coast of Brittany. This site is thought to have been a Celtic graveyard used by the Druids for worship of the sun god Mithras who was replaced by the Christian St. Michael, the leader of heaven's armies. One of many shrines to St. Michael in Britain and Europe (see also Glastonbury Tor), this dramatic Gothic architecture perched on a conical rock became a powerful religious center in the Middle Ages. It is now an island at high tide, and is still an important pilgrimage site for the French, comparable to the Great Pyramid in Egypt. Another pilgrimage beacon from the Middle Ages is situated on the site of five previous churches—the thirteenth-century cathedral of **Chartres** boasts 176 stained-glass windows that create an ever-changing play of colorful light in an ethereal interior honoring the Virgin Mary.

A small jump from the continent are the islands of **Malta** and Gozo, off the south coast of Sicily. Here the Neolithic temples dating from 3500 to 2500 BC suggest a cult of the Mother Goddess who was worshipped at one time or another from India to the Mediterranean. This nurturing earth mother was not only a fertility goddess but also ruled the unconscious state and provided healing and transformation.

Despite the tremendous variety of European sacred sites, of which only a very few are identified here, the theme of the earth as the teacher, provider, and mirror of the soul is again obvious. Surely the repetition of this theme since the beginning of known time tells us that some truth lies within, and that our search for oneness may also be satisfied through a nurturing relationship with the world around us.

India

Travelling in India

Despite our preparations for this first visit to India, our senses were assaulted by the impact of so much humanity. The color and vitality are powerful, as are the smells and the sights. As we drove from the Bombay airport at 3:00 AM, we didn't immediately realize that the dark shadows on the streets were poor people huddled like sacks, under a blanket if they were lucky. The outskirts of this modern city, with its wide boulevards, parks with cricket games, and classical colonial architecture, are crammed with tenement-style shelters, scraps of cloth and building materials improvised over the dusty earth. It is hard to imagine how these people fare during the torrential rains of the monsoon.

If you have back problems you may wish to be very selective in your travel. Other than by air, all local trips entail bumping around—even in the best taxis or rickshaws. Air India domestic reservations, booked from home, can still go awry so be sure to confirm everything. A good local Indian travel agent can save a lot of headaches. We had invaluable service from Kapadia Travel, 710 Rahaja Center, Nariman Point, Bombay 400021; Tel: 222–276 or 223–016. It is wise to contact the Government of India Tourist Office, in your country or at 88 Janpath, New Delhi 110001; Tel: 320005. They will provide detailed information about travel and accommodation, or refer inquiries to tourist organizations for each province in India, which have excellent brochures and contacts with local tourist offices, helpful to have while you are travelling. We also found the American Express offices in the larger centers (Bombay and New Delhi) very helpful. It is a good idea to buy area maps before you leave the larger cities; these are usually found in bookstores or even from street vendors.

When travelling by air, do *not* carry batteries in hand luggage. Pack them in your checked baggage or they will be confiscated and you will not see them again. The only consolation is that you can buy replacements at a reasonable cost, but not the rechargeables that we had stocked up on. Keep your luggage receipts to reclaim your bags at the next stop. Arrive before official check-in time, especially at small airports, as seating is often "open" rather than reserved, airlines are notorious for over-booking, and it seems to work on a first-come basis. Customs was surprisingly easy; despite our large amount of camera equipment (which needed to be itemized and which was checked as we left the country), their main concern is with video cameras. Airport taxis are usually on a fixed rate so are often cheaper for two people to share compared to two bus fares; in New Delhi we were told the bus was leaving in five minutes—it is *never* five minutes. Thirty minutes later it left and then made a multitude of stops along the way, including the domestic airport to pick up more passengers who were then delivered to their hotel before we were! Always establish the price first.

Train service is variable and unpredictable. Ticket queues can be long and people will try, and succeed, in slipping in front of you. There is often an extra quota of reserved first-class seats for tourists; ask for the station manager and try to apply for them. On the other hand, in practice we found that "reserved" meant nothing—we had to rely on a local person to evict people from our seats because the conductor was useless. Other travellers said second class can be better. In any case, stay close to your luggage and try to get a fellow traveller to help you watch for your stop. Trains always run late and you can't predict them by their arrival or departure times, stops are not easily identified in English, and hordes of people will be trying to get on as you try to disembark.

Bus service can be faster and easier than trains, and is also a more interesting way to see some of the countryside. Be aware, however, that roads are crowded and bumpy and filled with diesel fumes, although the trucks are very entertaining with their colorful paint jobs and decor with fringes, bells, religious insignias, and a variety of other paraphernalia. We nicknamed India the Land of Broken Trucks—everywhere one sees disabled vehicles stopped in the middle of the road, neatly surrounded by a ring of rocks, presumably to prevent other vehicles from colliding with them.

Banks can be infrequently available and painfully slow with foreign exchange which involves mountains of paperwork. Some large hotels will change dollars, or you can use the American Express Office exchange services in the large cities. Change enough so you won't have to go through the tedium too often, but remember that many hotels present bills in U.S. dollars and those in outlying areas often do not take credit cards.

Communications systems are variable. Telephones are often available but trunk lines can be very busy, especially within India. Sending a telegram is worth the price of admission. There are twenty-nine types of greetings to choose from, ranging from wedding/childbirth/exam or election congratulations, to public holiday, safe journey, and "thanks for your good wishes which we reciprocate heartily." Messages are on a priority system from (1) news of death, (2) arrival at railway or airport, (3) intimation of sickness or accident, and (4) application or offer of employment, or exam results. The system seems to work well as overseas messages were received and all our mail made it home too, including parcels.

Tourists will be plentiful in major destinations, including throngs of Indian tourists, and especially school children, all of whom are fascinated by foreigners and will try to include you in their photography. You will be accosted and surrounded before you realize what is happening; some will literally try to sit on your knee or cuddle like a bosom buddy. Courtney was awakened from a snooze in the shade to find his head being lifted for a picture, as he was surrounded on all sides. At the Taj Mahal, I had teenagers draped over my shoulder trying to read my notebook while someone took the snapshot. I suppose this is retributive justice for all the unannounced photographs that non-Indian tourists take of the locals.

You will be confronted by poverty and beggars. During the day we were approached by women holding out a hand and a wide-eyed baby as they blocked our way on the sidewalk or persistently banged on the window of our taxi when it stopped at a signal light. One feels caught in a dilemma, as local people told us not to give money unless the person is blind or lame, as it only perpetuates the problem. However, it is hard not to respond here, where the need appears so great, rather than donating to an organization at home to funnel money into a seemingly bottomless pit.

Another aspect of travelling in India is learning to dodge the garbage and dung piles that are particularly evident in smaller towns and on back streets. But even the wide sidewalks of Bombay and New Delhi will be painted with telltale red splotches of "pan"—a mixture of tobacco and spices commonly chewed for its narcotic effect. It is said to be addictive, much like smoking tobacco; the red debris is expectorated after use, leaving the evidence in the street and smeared over the user's teeth and gums. Most Westerners find this practice, along with the rather unsettling sight of people smiling with a mouthful of red teeth and gums, quite unappealing.

One learns to flow with the tide in India, or go crazy with the system. Just when you think you've had enough, you again recognize the vitality that is unique to this country, the variety of expressions of deep spirituality, and the many paths to enlightenment travelled in everyday life.

ELLORA AND AJANTA

February 18 . . . Many caves are dark and we strained our eyes to see the leftover glory of two-thousand-year-old paintings. The enormity of the task of carving these temples from the living rock is impressive enough, and becomes almost overwhelming when you examine the detail of the stone panels exhibiting every human emotion.

The caves of Ellora and Ajanta are considered by many to be the finest artwork in India and rival the best religious art in the world. Hindu, Buddhist, and Jain are all represented in these stupendous monuments glorifying divine intervention and guidance to earthly mortals.

Travel Tips

Both series of caves are in the province of Maharashtra, near Aurangabad, accessible by Air India, train, or bus from Bombay or New Delhi. If you have to budget your travel time, plan ahead as flights can be heavily booked. Our "on arrival" planning forced us to take a twelve-hour overnight bus trip because flights were full for a week, although we were lucky and got a return flight to Bombay, and a turn-around flight to New Delhi and onward to Allahabad (see Ganges section).

Local Resources

In Bombay we stayed at the YWCA International Guest House, 18 Madame Cama Road, Fort, Bombay 400039; Tel: 202 0445, which is central and adequate, although there is a wide range of hotels nearby. Take time for a pleasant day excursion to the caves of Elephanta on an island, a half-hour ferry trip from the main wharf in Bombay. This is a popular place for locals to picnic and enjoy the cave sculptures as well as the lively monkeys. The bus to Aurangabad leaves from the station beside the large Oberoi Hotel. The trip was tolerable and we were able to stretch over two seats and sleep before we were jolted awake at 2:30 AM going through Pune, where thousands of people were gathered for a concert! The Aurangabad bus station, adjacent to a tourist complex called Holiday Resort, sells tickets for bus tours to the caves. Luxury tours are run by the Maharashtra Tourism Development Corporation (MTDC) in Aurangabad (Tel: 4817); Ellora tours leave from the Holiday Resort at 9:30 AM, and Ajanta tours leave at 8:00 AM. Both tours return by 6:00 PM. Other companies offer less expensive tours—advertisements or representatives will be fully evident! We chose to stay at the budget Hotel Amarpreet which was clean, with air conditioning and a good dining room. Contact Hotel Amarpreet, Pt. Jawaharlal Nehru Road, Aurangabad 431001; Tel: 4615 or 4306. There are several luxury tourist hotels and some moderately priced ones as well as a youth hostel (Tel: 3801) nearby. Our work required us to hire a taxi and driver whom we met at the bus station. Ellora is 18 miles (29 km) northwest of Aurangabad, a half-hour drive; Ajanta is 60 miles (105 km), a two-hour drive. There is simple rustic-looking lodging available near both; most western tourists stay in Aurangabad. Ajanta is a larger center, the entrance road lined with stalls selling souvenirs and food. A government cafe at the site offers minimum respite and dirty washrooms. Bags may be checked, and guides can be hired as well as porters with sedan chairs to carry you up the steep stairs to the caves.

A surprise awaited us at the caves: no photography is allowed using a tripod without a special permit, which of course entailed a trip to New Delhi and a bureaucratic process we knew would take days. We discovered later that the proper channels are through the Indian High Commission in our own country, and if our request was approved, the commission would contact the Home Ministry of Tourism in New Delhi. The Archeological Survey of India, on Janpath, New Delhi 110011, would also be involved in the decision. We decided to do what we could, since flash photography was also denied, and the caves are so dimly lit (to protect the paintings) that a tripod wouldn't help much anyway. Some of the guards actually assisted us by shining light on the subjects, using a metal tray to reflect sunlight from the entrance.

The Sacred Caves

The rock temples of **Ellora** represent Hindu, Buddhist, and Jain faiths in harmonious coexistence which has not always been the case throughout history. Dating from the sixth to the tenth century AD, the caves are of two types: a chaitya or temple for worship, and a vihara or monastic center. Cave #10 is an eighth-century Buddhist chaitya with a grand architectural design incorporating a trefoil arched ceiling that magnifies the excellent resonance of sound, demonstrated to me by a monk chanting to the seated figure of Lord Buddha.

But the real glory of the sculptural art of Ellora is cave #16, known as the **Kailasa Temple**. Starting above and working inward, a 164-foot-long (50 m) complex series of rooms, passageways, niches, and a separate courtyard temple entirely covered with ornate carvings was hewn from the living rock. This central temple perched on a base of elephants contains the holy Hindu shiva lingam shrine, the stylized stone phallic symbol representing Lord Shiva, surrounded by flowers and lit by candlelight. The entire temple symbolizes holy **Mount Kailas**, the abode of Shiva and his Hindu deities. This temple has been called "an encyclopedia of mythology in rock," and is thought by some to surpass the Parthenon in Greece and Borobudur in Java in its conception.

The caves of **Ajanta** are located in a crescent-shaped valley, a series of thirty excavations, dating from 200 BC to 650 AD, that have been carved into the U-shaped cliff overlooking the Waghora River. This region of India was a flourishing trade center, full of agricultural and mineral resources, and the resulting political and economic prosperity it enjoyed fostered the creation of lavish artwork during a period known as the Golden Age of Indian Art. These exclusively Buddhist caves contain the most exquisite depiction of the life of Lord Buddha in India. Cave #26 with its pillared veranda and subsidiary chapels is monumental, but the focus is on the immense reclining Buddha who, on the verge of nirvana, is honored by a continuous flow of white-clad pilgrims. Ajanta has been described as a rare symphony of the three arts of architecture, sculpture, and painting; Ajanta paintings have been compared to the Italian frescoes at Assisi and Florence. Although many caves were dark and dreary, the glory of this creative genius honoring the spirit cannot be diminished.

THE GANGES

February 24 ... This river is the life force of India. The teeming humanity here is unlike anywhere else in the world. There is a continuous parade of activity against the background of rhythmic slapping sounds, as men and women knee-deep in the brown river water pound, scrub, rinse, and hand-wring a seemingly endless amount of daily laundry. Saddhus sit bolt upright in prayer and pilgrims perform morning ablutions, as smoke from the burning ghats wafts over it all and water buffalo step daintily around the amazingly colorful array of sheets and saris draped over the steps of the ghats.

The Ganga is the spiritual blood and lifeline of India, the most sacred of sacreds. Benares (Varanasi), where every Hindu desires to die and be purified, is said to be the oldest city in the world because of this unbroken tradition.

Travel Tips

Allahabad and Benares are separate cities sharing the sacred Ganges' waters in the province of Uttar Pradesh. Both are easily accessed by air from New Delhi.

Local Resources

During our visit, Allahabad was the site of the Kumbh Mela, the ritual bathing, held once every twelve years, which we attended along with fifteen million Hindu pilgrims. Hotel prices were inflated, but we were lucky to get a room at the Government Tourist Bungalow, 35 Mahatma Gandhi Marg, Civil Lines; Tel: 53640 beside the bus station, although there are many hotels nearby, including the luxury Regency on Tashkent Road; Tel: 56043. We would not recommend the Hotel Samrat where we were forced to stay for a few days because of tourist crowds. The regional tourist office is at 35 Mahatma Gandhi Marg, Civil Lines; Tel: 53883. For our departure a few days later, we stood in a variety of ticket lines for more than six hours until we finally secured reserved first-class seats on the train; we then waited sixteen hours for a train that didn't come because of political demonstrations on the track 100 miles (160 km) to the north. Eager to move on, we jumped on a bus to Varanasi, travelling four hours on tree-lined roads through dusty villages beside cultivated fields. Just as well, as we learned later that the next train didn't arrive for seven days!

The railway station and nearby bus station in Varanasi are hubbubs of activity where we were inundated with drivers of all types of vehicles wanting to deliver us to our hotel. We were lucky to find the new Hotel Malti around the corner on Vidyapath Road, Tel: 64703; it is bright, reasonably priced, and some rooms have hot baths! It is a good uptown location, although a twenty-minute cycle-rickshaw ride to the banks of the Ganges where there are also many hotels. The Garden View Hotel on Vidyapath Road was recommended and the government tourist office at 15B, The Mall, Varanasi 221002; Tel: 64189 can recommend a wide variety of hotels. In Varanasi, we experienced the real back streets of India: the dust, constant noise, blare of car horns and cycle bells, human and animal smells, exhaust fumes, raggedy children, and activity day and night. When you're walking, avoid the fresh dung piles drying in the sun.

The essence of Varanasi is the river. We spent three mornings in a small row boat photographing the activity that starts at dawn. Boats can be rented almost anywhere along the river, but first ask your hotel clerk or taxi driver what the going rate is; one fellow tried to charge us four times the normal price and was very persistent.

The Sacred Water

Allahabad (Prayag) is the holiest of the four sites for the Kumbh Mela. It is here that the holy waters of the Ganges, the Jamuna, and the mythical Saraswati rivers converge at the sacred point called the Sangham. Legend says a god carrying a pot (or kumbh) of nectar stolen from demons stopped here on his twelve-day journey to paradise, and it is now eternalized in this most important Hindu festival. The Kumbh Mela we attended was especially significant, being the last of this century and the last here for another forty-eight years. It was also celebrated at the time of a full moon and a complete lunar eclipse. The powerful interplay of these natural and legendary forces brought fifteen million pilgrims to take a ritual bath at this auspicious time. The month-long festivities were a riot of color as pilgrims from all over India and the Hindu world, many travelling on foot for hundreds of miles, arrived wearing traditional dress and carrying tents and goods to trade at the rows of market stalls set up for the event. A city of tents covered acres of land near the holy river, where different sects grouped themselves for festivities and rituals, as flamboyant holy men preached over loud speakers to attract followers. Every January or February, Allahabad is the site of an annual minifestival called the Magh Mela which follows the same traditions.

Varanasi, derived from the name of the mythical rivers Varun and Assi said to meet here below the Ganges, is also known by its ancient name of Benares, the soul-illuminating first city on earth, and the soul of Hinduism. It is also called Kashi, the City of Light, derived from the second-millenium BC Aryan tribe called Kashis, whose kings probably participated in the war immortalized in the great Hindu epic, the *Mahabarata*. Varanasi is guarded by Shiva, the supreme Hindu deity, to whom there are thousands of shrines, the most important being **Vishwanath Temple**. One winds down back streets and convoluted alleys to see the black-marble lingam, the symbol of the cosmos, which is given daily offerings of Ganges' water.

Millions of pilgrims crowd into this city annually; some stay to die. The pilgrims' focus is the river, and specifically the eighteen main ghats or stairways to the holy waters, of which **Dashawamedha** is one of the five most sacred points along the Ganges. It is here at dawn that the pilgrims begin their morning ablutions, pouring the sun-caressed river water over their heads and offering to Mother Ganga many garlands of orange marigolds and rose petals with a small candle on a leaf which float downstream. Nearby is **Manikarnika**, the most sacred place of the entire Hindu world, where Lord Shiva promised to remain present to liberate souls from the cycle of reincarnation. The wood cremation fires burn almost continuously, sacramentally liberating the bodily elements and freeing the soul for salvation, delivering the faithful to the holy river goddess Ganga, who purifies all.

Unfortunately most of this purification is symbolic, as the Ganges is probably the most polluted river in the world. It is not unusual to see partly burned corpses floating by because many families cannot afford to pay for enough wood to complete the cremation. The whole length of the river is used as a bathroom. The Indian government is developing a sanitation program and has implored pilgrims not to drink the water, but changing behavior based on strong belief systems is not easy, and the earthly reality of the unseen filth is far outweighed by the symbolic reverence for the Ganges.

Sarnath is the mother place of Buddhism, a twenty-minute ride by taxi from Varanasi. Here at the Chankhandi Stupa (shrine) is where Lord Buddha preached his first sermon, enshrining his teachings into law, and showing the way to nirvana. It is also here that he met his first five disciples. Once an extensive city, Sarnath was at the peak of its glory between the fifth and seventh century AD, before being levelled by Moslem invaders. The huge third-century BC Dhamekh Stupa is the only building that escaped demolition, but it is the reconstructed Mulgandh-Kuti Vihar Temple that enshrines the relics of the Buddha. The deer in the nearby fenced park are held sacred because of the tradition of Buddha's previous reincarnation as a deer.

There is also a wonderfully large Peepul tree, a graft from the original Bodhi Tree under which Buddha attained enlightenment. The larger-than-life-sized statues of Buddha and his disciples under this Bodhi Tree are colorfully painted, providing a cheerful note complementing the brilliant flowers lining the walkways.

Photo Tips   *Sunrise and Boats on the Ganges*

This photograph comes the closest for me to portraying the heart and soul of India. The theme is emergence: the first stirrings of the sun as it greets a group of laborers already at work on restoring the waterfront of the Mother Ganges. There is so much to see, to experience, and to photograph in Varanasi that one should try to visit for several days.

Leaving our hotel room about two hours before sunup, we pleaded with our boatman, a mere youth, to row faster against the current so that we could be in line with the boats and the rising sun. Then at the magic moment, he let go of the oars and we slowly drifted past this scene, at least 1,000 feet (300 m) away. I used a 500mm lens and made a long sequence of exposures, each with the sun in the picture. Only because of the mists muting the sun's usual brightness was I able to make exposures in which the contrast was within the tonal range of the color slide film, the soft warm hues (low tonal contrast), in fact, giving the photograph its visual appeal and portraying the gentleness of dawn on the Ganges. It is because I am photographing with a long focal-length lens from a considerable distance that the people and boats appear so small in proportion to the sun. Only seconds later the sun had risen above the cloud bank and was too bright to photograph. At that point I turned my back to it and concentrated my lenses on the warm frontal lighting of the opposite bank.

*Rising sun and Ganges River, Benares, India, February 1989/*Sacred Earth, p. 93

BODHGAYA

February 28 . . . The sacred tree was draped with silks of pure white and the rich orange color of Buddhism. Prayer flags fluttered in the slight breeze as the sun filtered down through the leaves. It didn't matter that the sacred lake was covered in litter—it provided a colorful foreground for the reflection of the statue of Lord Buddha, with the occasional white lotus flower stretching sky-ward from the slimy water, reminding us of the purity of this spiritual path.

Bodhgaya is the most venerated pilgrim center of Buddhism. It is here that the Buddha attained enlightenment, the culmination of a long journey by Prince Siddartha who, after giving up his family wealth to become a hermit, wandered for six years, and finally learned the secret of overcoming sorrow and suffering.

Travel Tips

Bihar state is generally poorer than neighboring Uttar Pradesh and has a reputation for bandits on the roads, although we had no problems. The nearest airport is 90 miles (145 km) north at Patna, or 150 miles (242 km) west at Varanasi, both entailing rather long train or bus rides to reach Gaya, 12 miles (20 km) away from Bodhgaya. We were glad to escape this rather dingy city where we spent a noisy uncomfortable night after a late train arrival. The auto-rickshaw ride to Bodhgaya takes almost an hour on a bumpy road, or by a very crowded bus.

Local Resources

There are about twenty Indian-style hotels in Bodhgaya, as well as pilgrim rest houses where you just walk in and ask for a room, such as the Burmese monastery where we stayed. The rooms are very simple—bring your own towels and mosquito coils. There are several government rest houses as well as the Travellers Lodge, Tel: 25. Write the Director of Tourism for Bihar, Secretariat Building, Patna 15, for listings. We couldn't find a proper restaurant; roadside stands offer food that looks questionable in cleanliness, but we had no problems.

The Bodhi Tree

This most sacred spot is now marked by a tree grafted from the Bodhi Tree in Sri Lanka, purportedly grown from the original tree under which the Buddha sat. This tree spreads its leafy branches as though protecting the adjacent first-century AD Mahabodhi Temple, the Shrine of Supreme Enlightenment.

It is easy to see why Bodhgaya receives hundreds of pilgrims daily. A simple dusty village similar to many others in India, somehow there is a special aura here. Away from the usual street hustling of western tourists to buy a variety of goods and services, the temple grounds offer a feeling of sanctuary unlike any other we experienced. Buddhist monks and pilgrims from Tibet, Thailand, Japan, China, Burma, and Sri Lanka grace the pathways of the square gardens as they honor the temple and tree, as well as the seven other sacred spots where the Buddha prayed. The murmur of the Buddhist mantra "Om Mani Padmen Hum" sits constantly in the air; the vibrational quality of this chant is said to induce a high spiritual state. Within the temple, offerings are continually renewed as groups of pilgrims await their turn to pray at the simple inner shrine. At the Bodhi Tree outside, which is surrounded by a decorative metal wall, the same groups chant under the silk-draped tree glowing in the ever-present candlelight. While we were there a special ceremony took place involving hundreds of pilgrims encircling the whole temple complex, chanting and ringing bells; their joy and smiles lit up the night in the reflection of the candles they held. One day we met the four-year-old boy who is considered the reincarnation of the tutor of His Holiness, the Dalai Lama. This sweetly smiling child-of-wisdom dressed in monk's robes is being groomed to take on his lifelong job.

Many international temples are found in other parts of Bodhgaya, each designed with the characteristic architecture of the country. Several have adjacent monasteries and will accept pilgrims. Another pilgrim site is near Dungeshwari, 7 miles (12 km) away at the cave of Mahakula, where Prince Siddartha is said to have fasted and meditated for a long period before accepting his first bowl of rice, thereby breaking his penance to follow the middle path to enlightenment. The two-hour walk across the dried riverbed through small villages and cultivated fields is well worth the reward of seeing this dark cave and basking in the gentle smiles of the two monks who offer tea and refreshments to tired pilgrims. The joy here is unmistakable. Don't miss it.

THE TAJ MAHAL

March 25 . . . It was in these gardens that Courtney was inspired to create his chapter on havens of renewal. From the muddy Jamuna River below and the chaotic back streets of the market place, this legacy of love graces the land like a white dove soaring to the heavens.

The Taj Mahal is the monument built by Shah Jehan, the fifth Moghul emperor, in memory of his deceased wife, Mumtaz Mahal. The splendor and setting of this jewel of architecture only enhances its sense of divinity as it speaks of eternal love to the thousands who pay homage daily.

Travel Tips

Agra is a three-hour ride by train from New Delhi. Driving took about the same time so we hired a taxi and driver thinking there would be places to photograph along the way, but we were disappointed to find only unpleasantly crowded roads filled with diesel fumes, and cars and trucks jockeying for superiority. It was a relief to stretch out in the gardens of the Taj, and inhale the almost-forgotten sweet smell of green grass. During visiting hours the grounds look like an immense garden party, draped with colorful saris, and bright-eyed children playing and feasting on a family picnic.

Local Resources

We stayed at the Hotel Mayur (also known as the government-sponsored Agra Tourist Bungalows) on Fatehabad Road; Tel: 67302; Cable: MAYUR. The hotel consists of attractive duplexes, surrounded by a lawn; rooms are clean, and there is inside or outdoor dining. Hotel bills are in U.S. dollars; no credit cards are accepted. The sumptuous Mughal Sheraton is a short walk down the street during which we were repeatedly hassled by rickshaw drivers and others as we tried to enjoy the night air. An interesting diversion is the Red Fort, a complex of red sandstone buildings started in 1565 by the great Moghul emperor Akbar, whose nearby tomb and deer park are another haven of greenery in this dusty noisy city.

The Monument

This most famous mausoleum was built for the "chosen one of the palace," the shah's favorite wife who died during the birth of their fourteenth child. The perfect symmetry of this building speaks of serenity. The white marble is still pristine, glowing with the precious stones set within the ornate carvings. Practically every inch is covered with inlaid floral designs and verses from the Koran. The effect is delicate and awesomely beautiful—even the most jaded tourist, coming with a ho-hum attitude of "I guess we should see this most famous monument in India," cannot fail to be impressed.

Completed in 1623 after twenty-two years of work by twenty thousand laborers, the Taj Mahal continues to be an inspiration to thousands of annual pilgrims of all faiths. The spectacular interior, with its highly carved tombs and pillars, glorifies eternal love with its intertwining of art and architecture. The outer gardens, away from the crowds around the central pools, echo the building's sense of tranquility, in the company of birds and chipmunks.

Photo Tips   *The Taj Mahal*

Every camera-toting tourist wants a picture of the classic view of the Taj, perfectly mirrored in the reflecting pool on the front terrace. As simple as it might seem, the task of getting that timeless view, uncluttered with tourists, is virtually impossible unless you are the first of the one hundred thousand daily visitors to the edge of the pool. Arrive at 6:00 AM and you will be the first through the gates. A quick sprint from the entrance to the pool will assure you the first shot, but you will soon be crowded not only by a continuous parade of humanity but also by a bevy of other would-be photographers, all vying for the perfect alignment that can only be achieved from the center of the poolside.

Procession in courtyard, Taj Mahal, Agra, India, March 1989/ Sacred Earth, *p. 51*

Though I did manage to arrive at the appointed hour, and did succeed in getting the cherished view, I also found the endless stream of pilgrims equally fascinating.

The problem was not in finding interesting subjects, but that there were simply too many people to get clear unobstructed views. Most of the time it felt like a sea of confusion; often by retreating and acting quickly I was able to record candid actions and brilliant color before the scene was obliterated and gone forever.

I had only one chance to record this row of Hindu pilgrims who happened to be among the first arrivals. I quickly moved away from the walkway, positioned the Taj in the upper right-hand corner, and watched for the magic moment when the group would be perfectly placed as they walked into the frame. When recording the decisive moment, it is better to make one deliberate exposure, rather than running off a series with a motor drive. The ultimate challenge is to keep an eagle eye on composition while hand-holding the camera, then to be ready for the precise moment.

THE LOTUS TEMPLE

March 27 ... This Baha'i Temple is a real jewel in the crown—a perfect white blossom floating above the sacred pools reflecting the great cosmos. It is easy to see why this symbol of eternal purity is fondly called The Dawning Place of Remembrance of God.

This Mother Temple of the Indian Subcontinent is located on the outskirts of New Delhi, India. The Baha'is see their temple as the central hub of a wheel; the wheel represents the city of people, which is constantly directed and supported by the center, the focus of community life.

Travel Tips

New Delhi is accessible by air on many international carriers, and by local air, train, and bus service. It is a huge city with a wide range of accommodation.

Local Resources

We felt most comfortable in a moderately priced western-style hotel in the heart of the city, the Hans Plaza, Hansalaya 15 Barakhamba Road, New Delhi 11001; Tel: 331 6868; Telex: 031–63126 HANS IN. There are also many choices for luxury and the budget-conscious traveller. A series of local buses will get you to the Lotus Temple, but the half-hour taxi ride is reasonable and more comfortable. The temple is open daily except Monday; shoes are taken off and left on supervised shelves at the base of the steps. Baha'is come here from all over the world, on personal pilgrimage, or to work at the temple, guiding visitors and taking part in services.

The Temple

The Lotus Temple is a perfect example of architectural symmetry and balance, but its secret lies more in the symbols of its shape, and the beliefs behind these symbols. The lotus is the utmost symbol of purity in many ancient cultural traditions; it grows in the slime but rises, untainted, above the filth of earthly reality. All the religions of India (and many others throughout the world) incorporate the lotus symbol. The Hindu creator god Brahma was born from the lotus that grew out of the god Vishnu's navel, and the Buddha is usually represented on a lotus seat. The lotus was also the symbol of the pharaohs of Upper Egypt (see Thebes). The lotus in art symbolizes divine birth, and is associated with the sun being the regenerator of life each day as it survives its nocturnal passage through the underworld. In this way, the lotus symbolizes eternal life as well as procreation.

The dome of this temple acts like a skylight, with light filtering down through the inner folds of nine central lotus petals surrounded by nine open petals and nine entrance petals. This lotus looks like it is floating above the nine reflecting pools, which act as an air conditioner and also represent the green leaves of the lotus floating on the water. The repetition of the number nine is also central to the Baha'i faith which embodies the nine major faiths of the world. Other ancient esoteric systems consider the number nine to be the number of completion.

The Baha'is are probably the most ecumenical religious group in the world today. The design of this temple has succeeded in symbolizing the cardinal principle of the Baha'i faith: the unity of religions. During the day, thousands of tourists and pilgrims wend their way to the Lotus Temple through the typically colorful surrounding gardens, emblematic and living proof of the Baha'i belief that all of nature is to be honored in its divine creation (see Haifa, Israel). At night, the lotus gleams from within, a beacon of divine illumination, like an exotic spaceship ready to travel to heavenly abodes. It is truly an inspiring experience to visit this temple, and as Baha'u'llah said, "Holy places are undoubtedly centres of the outpourings of divine grace . . . because one's heart is moved with tenderness."

Nepal

March 8 . . . Our screaming muscles strained up almost vertical paths as our porters, carrying an average of 80 pounds (36 kg), stopped to lounge over a cigarette which they jokingly called their "Sherpa oxygen"! Cultivated fields and wide-eyed kids and dogs lined this still-used ancient trade route to Tibet; we frequently stepped aside as yet another herd of heavily laden mules passed us, each beast wearing a different bell clanging from his neck, as the chorus of bells and ringing hoofs drifted back to us around the next bend.

Nepal is a country of sacred landscapes. Valleys, rivers, and mountains alike are treasured for their spiritual value, often marked with shrines and temples thanking the gods for their bounty and protection.

Travel Tips

Katmandu is connected by direct flights from India (New Delhi, Patna, Varanasi, and Calcutta), Thailand, Hong Kong, Sri Lanka, Singapore, and Burma. Thirty-day visas can be obtained on arrival for $10 U.S. If one is more adventurous, local buses travel to and from various points in India; one route passes the birthplace of the Buddha at Lumbini and the Royal Chitwan Jungle can also be visited along the way. Local buses service other major points such as Pokhara, the beginning of the trekking area around the Annapurna range, and Jiri, the starting point to the Everest Base Camp at Namche Bazar. Be aware that public buses have a reputation for being uncomfortable as well as unsafe; even our Nepalese porters were robbed of their money as they transported our camping gear by bus from Katmandu.

Credit cards and even traveller's checks are not universally accepted in Nepal; Nepalese rupees and U.S. dollars are preferred, and airline tickets are purchased in U.S. dollars.

Local Resources

Katmandu has five-star hotels on Durbar Marg near the Royal Palace, where all the airline offices and many tourist shops are located. Ethnic and western-style restaurants can be found here and in the colorful back streets of the Thamel area. At the airport tourist office we chose the Hotel Mayalu beside the American Express office because we were eager to pick up our mail. The luxury Hotel Sherpa, Durbar Marg, Katmandu; Tel: 412021 is nearby, and friends highly recommended the moderately priced Tibet Guest House in Thamel, Tel: 214383.

If you haven't arrived on a pre-paid tour it is really quite easy to arrange your own hotel and trek, but we chose the assistance of Above The Clouds which can be contacted in Katmandu, Tel: (4) 16909; information and bookings are best made from their North American office, PO Box 398, Worcester MA 01602; Tel: (508) 799–4499. They provided us with a congenial and efficient group of porters to carry all our camera gear, camping equipment, and food for our nine-day circle trek from Pokhara to Gorepani. You can do this on your own; there are many outfitters in Katmandu and in Pokhara where you can buy or rent equipment, maps, and local guides. Most trails are well travelled and a guide is not necessary, but we were glad to have porters to carry our big packs on the steep trails. The hiring of local porters is very inexpensive, and this work is a mainstay of employment for the Sherpas. In Pohkara these services are centered around the lake area where there is a proliferation of tourist hotels, shops, and a campground. Most of the popular treks go through villages that provide cheap cots, bottled water, and local food, which is the major risk for this venture.

If you go on your own it is wise to contact your embassy representative first to let them know your plans, and be sure to have current medical insurance, otherwise (we were told by other trekkers) you won't be rescued if you get into trouble. (Injuries and health problems are *not* infrequent occurrences, even with the most experienced hikers.) The CIWEC Clinic in Katmandu; Tel: 410983 is staffed by Americans who will renew your gamma globulin protection against the ever-present hepatitis threat, and give meningococcus vaccine (necessary to have against this prevalent bacteria) as well as look after any other ills. We were told anyone with a serious illness is flown to Thailand at their own expense.

Royal Nepal Airlines offers a one-hour scenic flight to view Mount Everest and the string of elegant snowy peaks of the Himalayas. This is well worth the price and can be arranged through any travel agent. Another popular excursion is to Chitwan National Park, the home of the Bengal tiger and one-horned rhinoceros. The best way to experience the park is to stay at one of the many jungle camps; we loved the relatively new Temple Tiger Wildlife Camp, PO Box 3968, KantiPath, Katmandu, Nepal; Tel: 2215855; Telex: 2637 TEMTIG NP. The tent facilities and cots are like minihouses, with showers in airy bamboo enclosures under the trees. Delicious meals are served in elegant style beside the huge fire in the center of the open-air thatched-roof circular meeting area, to the accompaniment of a screaming peacock or the "brain fever" cuckoo. Guides are superb and the atmosphere and ambience is more natural than in other camps in the area.

Sacred Nepal

Nepalese history dates to at least 1000 BC. The population is 90 percent Hindu, although Buddhism is also very apparent. The Hindu goddess of Katmandu is Kumari who was selected from a Buddhist clan. The Katmandu Valley is full of temples with ongoing festivals that reflect the deep spiritual forces at work in the daily lives of these people. The month-long Magha Poornima festival, for example, worships Lord Vishnu through fasting and daily bathing at the river ghats. The Akash Bairov Temple is the center of a week-long celebration of the god of rain. The Sway Ambhunath Temple, the oldest Buddhist stupa, is also honored by Hindus as the site of a blooming lotus that emitted five colored rays of Swayambu, the Self-Existent One. Holy books say the Katmandu Valley was originally covered in water before the Bodhisatva Manjushree used his sword to cut the Chobar Gorge to drain it; the nearby Jola Vinayak rock is worshipped by Hindus as the Waterside of Lord Ganesh, the elephant-headed god of wisdom.

But the **Pashupatinath Temple** in Katmandu was the focus of attention when we were there. This pagodalike temple to Shiva on the banks of the sacred Bagmati River is one of the holiest in the Hindu world, and the center of pilgrimage for the annual Shivaratri festival, celebrating Shiva's celestial dance of the Tandav. Only Hindus can enter the inner courtyard, but the burning ghats and the upper monkey temple are open to visitors with many saddhus (holy men) performing their ritual prayers and postures.

For us, the spiritual experience of Nepal was revealed in her mountains. The **Himalayas** are the abode of the gods, with many peaks named for gods and goddesses. It is from here that Shiva, as lord of agriculture, controls the fertility of the earth. **Everest**, the "Roof of the World" at 29,028 feet (8,848 m), is sacred to both Hindu and Buddhist. In India she is called Sagarmantha and is likened to the mythical Mount Meru, the center of the cosmos. In Tibet she is Chomo Lungma, the Mother Goddess of the Snows, and is thought to be a possible location of Shambhala, the ultimate mystical sanctuary described in ancient Tibetan holy books as the lotus-blossomed kingdom hidden by a rosary of snowy mountains. Here a golden life of peace and enlightenment awaits the spiritual traveller, like the modern-day utopia of Shangri-la.

Our trek took us to Gorepani, in the shadow of the Annapurna range to the northeast. The rain, hail, thunder, snow, and hot sun did not diminish our joy and the buoyant atmosphere we felt as we trekked through rhododendron forests in full bloom with the heady fragrance of jasmine permeating the clear air. Each morning our cook awoke us with hot tea that we sipped while watching the dawn turn to pink icing on Annapurna or **Machupuchare**, the sacred fishtail-shaped mountain home of twin goddesses which climbers respect by not ascending to the top. From Poon Hill, the highest point above Gorepani, we were awed by the whole panorama from the Daulagiri range in the northwest, to the peaks of Annapurna in the east. We only wished we could continue to the sacred hot springs at Tatopani and five days more past Jomson to the holy Muktinath Temple with its miraculous flame glowing from the earth. But the shrines are really not necessary; the natural glory of these peaks speaks of the reverence for high places all over the world as sanctuaries where the earthly mortal can feel one step closer to divine grace.

Back on the lowlands, we travelled by car to the Royal **Chitwan** National Park and spent a week in two jungle camps. Unfortunately we didn't see the Bengal tiger, but saw many one-horned rhinos from the safety of an elephant, as crocodiles and deer abounded nearby. This was a step back in time for us, walking and riding through tall grass sheltering some of the oldest wilderness creatures known to civilization. Four hundred species of birds sing throughout the valley where we had a picnic and gave the elephants their daily wash in the stream (which they followed with a mud bath!). We left on the final day of the Holi festival of colors, the spring celebration in honor of the coming harvest. We were also annointed with the red powder of the legend of Lord Krishna, as our hosts offered gifts and the same red ash to their shrine of simple rocks and earth at the base of a huge tree. We felt this honoring of nature was the essence of our Chitwan experience.

Photo Tips   *Mount Everest*

The entire chain of the Himalayas is a photographer's paradise, and a trek such as the one to the Everest Base Camp or around Annapurna is the best way to photograph here. Let the porters carry most of your gear while you hold onto your tripod, camera, and a few lenses. My camera did not come off the tripod except for a few candid photographs. For many of my mountain scenes I chose a 300mm lens and the tripod provided stability, reduced camera jiggle, and allowed me to arrange much better compositions than would be possible without it. But there is much more than mountain scenery; local village charm, domestic animals, mule trains, and colorful foliage along the route are all subjects for your camera.

We did not trek in the direction of Mount Everest, but we did fly over it several times. The panorama on a clear day is nothing short of spectacular. To enhance the magical look of Everest, Mother Goddess of the Snows, I used a polarizing filter on my lens. Combined with the color refraction effects of the airplane's window, the polarizer can produce striking results. As with any flight where I plan to photograph, I try to arrive early, determine the type of aircraft, and secure a window seat away from the wing. Generally it is preferable to shoot away from the sun, to reduce the effects of the reflections from the window; however, wonderful effects are also possible by experimenting on the sunny side of the plane. Photographing from the air also provides an opportunity to round out your trip with new and unusual points of view.

*Mount Everest from the air, Nepal, March 1989/*Sacred Earth, *p. 195*

Japan

Sacred Japan

The sacred in Japan is strongly connected to the world of nature and to Japanese history, social customs, and worship of the Imperial household. The name "Japan" comes from the Kanji characters meaning "root of the sun" or "sunrise," which explains the traditional symbol of this country. The sun goddess, Amaterasu, is honored as creator of the Japanese world, and the emperor is considered her descendent, thereby empowering him with the divine right to rule, not unlike the Egyptian pharaohs. Japanese shrines are always attended at sunrise, as well as at other times of the day.

The convergence of religious ideals with the activities of daily life is a predominant feature of Japan dating from the original tribal customs of the indigenous Ainu people.

Ancient Shinto philosophy espouses the awareness of form and right practice in the path of life. The basis of Shintoism is the concept of the kami; difficult to translate, it often refers to anything possessing spiritual power and inspiring awe. The kami are sacred and pure, requiring the devout to purify themselves before approaching shrines that house the kami spirits, these manifestations of divine power that occur in all of nature. This spiritual ambience in nature brings one into the presence of the transcendent aspects of existence, as long as one practises purity and devotion, not only by pilgrimage to specific shrines, but also by honoring the sun and the emperor.

By the seventh century AD, Buddhism was introduced in Japan and patronage by the powerful Imperial House has continued throughout history, but the important ancestral link with the sun goddess was never broken, and in fact the power of the Imperial Court probably increased through the joint worship of Buddhism and the Shinto kami that attended each Imperial clan. The Japanese world view acknowledged that the power and presence of kami spirits moved between levels in the manifest world and the underworld, affecting all aspects of life, especially ensuring the fertility of the earth. Ancient agricultural rites still persist today, along with the view that the eternal is best found in the grace of the natural world. Hence many Shinto shrines are rustic and simple, and are honored with the fruits of nature such as an orange or a few flowers. The Japanese tea ceremony, ikebana flower arranging, and the creation of a garden are other expressions of spirituality through engaging with nature.

Travelling in Japan

Japan is served by many international air carriers entering via Tokyo and Osaka. Tokyo airport was our first stop on a circular tour from Singapore; this airport at Narita is very busy. Although there is good train, bus, or taxi (expensive) service to Tokyo 40 miles (64 km) away, a lot of luggage can be a problem and it is often sent separately to your hotel (after you wait in a long queue to arrange this). My previous experience in Japanese train stations was marred by the memories of carrying heavy bags up numerous stairs (no elevators!), so we decided to short circuit the pain and fly directly to Osaka, especially as air travel is no more expensive than the bullet train (Shinkansen). We were lucky to get a flight almost immediately, landing in Osaka airport at 9:00 PM, just in time to grab a hotel list from the tourist information center that was closing.

Twenty phone calls later we finally found a hotel room for $125 U.S. All the budget hotels were full, and we soon realized how wise it would have been to plan ahead, as we adjusted our credit cards to the high cost of living in Japan. Speaking of credit cards, not all are accepted; neither MasterCard, VISA or American Express are universally accepted and many places in small towns take only local currency (no dollars). Watch for "Foreign Exchange" signs on banks—they may be few and far between, and not at all in some small towns like Futamigaura. Be prepared to wait up to forty-five minutes at the foreign-exchange counter.

Food is costly in Japan. One morning we paid the equivalent of $23 U.S. for one fried-egg breakfast, coffee, tea, and an apple. If you're on a budget, the cheapest meal that is both filling and delicious is the soup bowl. Almost all restaurants have "plastic food"; i.e., replicas of various dishes are displayed in the window with the price, so at least you have some idea of what is coming.

The Japanese bath is an important ritual to know about when travelling in Japan. Facilities vary, but the most important thing to remember is that you *never* take soap in the bath. All your washing is done first, sometimes in small cubicles, sometimes in an open bathing area with taps around the wall, using small bowls to lather and scrub. Only then, squeaky clean, do you climb into the steamy bath and soak as long as you can tolerate (temperatures vary). Baths may be private or communal (men and women separately). Some inns provide towels, often postage-stamp size, while others may charge extra for them or not have them at all. All inns provide sleeping kimonos (yukata), and larger inns (ryokans) may provide kimonos and wooden shoes for walking on the street.

Another important ritual of cleanliness is the slipper. Shoes are removed and left at the foyer of any Japanese-style inn; use the special (inevitably floppy) slippers to go to your room where you will find another pair to wear inside the room, and to the toilet room and the bath room where other pairs will be awaiting you.

Rail travel is the most efficient way to see Japan and there are several private railway lines (Nankai, Kinki Nippon, and Kintetsu) as well as Japan National Railways (JNR) to choose from. Travel connections vary, and the private lines can sometimes be more efficient than JNR but it offers tourists a Rail Pass. This pass can save a lot of money if you plan your time wisely; passes are for one, two, or three weeks, and they must be purchased from a travel agent outside of Japan (although in Singapore they didn't know of them). The pass is useful on the JNR Shinkansen, which is expensive if you buy individual tickets, but a journey on this train should not be missed. This is rail travel of the future, more comfortable than flying (unless you choose a busy time and have to stand), and smooth enough to eat your bento (lunchbox) of Japanese food, with chopsticks.

There are tourist information centers in all major railway stations. The best ones, however, are the Japan Tourist Bureau (JTB) offices in Kyoto (see Local Resources), at the Tokyo International Airport (Tel: [0476] 32–8711), or in Tokyo city at 6–6 Yurakucho 1-chome, Chiyoda-ku; Tel: (03) 502–1461. They will book travel as well as accommodation. They also provide a booklet on Japanese inns; ryokans tend to be larger than the family-run minshukus. Outside of the main centers there is often little or no English spoken (in Futamigaura and Fujinomiya, for example), so the JTB has provided a free tourist telephone (see JTB brochure as numbers vary with location). If you expect to make a lot of phone calls, telephone cards can be purchased from shops or the post office; this is especially handy for international calls, which are made from specially designated booths.

The Sakura Viewing Timetable is a display found in many rail stations and tourist centers in April, showing various cities and the degree of cherry blossom development, labelled by a partial or full-blown flower.

When we left Japan, we found it easier to take the speedy Shinkansen from Shizuoka to Tokyo, and change to a JNR local train (same station, but upstairs of course—and at the crazy rush hour—but it was the last stop so we didn't have to fight the crowds to get off). This local train took us to Narita City where we stayed overnight (much cheaper than in Tokyo), at the Kirinoya Inn, 58 Tamachi Narita-shi, Chiba-ken, Japan 286 (Tel: 0476–22–0724) and then took the half-hour bus ride to the departure lounge the next morning. Pay attention to airline rules; I was unable to confirm our reservations by telephone and on arrival at the airport found they had been automatically cancelled. We were lucky to find available seats on the same flight to Hong Kong.

KYOTO

April 5 . . . This old Imperial capital captured our imagination with its ring of resplendent temples and shrines reigning over the hillside and dotted through-out the modern city. Today it is raining cherry blossoms over the stately bamboo and bright pink azaleas sheltering the Ryoanji Temple. We sat beside the newly raked sand garden, its spiral patterns accented only by the few carefully positioned rocks that help to define its message of serenity and timelessness.

Kyoto has always been a place of pilgrimage for the Shinto and Buddhist devotee. A haven of holy shrines dating as early as the ninth century AD when it became the Imperial capital called Heian, Kyoto has not lost its spiritual essence despite the modern city that dominates it today.

Local Resources

Osaka is a large westernized city with many modern, expensive hotels and an efficient subway system with links to the main railway station (Umeda) which has a travel information center; we stayed at the Nakanoshima Inn; Tel: (06) 447–1122 or from Tokyo: (03) 578–8811. We were glad to escape on the half-hour train ride to Kyoto. The Kyoto Tourist Information is at the Kyoto Tower Building, Higashi-Shiokojicho, Shimogyo-ku, Kyoto; Tel: (075) 371–5649, one block up from the JNR station, which is also the local bus station. They will book accommodation and also provide a monthly visitors' guide to events. Buses travel everywhere and announcements are made in English. For Mount Hiei take #51 or #7 from the post office beside the JNR station. Taxis are also plentiful but don't expect the white-gloved driver to help you with your luggage. We found the Hotel Higashiyama; Tel: 075–882–1181, a minshuku on a canal lined with cherry blossoms, a short walk from the Heian Jingu. Here we had our introduction to sleeping on tatami mats and futons, sharing a toilet down the hall, and using a Japanese bath.

Around Kyoto

Springtime in **Kyoto** is the inspiration of poets and artists; even the rains cannot diminish its charms. It is a city of contrasts, with modern and elegant department stores displaying expensive designer imports and the most amazing array of foodstuffs ever seen in a market. Streets are a jumble of traditional sushi shops, private Geisha clubs, western-style bakeries with French bread and pastries, and crowded shopping arcades where you can buy everything from a hammer to a pet budgie. It is not unusual to see busy shoppers suddenly disappear down a back alley leading to a red torii gate. This gate signifies a Shinto shrine where an offering will be made as they clap their hands and ring a bell to catch the attention of the local kami spirit.

It is hard to choose from the profusion of sacred areas in Kyoto. The Imperial Palace is spectacular but requires reservations to visit. The Heian Jingu with its brilliant red torii gates is a frequent setting for weddings and has one of the most extensive and beautiful gardens in the city. The Ryoanji Temple is famous for its sand garden, raked daily into a new pattern that suggests the mobility of this "sea" against the timelessness of the heavy rocks that define its shape. The Shorenin Temple of the Tendai sect on Mount Hiei is noted for its imperial-style buildings, ponds of colorful carp, and the mosses in a garden that has not changed for eight hundred years. The nearby Chionin Temple has the largest bell in Japan, and still functions as a Buddhist monastery.

A visit to the Ginkakuji Shrine was a good starting point before we spent the rest of a beautiful day wandering down the Philosopher's Canal which could hardly be seen for the profusion of sakura blossoms. Here we watched an endless parade of Japanese people promenading in exquisitely gilded kimonos, business suits, or designer jeans and Reeboks, stopping at the expensive boutiques or French cafes for cappuccino and cheesecake! We finished our day at Maruyama Park, the home of the largest sakura tree in Japan, and the place of wild carousing to celebrate the advent of spring. Japanese picnics are an amazing tradition to observe; fifteen or twenty people (business associates or families) sit on large blankets (shoes off) and consume the most incredible amount of food and alcohol we have ever witnessed, taking breaks only to sing and dance to the music blaring from the inevitable ghetto blaster. However, even the inebriated young men vomiting in the nearby stream could not spoil the glory of the trees and the nearby shrines.

Northeast of Kyoto is holy **Mount Hiei**, an ancient center of Japanese Buddhism established by a young man named Saicho. He created a temple on the mountain to house a statue of the Buddha of Healing that he had carved from a log. In 805 AD, Saicho (also known as Dengyo Daishi) founded the Tendai sect, and the vast monastic complex that developed here was an important bulwark to protect the imperial capital from evil influences, traditionally believed to come from the northeast. Mount Hiei became a great spiritual empire, an alliance of church and state that was reinforced by the many ecclesiastics who came from aristocratic families. Although Saicho's intent was to create "people who illumine their surroundings," it is rather ironic that the monastery became so politically powerful that it was destroyed in 1571 because of the demands it was making on the government.

The Tendai sect of Buddhism teaches that all divinities are manifestations of the same unity, and that different forms of Buddhism are paths to this truth; this truth operates on various levels to accommodate the degree of spiritual preparation attained by an individual. The concept is mirrored by the many pathways leading around the wooded forests on Mount Hiei. The monastery was also an important force in incorporating Shintoism with Buddhist beliefs. The Hiyoshi shrine on Mount Hiei is the headquarters of the Shinto sect that worships the monkey as a divine messenger, although signs warned of the danger of being bitten by the local monkeys! The Sanno Shrine of the Mountain King at the foot of Mount Hiei is dedicated to the primordial divinity who ruled the mountain before Buddhism, and the restored monastery still seeks his protection.

The current monastery is an immense complex centering around Enryaku-Ji, central to the Tendai sect and sacred to Mahayana Buddhism in Japan. The Konponchu-do or central hall holds the three lamps known as "the inextinguishable Dharma Lights" which have been burning continuously for the past twelve hundred years. Ritual to protect the nation is practised here, and it is the main focus for the hundreds of white-clad pilgrims we saw on the day we visited. Ascetic monks continue rigorous practices such as the Sennichi-Kaihogyo pilgrimage in which they cover 2,500 miles (4,000 km) through the mountains and the city of Kyoto for one thousand days over a period of seven years.

We found another pathway above the parking lot leading up the mountain past a series of carved stone monuments exhibiting a variety of Buddhalike faces. This gentle ground covered in autumn leaves and green moss was, to us, one of the most spiritual places on Mount Hiei. We felt sure it was one of the many paths to the summit.

NARA

April 10 . . . Several deer nuzzled our pockets while others rubbed against the trees causing a snowstorm of cherry blossoms to whiten the temple gardens. Higher up on the hillside the early morning mist shrouded the evergreens in a ghostlike forest, the dew dripping from new green buds back-lit with the first rays of sun. The kami spirits seemed very close to us this morning . . .

Nara was the first Imperial capital, established in 710 AD, breaking the traditional practice of moving capitals following the death of each emperor because of the Shinto taboo against death pollution. Nara became a concentration of wealth and power, an opulent city of palaces and lavish temples honoring various gods. It is here that Buddhism was introduced early in the eighth century.

Local Resources

We travelled by JNR from Kyoto to Osaka where we transferred for the one-hour trip to Nara. For accommodation, see the JTB guides or book through the travel centers in Kyoto or Osaka; in Nara there is a tourist information office at the JTB train station and another larger one three blocks away on the main street, Sanjo-dori, Tel: (0742) 22–3900. We enjoyed the simple Ryokan Matsumae; Tel: (0742) 22–3686 near Sarusawa Pond, a short walk to the deer park. Nara is not a large city and many of the main sights are best seen by walking, although there is good bus service to the outlying areas.

Yoshino Mountain is a one-hour ride south (if you take the Limited Express train called the Tokkyu, on the Kintetsu line) with one change at Kashihara Jingu. This is a well-travelled route and easy to negotiate although few people speak English.

The Ancient Imperial Capital

The major focus in **Nara** is the old Imperial Deer Park, filled with pagodas and temples along with one thousand deer who regularly pilfer food from picnic lunches and hide behind the three thousand stone lanterns leading to the Kasuga shrine. This is the home of one of the founding clans of the city. The deer are held sacred, not only being reminders of the Buddha as a deer in a previous incarnation, but also because the imperial prince was said to have been carried to this shrine on the back of a deer.

The height of influence of Nara as the powerful Imperial capital for seventy-four years coincided with the leading edge of Buddhism which was integrated into the preexisting beliefs of nature shamanism predominant in the countryside. The Shinto sun goddess Amaterasu was also identified with Vairocana, the Great Sun Buddha who dominates the Todaiji Temple, the headquarters of the Kegon sect of Buddhism. Within this temple complex is the world's largest bronze statue of the Buddha. First cast in 749 AD, this 52-foot (16 m), 437-ton Buddha of wisdom and mercy offers salvation to all beings in the universe. The **Daibutsu-den** which houses him is only two-thirds the size of the original building, but at 508 feet (155 m) high, it is still the largest wooden structure in the world. The elegant statue holds the familiar lotus blossom, and is surrounded by huge 26-foot (8 m) Diva spirits, the four heavenly guardians who destroy all obstacles in the path of Buddhism.

But these famous shrines are not all there is to see in Nara. The old city has wonderful antique shops and private art galleries displaying contemporary Japanese arts in ceramics, painting, and sculpture. The **Arike Pond** near the deer park is a quiet haven to enjoy colorful carp swimming under lily pads ringed with necklaces of sakura blossoms. The wooded areas beyond the main temples of the park give sanctuary to an abundance of small Shinto shrines, often just a torii gate guarding tiny wooden structures holding a bright orange or a sheaf of colorful flowers honoring the attendant kami. We enjoyed the walk through residential areas to Shin-yakushiji Temple, then continued higher up the hillside behind a bamboo forest to **Byakugoji Temple**, the eighth-century villa of Shiki-no-miko, the seventh prince and son of Emperor Tenchi. The simple gardens and brilliant green grass were enhanced by a carpet of white and rose-colored camellia blossoms, one of the oldest flowering plants found in Japanese gardens.

From Nara we took a day trip to **Yoshino Mountain**, the site of the ruins of the southern Imperial Court in Yoshino Kumano National Park. A cable car delivered us to the village filled with tourist shops. This "mountain of the history and the devotee of a religion" is a prime spring pilgrimage site to view the cherry blossoms. (Try to avoid weekends when thousands of Japanese arrive to celebrate the sakura with phenomenal amounts of food and alcohol.) The Kimpusen-ji Temple was draped in colorful flags and the mountain was a blaze of pink and white with the profusion of blossoms from one hundred thousand cherry trees cascading their variegated colors from top to bottom. The variety of trees and the change in altitude guarantees a continuous show of color for several weeks (check the rating on the Sakura Viewing Timetable). We were lucky to see the full range of blossoms and colors, symbolic of the soul of Okuno Senbon, the kami spirit in the center of the mountain.

THE ISE PENINSULA

April 15 . . . The sense of peace generated by this setting was a powerful affirmation of the spirit of place . . . tall cedars swaying in the wind . . . gold emblems gleaming against the weathered wood of rustic buildings . . . copper-colored leaves gently falling on bright green mosses . . . the simple elegance of the man-made structures totally integrated with the land.

Ise is the abode of the sun goddess Amaterasu, the central mythological figure in Shinto ritual and practice. The shrine of Naiku is the Japanese Mecca, the holiest in the country, where Amaterasu brings the life and renewal that we felt in this marvellous forest, and again while watching the sun rise behind the torii gate at the Futami Rocks.

Travel Tips

Both JNR and Kintetsu (see Nara section) travel from Nara to Ise, onward to Futamigaura (twenty minutes), and to the great pearl ponds at Toba on the tip of the Ise peninsula. Pearls are the great souvenir to purchase here, although not at souvenir prices!

Local Resources

The Ise travel center is in the station. From here the #51 bus or the Kintetsu train delivered us to the station at Naiku. We enjoyed the seventy-year-old Ryokan Hoshide; Tel: (0596) 28–2377 with its delightful traditional garden and large dining room where we could get Japanese, western, or macrobiotic food. In Futamigaura, hotel prices can be very high, so it pays to shop around.

The Shrines

To the Japanese, nature reveals the sacred, and it is easy to see why the shrines at Ise are of central importance, receiving more than six million visitors per year. Like Mecca, the pilgrimage to Ise is a national passion; everyone desires to go once in a lifetime, and "Ise clubs" collect money to send a person chosen by lot to bring back a talisman, such as the shrine paper that denotes good fortune. These shrines to Amaterasu honor her as the ancestral goddess of the Imperial family and therefore the Japanese nation. It is here that Amaterasu emerged from the left eye of Izanagi, the great male creation deity.

Early shamanistic ceremonies probably took place at natural earth sites such as streams and mountains, but the feeling of nature is not lost at the man-made shrines of Ise. The forest of cypress and eight-hundred-year-old cryptomeria provide a natural cathedral for the grand shrine of Naiku. First built in 4 BC, this shrine is replaced on an adjacent site every twenty years as an expression of gratitude to Amaterasu for her blessings. The surrounding forest is replenished through an ongoing reforestation program to ensure a supply of wood, as only natural materials are used; unpainted wood, thatched roofs, interlocking joints, and dowels echo the rites of thousands of years ago. The nearby Uji Bridge over the sacred Isuzu River, where pilgrims first purify their hands and mouth with sacred water before visiting the shrine, is also rebuilt every twenty years.

Contemporary life at Ise includes one hundred male priests serving at the **Jingu** (the **Grand Shrine of Ise**) which is headed by the Sacred Priestess, Princess Kuzuko Takasukasa, who is the daughter of the recently deceased emperor. The most important annual ritual is Kanname-sai, the thanksgiving in mid-October held to honor the first bounty of rice. The emperor or his envoy attends at Ise several times a year. Female attendants participate in the sacred Kagura dances and a male dancer performs the Ninjo-Mai, which is offered only at Ise or in the Imperial household. Priests can be seen attending the shrines, their crisp white blouses enhanced by flowing skirts of white, purple, or blue, depending on their rank. The constant stream of pilgrims doesn't diminish even in the rain; instead it is augmented by a sea of colorful umbrellas.

We spent two days rejuvenating in this green haven. It is said the transformative powers of the holy seem very close to the earth at Ise. For us it was reminiscent of the thin atmosphere of Iona and the veil of Avalon.

The shrine at **Futamigaura** is called Meoto Iwa, the "Married Rocks," incarnations of the mythological creator gods, Izanagi and Izanami. Their marriage bond is symbolized by the rope that unites them in a sacred trust—the heavy straw rope is renewed in a sacred ceremony every January 5—and the torii gate on Izanagi's rock sanctifies the location. Somehow we expected to be alone to witness the Married Rocks at sunrise but we were joined by five hundred excited school children who came to honor the gods. The boardwalk and the bracing sea air were equally renewing, stimulating Courtney to propose marriage, which I accepted, but without the rope!

Photo Tips   *The Torii Bridge*

Much of my time at Ise was spent in the rain, and I was happier than a duck in water. Though rainy weather photography presents a special set of challenges, the results are often far more aesthetic than photography done in direct sunlight. Because color slide film lacks tolerance for wide tonal differences, rainy weather offers an even tonality of light and rich saturated colors, and the added moisture provides reflectiveness and life to the picture.

As important as it is to get out in the rain, though, it is equally important to keep your camera and lenses dry. I have learned to work with one hand, while holding the umbrella with the other, camera supported on the tripod. When I change film, I clasp the umbrella firmly under my armpit, and when I move about, I hold the tripod high so the camera and lens keep dry under the umbrella. (One of these days I am going to make a clamp to secure the umbrella to the tripod so that both hands are free to operate the camera controls.) Sometimes I work with an assistant holding a large umbrella for the three of us—photographer, assistant, and camera!

Rainy day photography lends itself to close-up work, to abstracting patterns in nature, and focusing on dew drops. Thus if there is little or no wind, working under an umbrella is not as difficult as it sounds. Dress warmly, use good waterproof footwear and rain pants, and give yourself more time than you would in dry weather. As few photographers really believe the benefits of rain for their work, try it and see the colorful results for yourself. Use slow film (ISO 25 or ISO 50) and small apertures (for complete depth of field); let the exposures run twenty or thirty seconds, then rejoice in the magnificent colors that are possible, even when the light appears dark and uninviting. Besides, here is the perfect opportunity to spend a day out photographing when other activities on your trip (like sightseeing) have been cancelled.

*Uji Bridge at Naiku Grand Shrine, Ise, Japan, April 1989/*Sacred Earth, *p. 241*

MOUNT FUJI

April 19 . . . The swans glide across Lake Yamanaka, effortlessly arching their wings to perfectly mimic the background shape of white-clad Fujisan. Together they echo the pristine quality of the natural world, the quiet solitude and the eternal presence of the spirit that is all around us. This seemed like the true kami presence.

Mount Fuji, or Fujisan, is the ultimate holy mountain, its name meaning "everlasting life." The indigenous Ainu people first called it Fuchi, after the fire goddess who created the frequent volcanic eruptions. Honored by both Shintoist and Buddhist, it is the duty of the faithful to climb Fujisan at least once in a lifetime.

Travel Tips

From the Ise Peninsula, the Kintetsu train is a two-hour journey to Nagoya, where we transferred onto the JNR Shinkansen to go to Shizuoaka, and then to the local JNR train to Fujinomiya.

Local Resources

From here a circular route can be taken around the Fuji Five Lakes; buses do connect each town but schedules may be erratic. We chose to rent a car in Fujinomiya;

the contract was completed in Japanese as we could find no one who spoke English! Don't rely on using credit cards here.

If you arrive by train from Tokyo at the Fuji Yoshida station at the northeast point of the circle route, the tourist center at the station is very helpful with maps, local information, and accommodation. The prime tourist season is summer, for water sports; I fear the area might be impossibly chaotic with tourists, although that is the only time to honor Fujisan with a climb to the summit. Consequently, thousands of pilgrims inundate this area during July and August, the only time when Fuji is free of snow and the temples are open for the pilgrimage trek (request JTB pamphlets for detailed information). Although some hotels on this route were open, many were closed. We chose to stay at the YMCA on Lake Yamanaka; Tel: (0555) 65–7721, a rustic setting that provided us with a wood cabin near the lake and group meals with young Japanese students on a variety of retreats. The simplicity of our days here enhanced the spiritual energy we felt in the presence of the mountain.

Fujisan is accessible by car to the fifth station most of the year. The northwest Suburu Road is a forty-minute drive from Kawaguchi-ko, which offered wonderful views through the drifting clouds. The Fujisan Skyline Road from the south was only open to the half-way station. The only access to the summit is by climbing in the summer, when buses bring pilgrims from Fujiyoshida or from as far away as Fujinomiya in the southwest, and deliver them to the starting point at the Fuji Sengen Shrine or to Go-gome, the fifth station half-way point.

Fujisan

Mount Fuji meets the Japanese ideal of a natural shrine, providing both a closeness to the mystical aspect of nature and an escape from the mundane reality of life to allow a deeper experience of the divine. Buddhists believe **Fujisan** is a gateway to another world, while Shintoists recognize kami spirits and build shrines to Sengen-Sama, the goddess of blossoms who can be seen in the form of a luminous cloud floating over the crater. Fujisan was active for twenty thousand years until 1707, but she is considered to be sleeping rather than dead. The Fuji Sengen Shrine, built by the Suijen emperor, is dedicated to the goddess Konohana Sakuya Hime, to pacify the volcano. This is the starting point for pilgrimages, with a July first ritual to protect climbers. Many other shrines grace the base and the climbing route, offering a haven and a place of prayer for the safety of the thousands of summer pilgrims.

Fujisan is definitely more impressive from a distance; many tourists choose to go only to the Lake Hakone area, and view her from 40 miles (64 km) away, but she can be finicky and is often hidden in the mists. We felt blessed to spend five days in her territory during which we experienced her many moods. This is a wonderful time to be introduced to this area when it is graced with a pink haze of sakura blossoms and the smell of spring buds on the many green trees.

Past volcanic eruptions have created dense lower material that does not allow the penetration of water, so the run-off from Fujisan creates nearby springs and falls such as **Shiraito Falls**. These semicircular falls, which look like the "white threads" of their name, are another popular tourist and pilgrimage destination. While we visited, two priests clad only in white trousers stood under the freezing cold spray, their arms raised in prayer, for more than forty minutes. Perhaps they practised the Buddhist folk cult of Shugendo, which is supposed to endow magical powers on those who undergo ritual austerities. We admired their endurance and their dedication to the spirit of Fujisan.

Photo Tips   *Mount Fuji and the Swans*

Unlike the Guilin Mountains of China, Mount Fuji is quite easy to photograph. Though it hides demurely behind cloud for days at a time, when revealed, it can be seen and enjoyed from long distances, portraying its classic shape and snow-capped peak. Summer is generally not the best time to photograph Fuji because the snows disappear, leaving a rather barren summit; April is ideal because the cherry trees are in full blossom. I believe Fuji is meant to be photographed from a distance as much of the pilgrims' path that leads to the summit is a gravel trail, and most uninspiring to the aesthetic eye.

There are several placid lakes nearby that offer an opportunity for mirrored images. One, shown here, is Lake Yamanaka, where we stayed for three nights and where one morning I found a number of swans preening and swimming close by. I used a normal lens, got as low as I could by lying on my stomach, and watched the swans at play. Only once did I see a display of outstretched wings so beautifully mimicking the mountain peak, but I was ready for the joyous moment. Taking time to be with your subject matter is so often the prerequisite to good photography, and the Sakura goddess, protector of Mount Fuji, smiles on those who take the time to pay homage to her beauty.

Swans on Lake Yamanaka, and Mount Fuji, Japan, April 1989/ Sacred Earth, *p. 165*

China

Sacred China

The spirituality of the Chinese is best reflected in their attitudes toward nature, not unlike the Japanese Shinto beliefs, in which all aspects of the spirit can be seen in the landscape. The identification of sacred geography has been influenced by mythology, natural features, philosophy, patronage, and economic and social issues.

The essential harmony of man and nature is seen in the creation myth of the god Shang Ti, a god of vegetation whose seed was the rain, and who created man as well as all living things on the body of the mother goddess earth (Keswick, p. 29). A later creation myth spoke of the god who died after living eighteen thousand years (surely this feat alone was impetus for the search for immortality!). His head became the sun and moon, his blood the rivers and seas, his hair the plants, his limbs mountains, his voice the thunder, his perspiration the rain, his breath the wind, and his fleas the ancestors of humankind. The legendary Immortals, called Hsien, were enchanted godlike beings thought to reside in the mythical peaks of the Kunlun (Himalayas) or the islands in the eastern sea, which melted into the mist as visitors approached. As early as the seventh century BC, Taoist thought showed reverence for the creative processes inherent in nature, revealing the divine immanence to which we owe our lives. Later Confucian principles related a similar philosophy with an overlying pragmatic system of ethics that also honored the earth, but primarily with agriculture as the basis of the state. The emperor was shown plowing the field, with the prosperity of the state seen as flowing from his personal virtue. The development of Buddhism by the last century BC allowed the incorporation of these ideas with the Buddhist view of the landscape as a symbol of the eternal void.

All of these philosophies were espoused by various ruling dynasties throughout history. Chronicles report that a third-century BC emperor sent an expedition to find the archipelago of the Hsien and the secret of eternal life. Unable to find them, he built a replica of their mountain abode to entice them to come to him. While the Taoist religious seeker wandered alone, an image of the sacred mountain hanging from his staff, the Buddhist built mountain monasteries to bring him closer to the Immortals.

This ancient cult of immortality continues to influence the mythologies built into the sacred landscape of China today. Perhaps the principles of the sacred can best be illustrated in Chinese gardens and the legacies of the Imperial parks. These were created not only as pleasure gardens, but for religious purposes as well, illustrating the contemporary world view and humanity's place therein, as each emperor tried to outdo his predecessors and reinforce his heavenly mandate in his private search for immortality. The nine sacred mountains of China (four Buddhist, five Taoist), the formal gardens found in every city, and the temples on the peaks of the karst mountains of Guilin are prime pilgrimage destinations of modern China.

Travelling in China

Hong Kong is the major entry port for most cities in China, and it is still a highly touted tourist destination with flashy electronic shops, designer clothes, and glitzy jewelry. Buses, trolleys, cabs, and Mercedes limousines compete for space on the garish shopping avenues and narrow back streets with their market stalls and tenement-style buildings, while floating villages of boat people dot the bay.

Our best-laid plans of reserving a hotel went awry so the tourist office at the airport found us one on Hong Kong Island, a five-minute ferry ride back to Kowloon. The moderately priced Emerald Hotel, 152 Connaught Road West; Tel: 5–468111, caters mostly to Chinese visitors, and is a ten-minute taxi or trolley ride from the ferry crossing the harbor. A good alternative on the other side of the bay is the YMCA at 41 Salisbury Road, Kowloon; Tel: 3–692211; Telex: 31274 HYMCA HX— but reserve well in advance as this central, hotel-style, moderately priced establishment is very popular. There are many more luxury hotels in this fast-paced city. The harbor cruise is a nice way to avoid the chaos of the streets and shoppers, although the waterways rival them for traffic!

Travel within China can be exciting, exasperating, and exhausting, even if you're on a guided tour. We chose to do it alone, but enlisted the help of Cultural Tours to get us there. They expedited our visas and managed to get us seats on a charter flight and a hotel in Guilin. They also offer a variety of excursions and extensive tours into China and Southeast Asia; contact them at 11C Cindic Tower, 128 Gloucester Road, Wanchai, Hong Kong; Tel: (5) 8346382; Fax: (5) 8346391; or through their Canadian office at #306–2600 Granville Street, Vancouver, B.C. V6H 3V3, Canada; Tel: (604) 736-7671; Fax: (604) 736-5603.

Our first inkling of the hassles of travelling alone in China came when we arrived at Guilin at 10:00 PM. We waited an hour in a non-queue to clear immigration (no questions), and when we finally found a taxi driver who could understand where we wanted to go, he charged us double the going rate (we discovered later) in Hong Kong dollars because there was no exchange office open at the airport. This was not a great introduction to this gray city that looked even more drab in the constant rain, relieved only by the colorful array of plastic capes whizzing by on the endless stream of bicycles. People did not seem friendly here, although the CITS (the China International Travel Service, the official government service) was very helpful. In general, CITS is the only way to arrange travel, but some of their offices could not provide reliable information out of their own area. We still don't know if the airport at Shouzhou is open! Many places gave us conflicting information and the only solution was to get to our destination and try to figure things out there. The constant uncertainty can be wearing. The official government airline, CAAC, has offices in most tourist-oriented cities, but it is a toss-up whether they or CITS are more efficient. The first thing to do on arriving in any Chinese city is to start planning your departure, as air and train tickets can be difficult to reserve.

All modes of transportation in China are crowded, and confirmed flight reservations can be bumped because of overbooking—even organized tours have been known to go amiss. Train travel is on "hard" or "soft" seats, the former just being a wooden or metal bench with little padding. CITS in Chengdu was very helpful in getting reserved soft seats for our overnight trip to Chongqing—you can try to negotiate the purchase alone but the system seems to operate on a request basis, and only then does the official CITS get first choice. There was a minimum two-day wait when we were there. My experience in buying hard seats to Mount Emei would not make me confident about negotiating *anything* in the railway station! Unable to book ahead, in Chongqing we were able to arrange our own cheap three-day Yangzi River cruise; we felt lucky that one young man spoke some English and found us second-class reserved seats in one of about ten two-berth private rooms. The other five hundred travellers slept in bunks in dorms of ten to fifty beds per room below deck. Most mainstream tourists take the luxury ships, but there were a dozen other western tourists with us, one of whom spoke Chinese.

One of the biggest hassles for the individual traveller in China is dealing with the "staring squads" as one travel guide has aptly described them. Everywhere we were surrounded and gawked at. If Courtney stepped away from his tripod, he frequently had a crowd looking through his camera; locals often tried to gaze over our shoulders to read maps, and asking for information always produced a large crowd with diverse opinions (in Chinese) of what to do. Luckily we were always rescued by someone who spoke enough English to assist; a dictionary or phrase book with Chinese characters is invaluable. We also had English-speaking contacts write down useful information in Chinese characters, such as directions for taxi drivers, our favorite foods, and basic information about us so that we could communicate our needs to new people. This was vital in smaller towns where no one speaks English, and even in larger cities or big hotels where communication is often carried out on a very basic level.

A more unpleasant and constant occurrence is the spitting and hawking—on the street, in buses, in hotels—everywhere; being exposed to this can bring one to the point of nausea. Perhaps the air pollution is to blame. One frequent visitor to China told us he never goes home without a respiratory infection and unfortunately his experiences held true for us. This uncomfortable exposure to droves of people is compounded by the general noise level. People *shout* in China, for every aspect of communication. It is all-pervasive and can be very uncomfortable for the westerner; in one private bus, even my earplugs didn't help. The shouting is compounded by drivers of cars, buses, and bicycles constantly leaning on their horn, which unfortunately seems to be necessary as people wander obliviously about the streets.

In most places we stayed in larger hotels as we needed the comfort away from the daily chaos we experienced travelling. Most of the time we found hotels when we arrived in a place, as CITS would not book them ahead for us, and it was difficult to telephone; we just arrived by taxi and always found accommodation. As most westerners and tour groups use five-star hotels, moderately priced and budget accommodation is probably usually available, so most hotels are listed here only with the street location and the telephone number. The western-style hotels in the largest cities provide telephone, telex, or Fax services. In other places telephone services are minimal and a Chinese translator is usually necessary. Postal services seem reliable, although the stamps always need glue!

Large hotels tend to offer both a western (expensive) and Chinese menu which we found delicious. In small towns we took our chances and ate local food from streetside stalls or small cafes and never had any digestive problems even though the sanitary conditions were often questionable. In many small places there are no bathroom facilities, or at best a pit toilet; always carry toilet paper and don't expect water to wash in even if there is a toilet. A most common sight is kids up to four years old with their pants split from stem to stern so they can relieve themselves anywhere. Although we could appreciate the difficulty in providing facilities in rural areas, it was distressing to see the lack of regard for basic sanitation and the subsequent stress on the environment, a situation we found in many countries.

As for money, all foreigners are supposed to purchase goods and services with FEC (foreign exchange certificates) obtained in banks or hotel exchanges. However, in small towns we found it common practice to use RMB (the local currency, which is exchanged on the black market in larger towns at half the cost). This is probably quite risky, and it is not possible to change the RMB back as foreigners are not even supposed to have it! It is probably best to stick to FEC as costs are not that high anyway. In our Chengdu hotel we were able to get cash advances on credit cards, but don't rely on cards for expenses.

CHINA

May 10 ... Travelling alone in China left us waxing eloquent and groaning in total frustration. We bicycled along the back roads of Yangshou, watched the sunrise over the Li River at Xing Ping, shivered in the snow on the Golden Summit of Emeishan, had lunch on the great toe of the largest Buddha statue in the world, and searched for the Immortals in the mists of the Yangzi ...

The sacred sites of China are based on Taoist, Confucian, and Buddhist beliefs. The world of nature is the embodiment of immortality, and the pilgrimage has long been practised as the vehicle to the sanctuary of heaven.

Local Resources

Guilin, a favorite tour group stop, has a wide range of hotels, from the luxury Holiday Inn (14 South Ronghu Road; Tel: 3950; Telex: 48456 CLHCL CN) to the moderately priced favorite, the Guilin Osmanthus (451 Zongshan South Road; Tel: 2261; Cable: 0030). The Garland Hotel on Zongshan South Road across from the railway station was also good. The CITS office is at 102 Wen Ming Road; Tel: 223224, but have your hotel show you on a map as street signs are nonexistent. Boat tickets for the five-hour Li River cruise can be bought here or in larger hotels; the tour bus delivers passengers to the dock, and returns them from Yangshou the same day. In Yangshou, the Moon Hill Sheraton (opposite the bus station, a few blocks from the river dock) did not live up to its borrowed name but has basic facilities and is popular with budget travellers, although the official Yangshou Hotel on the lake near the CITS office, at 102 West Street; Tel: 2256; Cable: 0948, is probably more acceptable to the average tourist. Hotel representatives meet all the boats on arrival so you will have no problem finding accommodation. Most people make the cruise a day trip, but we felt our week in Yangshou was one of our best experiences in China as we were able to relax and use it as a base to explore nearby small villages on bicycles. Along the way we met very friendly young Chinese people who were accustomed to adventurous western travellers, and eager to help by getting boat or bus tickets, or stamps, or by guiding us to out-of-the-way places.

In Chengdu, the JinJiang Hotel at 36 Renmin Nan Road; Tel: 24481; Telex: 60109 JJH CN, has long been popular with westerners so try to reserve ahead. It is on the busline (#16) and has a friendly CITS office (Tel: 29474; Cable: 8225 CHENGDU), as does the large new luxury Minshan Fandian Hotel directly across the street. Use these CITS offices for travel information to all major areas in China; pick up a local map and a map for Mount Emei here, but you will have to purchase your own tickets from the train station at the end of Renminbei Lu, a ten-minute taxi ride or a twenty-five minute bicycle ride from the hotel. It is wise to have someone write out what you want in Chinese; I was the only westerner in this huge crowded station and I found it extremely difficult to find the right wicket and to be understood, while a huge queue of people stared at me.

If you choose to climb the mountain, there are several monasteries on Mount Emei offering accommodation on three different routes (detailed in the pilgrimage map provided by CITS). Local taxis or rickshaw drivers usually meet the train and will deliver you to the starting point or to the bus that goes to the cable car. Do not underestimate the climb; a good hiker travelling light (the Chinese carry only a walking stick and a small shoulder bag) can do it in a day and a half up, and one day down. Some of the trails are very steep, even with stairs cut into the pathway. At more than 10,000 feet (3,048 m), the summit can be very cold and misty, but you can rent a heavy coat. If you are not hiking, there is a decent hotel where the cable car starts, or you can take the five-minute cable-car ride and stay at the top, although accommodation at the summit was very spartan. It is rare to see westerners here, and we were lucky to meet a German girl who could speak both Chinese and English and negotiated a room for us. This "hotel" was really a shacklike structure with the wind whistling through, but a definite improvement over the dormitories in the main building down the hall from a filthy open lavatory. Our saving grace was the great coats that were supplied, and even though the room was lit only with a bare light bulb, we had the amazing luxury of an electric heating pad on the thin bumpy mattress! A new pavilion with accommodation is apparently planned for the future. The food in the canteen was good, despite the uncertain sanitary conditions.

In Leshan, we stayed at an unnamed new hotel, a five-minute walk through the gardens behind the Buddha statue, past the Dafu Temple (which also has rooms) and up the stairs overlooking the valley. It is also accessible from the main street down from the ticket office, past all the shops, and up the steep hill. Here we had a room with a balcony over the evergreens which provided a peaceful respite for four days. The hotel bus took us back to Chengdu and it was a blessing not to have to negotiate public buses with our luggage; we took the overnight train to Chongqing but bypassed the glamorous and expensive Chongqing Hotel (41–43 Xinhua Road; Tel: 43233) and opted for the Chinese-style Huixian near the Jiefang memorial on Minzu Road, which offers budget private rooms as well as hostel-style beds. The Renmin Hotel at 175 Renmin Road; Tel: 351421 also has the local CITS office, which may be helpful to get boat tickets for the Yangzi River cruise. Be aware that it usually takes at least one day to get tickets, and may be much longer if there are a lot of tour groups (April through September).

Our tour of China coincided with the political upheaval that led to the student demonstrations and military confrontations in Beijing's Tiananman Square in 1989. We witnessed large demonstrations in every large city and were invited to political gatherings; in one city we saw thousands of people march down a street at 3:00 AM, arm in arm, singing songs of brotherhood. By the time we arrived in Wuhan, the end of the most popular section of the Yangzi River cruise, the situation was so uncertain that we decided to leave, but travel information was difficult to obtain by then. The political demonstrations had closed the bridge to the airport and the CAAC office, and CITS was useless, but we miraculously found our way to the westernized Yangzi Hotel (on Jie Fan Da Dao, Hankou, Wuhan; Tel: 562828; Fax: 353759) and treated ourselves to some comparative luxury, as by this time we were both suffering with the dreaded respiratory ailment. Even the travel agent at this large hotel could not guarantee any tickets out of China. We finally took a local ferry across the Yangzi and waited all day at the airport, where contrary to prevalent opinion, and to our amazement, we got seats on a flight to Guangzhou (Canton). Here we transferred to a direct train to Hong Kong, which turned out to be a fast and a most comfortable way to cross the Chinese border.

Sacred Sites

In **Guilin** the Seven Star Park is a main focus of social and pilgrimage activity, with its extensive ponds and network of temples named after mythical beings. The bonsai garden reflects the idea of miniaturizing nature to focus on its magical quality; the dwarfed trees are made to look aged like the elusive Immortals, allowing the viewer to use his imagination to access the spiritual world. The carefully placed rocks are another symbol of the secret of eternal life, the timeless quality of their long endurance perhaps endowed on the viewer through a kind of sympathetic magic.

This garden also illustrates the ancient science of Feng Shui or "wind and water," which is still employed in all aspects of Chinese living. The knowledge of earth energies is used in the planning of cities, especially in the placement of temples and homes in relation to specific landscape features such as trees and water, as well as the interior relationship of furniture and fixtures. Even in North America it is common for Chinese people to consult a geomancer before purchasing or building a home, and many real estate contracts have gone awry because the lay of the land is incorrect and would bring misfortune to the family.

The related philosophy of Shan Shui, which literally means landscape, is also illustrated here, involving the combination of mountains and water which is thought to invoke the isles of the Immortals. Rock worship was popular in the eleventh and twelfth century AD as seen in the building of false mountains in gardens; the yin-yang balance of nature was achieved by harmonizing the hard male aspects symbolized in the jagged rocks with the flowing feminine element of water which also symbolized purification and offered repose to the spirit. Mountains were also analogous to the earth's skeleton, while water symbolized the life-force of blood flowing through her veins (Keswick, 1978).

These concepts are illustrated through the unending adoration of the **Guilin Mountains**, the karst formations with names denoting legendary beings or associated with experiences of the Imperial rulers. Each hill around Guilin is graced with a temple to be honored. The cruise down the Li River is a lesson in mythology and social history, and every Chinese teenager can recite the important features of each historical dynasty. This popular cruise is also a lesson in the philosophy of yin and yang, illustrating the harmony of the elements of opposites in the natural world, as the jagged land formations are perfectly balanced by the gently flowing green river.

After visiting the **Reed Flute Cave** in Guilin, it is easy to see why caverns are also thought to be the home of the Immortals and the access to heaven. Every turn of the convoluted 1,640-foot (500 m) path down to the caverns suggests mythical beings, with dripping stalactites that were thought to nourish legendary kings during their grotto searches for the juice of immortality. Since its discovery in the seventh-century AD Tang Dynasty, the vast inner grotto called the Crystal Palace of the Dragon King has often been used as a refuge; the legendary battle of the Monkey King who destroyed the Dragon King's army of snails and jellyfish, leaving them petrified on the floor of the cave, has not deterred the use of this haven. The multicolored electric lights enhance the mythology, making this a popular tourist destination for the Chinese populace.

The village of **Yangshou** is the popular terminus of the **Li River** cruise but for us was an extension of the experience of rural China as we took daily cruises to small villages and bicycled back to our base. The early morning mists revealed the eternal image of the fisherman quietly poling the green waters, looking for his daily catch to feed his family. One day we took the ferry to Xing Ping where we bought huge straw hats to protect us from the hot sun as we pedalled for hours in the countryside looking for the sacred Lotus Cave. When we finally found it, the entrance was barred with a locked grate and locals told us we needed a "visa" (the only character in the phrase book which came close to "permit"). We were disappointed, but the lush valley and the exquisite red sunset we witnessed at Xing Ping helped to assuage our feelings. Another forty-five-minute bicycle ride from Yangshou took us to Moon Hill, where a strenuous climb of hundreds of stairs delivered us to this natural formation which is seen as a symbol of perfection and heaven.

Humanity's role in the world is often shown in the placement of a pavilion amidst the elements of nature. Many karst formations along the Li River have pavilions dedicated to the immortal beings, perhaps as an enticement for them to stay. These pavilions are not just tea houses, but are situated to show us our tiny but essential niche in the order of the natural world. The **Wanjian Loo** (River Viewing Pavilion Garden) in **Chengdu** is a good example, elegantly set overlooking the pond surrounded by great stands of bamboo. Perhaps we are to learn something from this bamboo, a Confucian symbol of virtue, which, like a true gentleman, shows its resilience by bending with the wind.

Later, I biked through the back alleys of Chengdu, past market stalls hanging with fresh meat as dozens of ladies sat nearby, bent over their knitting. My destination was the highly touted Chengdu Zoo which, unfortunately, was not at all exemplary of the beauty of nature as Wanjian Loo had been; garbage and cement surrounded the two pathetic-looking panda bears hiding from the heat in the back of a barren cage. Hoping to experience these entrancing beasts in the wild, we spent two days dealing with the bureaucracy trying to get permits to go to the Wuolong Panda Reserve, advertised on a poster in our hotel. However, the red tape won out, and our disappointment was only partly mellowed by the comment that all we would see is pandas in research cages.

From Chengdu we took the local train with "hard seats" to **Emeishan**, one of the four sacred Buddhist mountains. This is a very popular place of pilgrimage; one tourist pamphlet reports "the state of Shu abounds in fairy mountains, but none can match Mount Emei in beauty . . . the most well-known mountain under heaven." People of all ages struggle up thousands of steps on the two-day hike; on the train we met a group of teenagers from a candy factory who urged us to climb with them and offered to carry our equipment! We chose the bus and cable car route but met them again at the summit.

Taoists and Buddhists competed for superiority on **Mount Emei** but finally the Buddhists prevailed, as evidenced by the 151 monasteries at the height of influence in the fifteenth century AD, 20 of which are in use today and provide pilgrims with overnight accommodation. Temples with names such as Loyalty to the Country, Elegant Sound, Fairy Peak, and Thundering Cave allude to the sacred relationship with nature and the influence of social customs. The patron deity of Emeishan is Pu Hsien, the Buddha of Universal Light, who is said to have appeared once on an elephant while holding a lotus, perhaps near the popular Elephant Bathing Pond which provides a symbolic cleansing of the mind. This mountain, rising over 10,000 feet (3,077 m), is considered a natural museum, touting three thousand species of plants. The Golden Summit of Ten Thousand Buddhas promises a view of the Buddha's Halo, a particular combination of light on water crystals that produces a luminescent effect which, according to the tourist pamphlet, will leave the visitor "inspired, as if you were right in the clouds, as happy as an Immortal." Our view of this phenomenon was brief, and the beauty of the summit was marred by the shacklike hostel, filthy latrines, and freely strewn garbage. We found it hard to understand how the Chinese people could honor this place while at the same time creating such a physically offensive environment. Pilgrims seemed oblivious to their surroundings, other than the "ahs" of appreciation as the light changed on the mists. Despite being constantly cold, we were delighted when it snowed overnight, and we woke to a fairyland of white crystals which graced the rhododendron bushes and nicely covered the garbage. The invigorating air and layers of view over the valley then produced the appropriate awe for us.

From Emeishan we crammed all our bags in the already crowded local bus for the one-hour ride to **Leshan**. After helping our driver push his cycle rickshaw up a hill from the Leshan bus station, we spent four days in the aura of the largest Buddha in the world, who overlooks the confluence of the Dadu, Quingyi, and Minjiang rivers in this three-thousand-year-old city. This 230-foot (71 m) statue called **Dafu** was carved from the living red rock over the course of ninety years in the eighth century AD. Created to protect the boatmen in the swirling waters below, the Buddha offers not only spiritual protection; surplus rock from its construction was used to fill the river eddies, thus calming the waters, and a water drainage system is concealed within the statue.

Dafu is a glorious example of the Buddhist relationship with nature; ferns grow around his canonical curls (topknots) as though he is listening to nature with his

23-foot (7 m) ears, and flowers emerge from his chest and hands. It is said that Dafu is so old now that the foliage is trying to reclaim him. The Grand Buddha Temple stands on top of the promontory near his head, and layers of gardens spread over the surrounding grounds which are graced with temples. Aged ladies with bound feet lean on their wooden walking sticks as they push themselves up the hundreds of narrow stairs from the river level, where others choose to picnic on the Buddha's 26-foot (8 m) toe. Despite the crowds of pilgrims, this sacred place is one of the most peaceful we found in China.

Rather than rely on local buses from Leshan, we returned to Chengdu and were lucky to get reserved berths on the overnight train to **Chongqing**. The **Yangzi River** ferry terminal was not hard to find and a friendly man found us tickets for the next day on a boat crowded with local travellers who continually played mah-jongg and cards in the smoky upper lounge. The trip was comfortable and pleasant except for the restaurant staff who tried to triple the cost of our meals, until a Hong Kong tourist negotiated for us to pay only twice the price—which was still very cheap! This River of Golden Sand is the third largest in the world (after the Amazon and the Congo), a total length of 3,237 miles (5,179 km) with a navigable length of 1,800 miles (2,900 km). Still the primary river of commerce connecting the western Sichuan Province with the sea, it has only one bridge on its entire length (at Wuhan). The old saying "like walking into a Chinese painting" seemed appropriate to this scenery, and we wondered if this was the eastern home of the Immortals, with Hsien hiding in the mists. In medieval times it was said that the Rainbow Woman, guardian spirit of the Yangzi Gorges, was veiled in the drifting rain until her supernatural powers of fertility emerged in the form of her rainbow.

Our China experience stands out as unique in all its glories, despite the difficulties. We only hope that the Chinese people can retain their spirit and find a peaceful life in the land that nourishes them with a long history of the sacred.

Photo Tips   *The Guilin Mountains*

The Guilin Mountains offer the photographer the ultimate experience with stylized shape and form, but getting a strong bold portrait of these formations is not as simple as it might appear. The range spreads itself along the Li River Valley where, for my tastes, there is too much evidence of the twentieth century to be able to capture the unblemished majesty of the formations. There are several techniques to isolate Guilin's natural beauty in your photographs. One is to take the boat trip from Guilin to Yangshou and choose your foregrounds with care and dexterity while shooting quickly from the deck. Though I have some views I am quite pleased with, I preferred to climb and photograph more asymmetric compositions of three or four peaks using a tripod and an 80–200mm zoom lens.

For this photograph of the river bank at Xing Ping, I carefully composed the scene of ferns and mountains using the same zoom lens to fine tune the exact framing. Then I waited as the smoke from a nearby cooking fire wafted over until just the right blend of hues complimented the scene. When you have already dealt with framing the picture by zooming to the exact composition you desire, and have made decisions on exposure, depth of field, and shutter speed, the task of watching and waiting for the precise moment becomes relatively easy. And the mountains, which have attracted painters and poets for centuries, are always there, to give charm and mystique to your images.

Karst formations and ferns, Xing Ping, China, May 1989/ Sacred Earth, *p. 171*

Photo Tips   *The Grand Buddha*

The Grand Buddha in Leshan was so colossal that, from the viewing areas on each side, no traditional lens could encompass the entire carving. Only by using my 16mm fisheye lens, reaching 180 degrees from corner to corner, was I able to get the whole statue in the picture. I waited until a person approached the statue at the Buddha's foot. The tiny dot, once recognized as being a person, adds a marvelous sense of scale to this enormous figure. Although fisheye lenses do distort the image by curving straight lines near the edge of the frame, the distortion here appears minimal. The good news about fisheye lenses is that even though they have limited use, they are small and light, tucking easily into the camera bag and always ready for those special occasions when you feel in a squeeze.

If you arrive in Leshan without a fisheye lens, there is still one other opportunity for photographing the Grand Buddha in its entirety. You can take a boat trip on the Min River and record it from the water. The boat even stops on a sandbar and allows enough time for serious photo buffs to set up their tripods, where a 200mm lens is the order of the day.

But Leshan offers much more than views of the Grand Buddha, as wonderful as this is. The gardens surrounding the statue present a haven for those wanting to relax from the pace of travel through China. They are rich with ferns and mosses, and provide vignettes of abstract color, the beauty of which I have rarely seen.

The Grand Buddha,
Leshan, China, May 1989/
Sacred Earth, *p. 11*

Indochina

ANGKOR

February 10 . . . The jungle silently encroaches on the glorious
stone . . . banyan roots envelop the ancient entwined arms of the voluptuous
apsaras, and the brilliant red kapok flowers adorn the bodhisattvas now
honored by orange-clad Buddhist monks . . .

Angkor is the Kampuchean city of temples built by the ancient Khmer god-kings between the ninth and thirteenth century. Despite years of decline in the forest, the restored Angkor Wat is awesome—the largest temple complex in the world— and nearby Angkor Thom struggles to emerge from its wilderness shelter to regain its place as the symbolic center of the Khmer cosmos.

Travel Tips

Angkor is located in northern Kampuchea (Cambodia) not far from the Thai border, near the town of Siem Reap, 150 miles (242 km) northwest of the capital city of Phnom Penh.

Local Resources

At the time of writing, it is literally impossible to travel into Kampuchea without an organized tour group, which is best arranged from your country of origin. Although individual tours are rumored to be available from Bangkok, friends of ours could not obtain visas, and even if you could arrange entry visas, you would be required to join a tour on arrival. Others recommend Diethelm Travel, Kian Gwan Bldg 11, 140/1 Wireless Road, Bangkok 10500; Tel: 255–9120; Fax: (662) 256–0248. Abercrombie and Kent also has an office at 491/29–30 4th floor, Silom Plaza, Silom Road, Bangkok 10500; Tel: 235–3545; Fax: (662) 233–1864. Most tours also include Viet Nam, Laos, Thailand, and Burma, and are very expensive, but they are the only way to access some of these places. U.S. tour operators are not allowed into Kampuchea or Viet Nam; Orbitours, 7th floor, Dymocks Bldg, 428 George Street, Sydney NSW 2000, Australia; Tel: 221–7322; Fax: 221–7425 arranges overseas bookings and has many tours to choose from (see Parkes, *Southeast Asia Handbook*, for detailed information). Hotels are good and food is generally inexpensive and delicious. The best time to go is between November and April, when there are no monsoon rains to compromise landing in Siem Reap, a one-hour flight from Phnom Penh. Black market trading is very risky, and Khmer Rouge guerrilla factions still hold many areas of northwest Kampuchea and around Angkor, so be sure you are travelling with a reputable company that will not compromise on safety.

If photography is one of your prime goals, be aware that it is generally difficult to gain access to these sites at the most desirable times for photographing. With great persistence, Courtney was able to arrange a private guide from Siem Reap into Angkor Wat and Angkor Thom for sunrise photography, but he was not allowed to go to the outlying temples because of the high security risk—soldiers posted in the jungle shoot on sight and ask questions later.

Burma, now called Myanmar, is even more difficult to enter as an individual traveller. There is no land access; all visitors must enter Yangon (Rangoon) by air, serviced by Thai Air, Burma Air, Royal Nepal, Aeroflot (from Vientiane, Laos), or CAAC (from Kunming, China). All onward tickets must be confirmed, and inland travel is complicated by ancient vehicles, the poor condition of roads and train routes, and lack of information in an exceedingly bureaucratic system (see Parkes). Unless you are a *very* patient and experienced traveller, an organized tour is the best choice. Myanmar has a history of isolation and is now highly controlled by a military government, with a thriving black market and internal unrest, so a travel company specializing in the area is suggested.

However, the people of Myanmar are a generally friendly and interesting ethnic mix that includes the Mons from south Burma, groups from Thailand and Cambodia, Burmans from the Tibetan plateau, and Shans from China, resulting in more than eighty different dialects. Myanmar is primarily Buddhist, and hundreds of thousands of orange-robed monks can be seen daily walking the streets. The ancient temple city of Pagan is surrounded by a thriving contemporary city so travel, in general, is easier here than around Angkor. The main tourist hotel overlooks this site on the Irrawaddy River 90 miles (145 km) southwest of Mandalay. Most tour groups fly from Yangon to Pagan, and thence to Mandalay, although the Hollywood-immortalized steamer service on the Irrawaddy from Mandalay to Pagan still operates twice-weekly, taking 12 hours to complete this romantic river journey.

The Ancient Sacred Temple Cities

The Mon-Khmer civilization, the most significant of ancient Indochina, thrived for at least ten centuries in Kampuchea with a wealth of natural resources in a world dominated by supernatural beings. This monsoon civilization depended on fertile plains producing rice, fruit, and spices, and bountiful coastal fishing. Eight centuries of contact with India led to the gradual absorption of Indian art and culture and the fusion of Hinduism and Buddhism with native beliefs. The hierarchical chiefs of the resulting highly refined Funan state eventually split into several political units, and by the end of the eighth century the first great Angkor dynasty was established by King Jayavarman II on his return from exile in Java.

The name **Angkor** comes from the Sanskrit word "nagara," meaning "the city." Angkor became the crossroads of trade to Siam, Burma, India, and China, in a land of natural bounty fertilized by the waters of Tonle Sap, the huge northern lake draining into the great Mekong River system which facilitated transportation and communication to the southern sea gulf. Here Jayavarman II set up the concept of the god-king cult whose power was mediated through priestly brahmans. The monarch's power was further reinforced by his ownership of the soil. Thus he also became the vehicle for the populace to communicate with the powerful indigenous spirits embodied in natural phenomena. This civilization's dependence on the natural environment echoed in the plan of the temples of Angkor, where an extensive network of canals and reservoirs became part of the architecture, controlling the monsoon waters to maintain the fields. The indigenous concept of the high places being the abode of the gods was refined in these great temples built as symbols of the accepted cosmology, where each temple was constructed as a replica of Mount Meru, home of the sky god Indra and the center of the world, and was accessed by a series of terraces echoing the shape of the nearby landscape.

Angkor has been described as a journey through the universe. Here pilgrims cross moats and waterways, stretching like the mythical cosmic oceans, and follow the terraces and galleries symbolizing successions of earthly worlds and islands; the pathway is like a ritual compass leading to the temple towers that mirror the foothills of the five peaks of Mount Meru, the central sacred mountain and the navel of the earth where the god-king showered blessings from above. Each of the many temple complexes at Angkor echo this concept. The first great temple-mount of Bakong built in 881 AD by Indravarman was followed by Yasovarman's construction of his temple on the mountain of Bakheng, 6 miles (10 km) to the north. Each successive king built his own temple as a monument to himself and as a mortuary abode.

Angkor Wat is considered the perfect expression and pinnacle of Khmer art employed in the service of the liturgy. Built by Suryavarman II, this is the only temple facing west, symbolic of death and evidence of the elaborate burial practices of these god-kings who sought to escape reincarnation. Dedicated to Vishnu, the great Hindu preserver of the cosmos and the destiny of man, this greatest temple rises 213 feet (65 m) through a succession of terraces draped with galleries, pavilions, and towers which accentuate its subtle rise like a pyramid. The 492-foot (150 m) causeway incorporates balustrades in the shape of the naga-serpent to symbolize immortality. Every inch of space is covered with a re-creation of the godly abode in stone; bas-relief tells the stories of the Hindu epic, the *Ramayana,* with curvaceous apsaras (heavenly nymphs) in great abundance to welcome one from the lower hells and the steep steps confirm the effort required to attain spiritual heights. Angkor Wat is so extensive that its divine plan can only be completely visualized from above— like a magic diagram on a plain that, it is suggested, could only be seen from the vantage point of the gods.

The concept of the temple embodying an idea rather than just a place of worship becomes most apparent in the brilliant construction of Angkor Thom, attributed to Jayarvarman VII in the twelfth century. This last great king was a devout Buddhist, but his friezes incorporated both Hindu and nature gods with the Buddhist bodhisattvas to guide his people to heaven. The central Bayon is the omphalos or navel of this stone cosmos, surrounded by fifty-four towers with colossal Buddhist faces addressing the four cardinal directions. The total concept is symbolic of the great Hindu myth of the "Churning of the Sea of Milk"; here the outer moat and balustrades depict twenty-seven giants grappling with the naga-serpent that also symbolizes the rainbow—the magic bridge to the gods in the central Bayon. The gods and demons encircle Mount Mandara and the serpent Vasuki, the god of waters, pushing and pulling him around the Sea of Milk (the primal void), to release the amrita or ambrosia that confers immortality.

Even these great temples, however, could not guarantee immortality. Subsequent kings reverted to Hinduism and as the great god-king cults disintegrated, so did the waterworks that maintained a population estimated to be five hundred thousand during its prime. Some scholars suggest that the absence of another philosophical system led to the downfall of Angkor; it was gradually taken over by the Siamese who deported workers as slaves and abandoned the city by the early fifteenth century. Although reports of a glorious city filtered down through the centuries, it wasn't until 1850 that a French missionary stumbled on the disintegrating stone reclaimed by the jungle. In 1907 Siem Reap was restored to Cambodia, but major reconstruction at Angkor was halted by the recent years of war in Indochina. The stone is showing its mortality as the elements invade, the Bayon of Angkor Thom barely surviving its struggle with immense fig and banyan tree roots, but hopefully the hand of humankind will soon be able to restore a semblance of the glory of Angkor.

In Burma (Myanmar) the first great dynastic empire was **Pagan**, the temple city of the kings of the Golden Age that thrived in the eleventh and twelfth century AD. This walled city on the west bank of the Irrawaddy River has been a place of pilgrimage for more than a thousand years. Buddhism, Hinduism, and the indigenous Burmese cults came together in Pagan when King Anoratha brought the Mon royal family here in 1056 AD and started a two-hundred-year spree of temple and monastery building by dedicated slave labor. This sacred dynastic fortress of five thousand temples was protected by a two-and-a-half-mile circumference wall, and its inner moats were fed by the waters of the Irrawaddy, which also provided the means for overseas trade.

The primary architecture of Pagan is the Buddhist stupa, the terraced pagoda topped with a solid bell-like structure containing the enshrined relics of saints. The early Schwezigon Pagoda with its pyramidal shape crowned by a traditional bell-shaped Mon stupa is identified by a huge golden umbrella encrusted with jewels. In contrast, the hollow temple structures can be entered to meditate upon the statue of the Buddha. The Mahabodhi Temple is a copy of the most revered temple at Bodhgaya, India (see India section). Built in 1144, the Thatppyinnyu Temple with its two-staged pyramidal structure illustrates the later development of spacious interiors and combinations with Hindu shrine towers, porticos, interior arches, and vaults.

But the Ananda is one of the most glorious of the temple-mountains, built in 1090 on a site legends say was chosen by Indra, the Hindu sky god and founded by the famous King Kyanzittha, whose name translates to "he who survived the search." It seems that the previous King Anoratha, fearful of overthrow by a child who would be king, killed many children to protect his position. Kyanzittha became a Buddhist monk and eventually a minister and warrior to the king, who finally recognized the warrior and was not threatened by him. Kyanzittha's Ananda Temple was said to be made from the waters encircling Mount Meru and the earth from Bodhgaya. Its Greek cruciform base is topped with a multitude of terraces, a typical Indian conelike sikhara structure or spire, a stupa, and internal arches with flamboyant ornamentation, four 31-foot (10 m) Buddha statues honoring the four directions, and the largest collection of Buddhist stone relief and sculpture in Burma.

Pagan also contains many temples dedicated to ancestral and other spirits honored through the nat cults, the traditional religious system that identifies a multitude of spiritual beings. Personal and house spirits, communal spirits, spirits of the dead, and nature spirits are some of the many who are honored with wooden shrines which glow with lamps to honor and keep their favor. Some suggest that these indigenous cults provide an outlet for human drives frustrated by the puritanical aspects of Buddhism; the Gawdawpalin shrine at Pagan, dedicated to ancestral spirits, is surrounded with minipagodas and its interior displays lavish ornamentation. Contemporary nat shrines and festivals are supported by the government and by Buddhist doctrine which also acknowledges supernaturals as being important for the attainment of earthly goals, whereas Buddhist worship is the means for spiritual benefit.

Although a 1975 earthquake severely damaged many temples, Pagan is still a glorious site, continuously awash with smiling pilgrims revering its multitude of temples.

Indonesia

JAVA

June 5 ... From the steamy grandeur of Borobudur, we escaped the enervating heat to wander past bubbling geothermal pools wafting their sulfurous hazes through the dank temples of the Dieng Plateau. This respite prompted us to follow our intuition to Bromo Crater where we basked in cool mountain air and awoke every morning at 3:30 to glory in the misty dawn vistas of Semeru, reminiscent of the legendary cosmic center of the earth.

The island of Java, Indonesia, is famed not only for its coffee and batik, but as the haven of Borobudur, the Buddhist shrine named from the Sanskrit words Vihara Buddha Uhr, meaning Buddhist monastery on a high place. Here, Buddhist pilgrims experience the life of Prince Siddartha in the twenty-seven hundred pictorial panels and sculpture contained in the largest Buddhist stupa in the world. Other Hindu temples and natural sanctuaries have made Java a long-standing place of pilgrimage.

Travel Tips

The easiest access point to Java is through Singapore, the independent republic at the tip of the Malaysian peninsula, which is serviced by many international airlines. Singapore is a mini-Asia, offering the culinary, social, and souvenir experiences of a major excursion. It is also another electronic and shopping capital, easily rivalling Hong Kong in variety and prices. A word of warning: do *not* take drugs into Singapore—this is punishable by death, and they are *not* joking. Singapore is the squeakiest-clean city in Southeast Asia: from the efficient airport, immaculate and smoke-free taxis, broad tree-lined avenues without a speck of garbage (but very congested with traffic) to the new subway system which is air conditioned, brightly lit, and spotless. The efficiency continues in the postal and telephone system. There is a wide range of deluxe to budget accommodation; we enjoyed the Orchard Road YMCA with its hotel-style rooms and roof-top swimming pool. This is the best of the three YMCAs in Singapore, as it is central, moderately priced, and comfortable accommodation—contact 1 Orchard Road, Singapore 0923; Tel: 337–3444; Telex: RS 55325 YMCA.

Indonesia's Air Garuda flies to Jakarta where we cleared customs (easily) and opted to fly on to Yogyakarta to visit Borobudur. Although public bus service is extensive throughout Java, both locals and tourists told us horror stories about tourist rip-offs on buses; one friend had her traveller's checks cut out of her money belt secured under her jeans—a razor blade was used to cut through both layers on a crowded bus in Jakarta.

Local Resources

Yogyakarta is a charming former Dutch colonial stronghold that became the seat of the first Sultanate in 1755. It is an artistic center, boasting a fine arts college and a batik research center, as well as a bustling tourist town. There are many good hotels in town, but we chose to stay a ten-minute ride away, near the airport at Sahid Garden Hotel, JL Babarsari, Yogyakarta, Indonesia; Tel: (0274) 87078. The Ambarrukmo Palace Hotel on JL Laksda Adisutjipto, PO Box 10; Tel: 88488; Telex: 25111 is more luxurious and closer to the city center. Hotel representatives meet flights, and this hotel offered half-price rooms, good service, and an outdoor pool which was very welcome. Transportation is by hired car and driver, or locally by cycle rickshaw. Buses are available to Borobudur but their timing was too erratic for our needs, so our driver took us on the one-hour drive there and on the two-and-a-half-hour excursion to Dieng Plateau. The Tourist Information Center has an excellent handbook that meets all tourist needs and can be found at 16 Malioboro Street (Tel: 2812) in the center of town, two blocks south of the railway tracks. Indonesian rupees can be purchased in larger hotels, at special exchange kiosks, and at some banks. Credit cards are accepted in larger hotels in Yogyakarta, but not at Dieng or Bromo. Many tourists use Yogyakarta as a base to explore the seaside resorts to the south, and the cool mountain hill resorts on Mount Merapi northeast of Borobudur.

From Yogyakarta we flew to Surabaya, and rented a taxi (fixed rate, with or without air conditioning) to take us to Bromo Crater which involved a one-and-a-half-hour ride to the north coast resort town of Probolinggo, then a further hour on a good road winding up the mountain through the lush vegetation of fertile terraces to the village of Ngadisari. Guest houses are available here but we preferred to go another 1.5 miles (2.5 km) up the hill to the Hotel Bromo Permai (reserved through East Java Booking Office, JL Pang, Sudirman 237, Probolinggo; Tel: 21510–41256) where we had a rustic two-bed bungalow with a shower, and our own porch with bamboo chairs to enjoy the fresh mountain air. From here we walked forty minutes (or you can rent a horse or jeep) over a miragelike landscape, and trudged up two hundred and fifty wooden stairs in swirling sulfur mists to the crater rim. Tourists routinely stay one night, arising in the cold darkness at 3:30 for hot chocolate before the one-hour jeep ride to the Mount Penanjaken outlook (or to the crater) to see the sunrise. A local bus or taxi will take you back to Probolinggo, and the same options are there for return to the airport at Surabaya, or westward to Bali via the ferry from Ketapang. Be sure to bargain with local taxis as rates can vary tremendously.

Sacred Sites of Ancient Java

Borobudur is the Javan masterpiece of Mahayana Buddhism, its ornate sculpture comparable to the best ornamental wonders of Indian, Mayan, or Moorish architecture. The stupa is unique to Buddhism; this ninth-century AD structure is built on a natural mound similar to prehistoric earthworks found in other parts of the world. It consists of a square base topped with a sequence of concentric terraces that the pilgrim can circumambulate to experience the different stages of Prince Gautama's wanderings in his quest for enlightenment. The gradation symbolizes the levels to attain perfection, from the square base of the world of sinners in the sphere of desire (Kamadhatu), through the five hemispheres symbolizing form (Rapadhatu), to the final pinnacles of formlessness (Arapadhatu) which lead to salvation through the release of earthly bonds. At this ultimate height one meets 432 images of reincarnated Buddhas that display a multitude of hand symbols, or mudras, signifying the way of the Buddha through postures of charity, meditation, fearlessness, reasoning, and the wheel of dharma (the law). Housed within latticed bell-like stone chambers, most of the Buddhas are only partially visible, symbolic of the formlessness achieved on this level.

This amazing illustration of Buddhist cosmography teaches that assisting others to reach nirvana is the way to be delivered from one's own suffering in the cycle of samsara. This eternal message in stone is delivered to hundreds of thousands of pilgrims who annually descend on Borobudur.

Ten miles (17 km) east of Yogyakarta, past the Valley of Kings housing the temples of the royal mausoleum, is the **Temple of Prambanan**, the ninth-century AD monument illustrating the great Hindu epic of the *Ramayana*. The highly ornate pyramidal spires of the main temples soar above ground that is littered with ruins from other structures awaiting restoration. On every full moon evening between June and October this becomes the setting of an open-air theater where the *Ramayana* tale is recreated in ballet with the traditional Indonesian gamelan music.

The 6,000-foot (1,828 m) **Dieng Plateau** to the northwest is a welcome relief from the sultry heat of Yogyakarta. This haven treasures some of the oldest Hindu temples on Java, as well as a geothermal earthscape of gurgling mud pools and sulfurous steam vents which soon left us light-headed. The tiny temples sit like dollhouses, misted with swirling sulfur fumes from the crater floor that last expanded in August of 1988. The nearby Telaga Warna (Colorful Lake) harbors caves and legends that made it an ancient pilgrimage destination and it is still a favorite place of meditation. The meaning of "Dieng" is translated variously as "Home of the Gods," "Dawn Horizon," and "Spirit Place," but the linguistics don't really matter as it is one of the most tranquil spots we found in Java. The nearby "Spring of Youth" is another reason to make the effort to come here—our guide guaranteed results if we washed in both fonts (and we did)!

This physically and spiritually refreshing sojourn in the mountains inspired us to follow our intuition to **Mount Bromo**, another home to the gods in east Java. Although promoted for its sunrise view, we discovered from locals that "Bromo" is the Javanese anglicized version of "Brahma," the supreme deity of the Hindu trinity. East Java is the land of the old Hindu kingdoms that eventually penetrated into the island of Bali after the invasion of the Mongols and the resulting dominance of Islam in Java. The local Tenggerese villagers still make frequent offerings to Dewa Kusuma, god of fire, deep in this volcano, and the annual Kasada festival (December or January) is the peak pilgrimage season for Bromo Crater.

And the sunrise was not a disappointment. On three consecutive mornings we dutifully arose at 3:30 for the hour-long jeep ride in the dark across the sandy crater floor and up the steep bumpy trail through heavy mists to the lookout at Mount Penanjaken. Bromo is one of several craters within the larger Tengger caldera which seemed constantly veiled in swirling mists, creating a different panorama for us each morning. The changing angle of the sun rising through this haze produced a series of miragelike vistas through which the distant belching of the active volcano of Mount Semeru entertained us with mushroom clouds of ash every twenty or thirty minutes. Semeru, the highest mountain in Java at 12,060 feet (3,676 m), is also known as Mahameru, "Great Mountain," reported in myths to have journeyed from the Himalayas. The view from the rim of Bromo was equally spectacular, complemented by the brilliant yellow sulfur stains deep within the cavernous crater and the wafting sulfur smell which left us feeling quite heady at times as we walked for an hour on the narrow pathway circling the huge rim. The walk to Bromo over the "sea of sand" of the caldera floor provided another moonscape of images as we approached through the ancient lava formations.

We also loved the **Widodoran Cave**, hidden in a sheltered green area of regrowth on the backside of Bromo and a twenty-minute hike up from the caldera floor. Known as "Angel Cave," a local man told me that pilgrims pray here every "sweet Friday," and we met several women from other parts of Java who had come to bring back the healing waters of the nearby spring. We found the cave draped in lush greenery, with water gushing through the ferns and mosses to form the holy stream below, as drips inside the cave plunked into a smooth pool garnished with recent flower offerings. This place felt like another haven of meditation, with a vast outlook over the desertlike floor of the larger caldera.

Photo Tips   *Bromo Crater Lookout*

There are times when the atmospheric conditions and quality of light combine to produce a landscape that beckons to be called sacred. It is sacred because of its

*View at Bromo Crater Lookout, Java, Indonesia, June 1989/*Sacred Earth, *p. 188*

power to alter our minds, stir our imaginations, or fill us with awe. There may be a geomantic component to the landscape, a measurable physical quality of electromagnetic power, but I believe the more potent force is in its potential to excite those willing to be transported by its beauty.

In these rare moments of union between light and form, the call is not to master the camera, but to be open to and in touch with the harmony. If technique comes into play, it is only to isolate the perfection from its surroundings: the more familiar you have become with camera controls and relaxed with the mechanics of tripod use, the less the photography will interrupt the sheer joy of being there.

If you don't use a tripod regularly, be sure to resurrect it well in advance of your departure date. Get comfortable with setting it up quickly and using a ball-and-socket head, and be sure that the legs and the head firmly support your camera and heaviest lens. When planted in one location for more than a moment or two, I will remove the weight of my camera vest from my shoulders and hang it on my tripod. Transferring this weight helps to steady the tripod, especially when it is exposed to the wind, and leaves me free to compose, searching to portray the mystical in landscapes such as this at Mount Bromo.

Photo Tips   *Bromo Crater, Interior*

Standing on the rim of Bromo Crater is an awesome experience. In the depths below, gases and steam hiss and gush, seemingly from the very bowels of the earth. Yet it is difficult to make images that portray the feeling that the crater evokes; a wide-angle lens makes the chasm seem remote and unthreatening, while a normal lens fails to capture its enormous size. The smoke and steam that emanate from the fumeroles tend to obliterate the bottom of the crater from view, and standing on

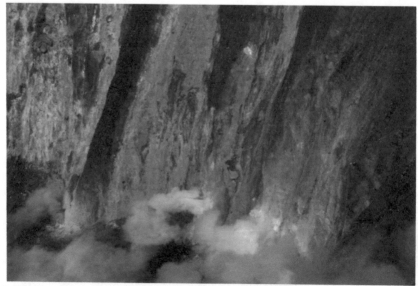

Sulfur deposits and steam vents, Bromo Crater, Java, Indonesia, June 1989/ Sacred Earth, *p. 187*

top of the crater rim exposes one to wafts of heady sulfur gases which may cause dizziness and coughing. When the sheet of white did clear for brief seconds, I could see brilliant yellow swatches—sulfur deposits at and adjacent to the crater floor. A two-hour return hike back to my hotel to fetch my 300mm lens proved to be the answer. It reached to the bottom, providing tight, compact scenarios of the action and drama. I waited patiently for the smoke to clear, then grabbed the moment when the brilliant streaks of yellow revealed themselves.

But there is much more to Bromo than its colorful interior. The mists that tease among the crags and boulders in the early morning light produce spectacular effects, and locals and tourists riding horses across the sea of sand appear and disappear in these mists floating across the larger inactive crater that holds Bromo. Be ready for these "other-world" effects by arriving before the first light and setting up your tripod near the bottom of the giant staircase to the crater's rim. One moment you are shrouded in a garment of mist, the next instant it evaporates to give you fleeting glimpses of a surrealistic world. Put your camera on automatic, set the manual override for slight over-exposure, and prepare to react quickly as the drama of horse, rider, mists, rocks, and sunlight unfolds on the stage before you.

BALI

June 15 . . . Our first walk on the beach was under a full moon, the warm water gently lapping over our toes in the golden sand. But the heart of Bali is not her beaches—it is her mountains and lush valleys, her mist-shrouded temples draped with garlands of flowers, and her gentle people who serenely honor their gods with every step of the day.

Bali is the most openly spiritual culture we experienced. There seems to be a perpetual atmosphere of religious festivals honoring the Hindu gods who have joined with the ancient Balinese gods to influence every level of daily life.

Travel Tips

Denpasar is the capital city of this tiny island which is the Indonesian mecca for sun worshippers who arrive on international flights from North America, Europe, Australia, and Asia. A convenient departure point to Guam and Micronesia via Continental Airlines, which continues its flight to Hawaii and Los Angeles, it is also a short air hop to enter Australia via the northern coastal city of Darwin. A series of ferries or small private boats connect it to the eastern islands of the Indonesian archipelago.

Visas are automatically given on arrival, but if you have a punk or hippie style of dress be advised that immigration officers will question you in detail; every visitor is expected to have an ongoing ticket or proof of ability to buy one.

Local Resources

Denpasar is defined by its beaches with Kuta being the long-time favorite even though it is more crowded than nearby Legian. We chose to stay at the Legian Village Hotel, Jalan Padma, Legian-Kuta, Bali, Indonesia; Tel: 51182. Rooms are large, with big comfortable beds, air conditioning, open-air bathrooms so you can star gaze as you bathe, a large swimming pool, and great dining, all five minutes from the beach. This area is also crowded with shops and hotels but seemed a little quieter than some other streets. The more expensive Bali Mandira cottage complex down the street on Jalan Padma (write Box 1003, Denpasar; Tel: [0631] 51381) will rent tennis court time. Hotels at Sanur on the southeast coast, and Nusa Dua where the Club Med is located on the peninsula south of the airport tend to be more luxury oriented. The Government Tourist Board at Jl. Surapati, 7 Denpasar, Bali; Tel: 23399 publishes a free monthly tourist guide filled with information about festivals and arts across the island.

Local transportation is by bemo—a small truck that crowds as many people in as possible. Service varies from village to village, and prices are negotiable but generally inexpensive. Jeep rentals are also comparatively reasonable and having one gave us a great sense of freedom to explore the back roads. Many shops and hotels have rental vehicles and are competitive in their prices, so be sure to bargain. Motorbikes are also popular and cheap, but drive defensively; Bali roads have a reputation for many accidents and tourists are killed every month. Also keep track of the infrequent gas stations.

A branch of the government tourist office is beside the Kuta Beach Club, as is the local Garuda Airlines office, which had thirty-five people waiting the day I went in, and no computer to confirm reservations. I found it easier to take a taxi to the Bali Beach Hotel at Sanur where the Garuda office has the main airline computer (there is also one in the Denpasar office). This same complex contains the Continental Air office, as well as American Express if you are picking up mail or need other services; they also provide an excellent free guidebook to Indonesia. The streets of Legian, Kuta, and Sanur are lined with numerous travel companies who will arrange bus tours of Bali, or excursions to the other islands; Komodo is becoming a popular destination to see the ancient Komodo dragons (huge lizards) devour freshly killed goats. All of these trips can also be done without guides, but be aware that some of the outlying islands are little visited, facilities are minimal, English is sparse, and we were told malaria is highly prevalent.

The heart of Bali is in the mountains and valleys outside of Denpasar. We did not need to pre-book any of the following hotels, although a travel agent in Denpasar may be helpful; accommodation is very inexpensive, often with breakfast included. The southeast coast lagoon and beach at Candi Dasa is a growing resort with excellent restaurants. The losman (small bungalow-style hotel) at Tulamben Beach on the east coast (watch for the sign to turn to the water in the village before Kuba) has rustic cabins in a lush garden setting with excellent offshore diving and fishing. The lookout at Putung over the Strait of Lombok and the eastern islands is worth the trip, with A-frame cabins and a wonderful restaurant at Putung Bungalow, Selat Karangasem. The Losman Gunawan at Penelokan has a good dining room and a fabulous view over Lake Batur with Gunung Batur and Agung in the distance. The rooms are very rustic, but the nearby Astina Inn, about .5 mile (1 km) east off the main road at Kintamani, has fabulous rooms and dining room. On the north coast, the Jati Reef Bungalows, PO Box 52; Tel: 21952, at Happy Beach a few minutes east of Singaraja is comfortable. From here we drove 9 miles (15 km) east of Singaraja to the hot pools of Air Sanih, and west to the sacred springs of Air Panas near Dencarik, on the first road south of the highway, 5 miles (8 km) west of the popular beach of Lovina. The main road south out of Singaraja took us back into the mountains, where we enjoyed the wonderful gardens and tennis court at the Pancasari Inn north of Bedugal. Ubud, the popular tourist center outside of Denpasar, is crowded and noisy but we found a haven at the Hotel Tjampuhan (or Champuan; contact PO Box 15, Denpasar, 80001, Bali; Tel: [0361] 28871) on the hilly Jl. Raya Road east of town. The hotel overlooks the sacred river and temple which had a festival when we were there; every room has a view, and an excellent breakfast is served on your private balcony.

The Sacred Places of Bali

Hinduism is the basis of Balinese life but it is rooted in the ancient animistic beliefs of the Bali Aga culture. This integration, along with aspects of Buddhism, has resulted in a unique Hindu-Bali world view which is reflected in the thousands of temples (pura) that structure daily life.

Although tourist Bali means the beaches, sacred Bali is dominated by the mountains. It is here that deified ancestors are enshrined, and holy lakes and rivers provide the source of the fertility of the land. The four sacred mountains of Bali were the focus of our visit, as we searched for images that would mirror the depth of spiritual beliefs in this culture. **Gunung (Mount) Agung** in east Bali, known as the "navel of the world," dominates the sacred landscape on the whole island. At 10,000 feet (3,140 m), it is the highest point on the island and is frequently covered in mists which swirl around the huge temple complex of Besakih, the Mother Temple of Bali. The five-story Pura Panataran Agung is the permanent sanctuary of the three-seated shrine of Brahma, Vishnu, and Ciwa (Shiva), draped in their symbolic red, black, and white colors. This is the holiest of all temples, containing thirty subtemples representing villages all over the island, which results in continuous festivities as each temple celebrates its own deity. These celebrations culminate at the full moon of the tenth month of the ancient Balinese calendar when the entire temple complex holds a week-long celebration of the annual visitation of the gods.

We approached Gunung Agung from the east coast, after living in her shadow for several days. Near the old royal courts at Karangasem we stopped for a funeral procession which we were invited to join. The large gathering sat in an open field as drums and gamelan players accompanied the open-air gas-fired cremation of the body of a young man. The faces of these people reflected the joy and serenity of the belief that his spirit was transcending into a better life in his next reincarnation. We carried on to the Water Palace at Ujung where floating pavilions represent the sun and moon, and then to the Royal Bathing Pools at Tirta Ganga, symbol of the healing powers of the Ganges River in India. Continuing northward on a rather deserted road, we turned to the ocean just before Kuba, and found the gardenlike bungalows of the losman at Tulamben Beach. The ferocious waves of the Bali Sea crashed all night in the pouring rain, reminding us of the Hindu-Bali belief that the sea is an impure place full of demons.

Every village has its guardian spirit and special holy days when temples are decked with offerings of food, flowers, and graceful bamboo poles called penjors, a symbol of village prosperity. Each village has a five-story pagoda symbolizing Gunung Agung, and a myriad of other temples specifically designed to honor other deities and ancestors. A pre-Hindu system of magical orientation still prevails, exemplified by homes and village temples that face the holy mountain of Agung. The lunar calendar also supports these beliefs, as fasting days are guided by the mystical significance of the earth's rotation around the sun, Surya, who gives life to all beings and influences the wind and rain and all aspects of the climate. The most sacred time of the year is Tilem Kasanga (in March) when the sun turns north on its positive course, a symbol of purity when the soul is directed toward heaven. The agricultural base of Bali's economy reinforces the significance of cosmic events in daily life. Small roadside stone shrines are honored daily, covered with checkered cloths and a fresh bowl of flowers shaded by a colorful tassled umbrella on a bamboo shaft.

Leaving Gunung Agung, we travelled across the valley and up the next ridge to Penelokan, the "place to look" at **Gunung Abang** and **Gunung Batur**, the two sacred mountains northwest of Agung. Gunung Batur is the home of a fertility goddess, whose twenty-five hundred temples have been twice destroyed by volcanic eruptions in this century. Sixty-five thousand homes were lost and one thousand people killed in 1917, but the locals seemed undeterred, building higher up the mountain, maintaining the legend that Pashupati divided the sacred cosmic mountain of Meru and placed its two halves here, creating Agung and Batur. We spent hours in the predawn light watching the swirling morning mists variously reveal all three mountains, with sacred Lake Batur in the foreground. A short distance north is the temple of Penulisan. Bali's highest temple, it was a sanctuary of the ancient god-kings of this area of Pejeng, hidden in the mists and surrounded by evergreens and graced with the pure white trumpets of the deadly datura blossoms.

The north coast of Bali seems like one continuous beach, from the swimming pools of the sacred springs of Air Sanih in the east, past the port of Singaraja, the bungalows at Lovina, and the sacred pools of Air Panas near Dencarik. These springs are fed from **Gunung Batukau**, Bali's fourth sacred mountain, whose spirit lives in the seven-tiered temple of Mahadewa. These pools are more natural than Air Sanih, tucked into a primordial vegetation of cascading ferns and riotously colorful ti plants with the mineral-rich warm water turning rocks to bronze.

Then it was on to the central interior. The steep road winds through sacred nutmeg trees and lush terraced hillsides often hidden in the mists of the sudden torrential rains which can create a temperature change of as much as twenty degrees (Fahrenheit) within ten minutes drive of the coast—this geographical and climatic diversity is an exhilarating experience. The wild monkeys on the roadside play and beg for food, but at the monkey forest at Sangeh, which commemorates the spot where the legendary Monkey King lifted sacred Mount Meru and broke it in half, they will steal your glasses and anything else they can grab. Continuing to **Ubud**, we explored the sacred rivers of Pekrisan and Petanu and the pilgrimage springs of Tirta Empul, and were reminded that the Balinese refer to their religion as Agama Tirta, religion of the waters. It was at the nearby Tampaksiring Spring where, according to legend, the god Indra pierced a stone to produce the source of amrita, the elixir or ambrosia, of eternal life with its magical curative powers. Despite the tourist bustle in Ubud, we could escape to the luxuriant green hills stretching down to the riverside temples, where the temple pools floating with the sacred lotus were a gentle reminder of the nourishment provided by Ubud's name which means "healing medicine." Rejuvenated, we then returned to the over-stimulation of Denpasar, to fly on to Micronesia in search of our next sacred place.

Micronesia

NAN MADOL

June 28 ... Up 4:30 AM to catch the tide ... gentle breeze caresses bare skin as we motor across this big warm bathtub, threading our way between coral castles illumined only by moonlight and starlight shining to the depths ... weave past reeds and tangled mangrove roots until we finally run out of water and resort to sloshing through the low tidal channels, pulling the dinghy to the gateway of Nan Madol ...

Nan Madol, an elaborately fortressed city built on ninety-two man-made islets covering 18 square miles (47 km²) off the west side of the island of Pohnpei (Ponape), reached its peak between 1300 and 1600 AD. A place of political, social, and priestly ritual ruled by a tyrannical royal dynasty called the saudeleurs, this stone city linked by a myriad of canals has earned the title "Venice of Micronesia," and is considered on par archaeologically with the Mayan ruins of Mexico and the stone statues of Easter Island.

Travel Tips

Micronesia is suitably named, a group of twenty-one hundred "small islands" scattered throughout the North Pacific between Hawaii and the Phillipines to the east and west, and Japan and Papua New Guinea to the north and south. Guam is the jumping-off point for all of these islands grouped into three geographical archipelagos: the Marshalls, the Carolines, and the Marianas. Air service is best from Tokyo (Japan Air, Northwest Orient, and Air Micronesia), Hong Kong via Manila (Air Nauru), and Los Angeles or Denpasar, Bali (Continental Air). Be aware that there is an expensive government tax on international air tickets bought in Japan, and flights are often booked because the Japanese love to holiday in Guam.

A valid passport is needed by all except U.S. citizens; no visas are required for stays under thirty days. Because Guam flights frequently arrive between midnight and 6:00 AM, reserving a hotel room is advised as the cheaper airport hotels often do not answer their telephones during these times, or are full if you arrive at the door. Beachside hotels are *very* expensive, although exotic if you want a decadent stopover. Island flights leave later in the day so one alternative is to rent a car at the airport to tour and relax on the beaches until departure time. There is no departure tax, but allow lots of time to go through security. Each flight is called at one specific time, after which the gate is closed; if you miss that time, they will not let you through, even though your flight hasn't left!

Local Resources

Air Micronesia (fondly called Air Mike), a subsidiary of Continental Airlines, flies to most of the smaller islands on a variable basis. The 1,017-mile (1,636 km) three-hour flight to Pohnpei goes three times per week, including a stop at the island of Truk. Hotel representatives meet the flights arriving at the main (and only) town of Kolonia, and we were easily able to rent a thatched-roof cottage at the Hotel Pohnpei (Box 430, Kolonia, Pohnpei, Micronesia 96941; Tel: 329), perched on a hill with ocean view, three beds, shower, fan, and mosquito coils! There are four other similar hotels nearby, plus the Joy Hotel (PO Box 484, Kolonia, Pohnpei, Micronesia 96941; Tel [691] 320–2447; Fax: 320–2478) in the main part of town which is newer and more conventional, and a more expensive resort-style hotel, The Village, located 5 miles (8 km) out of town, which can be reserved at Box 339, Kolonia, Pohnpei, Micronesia 96941; Tel: 797; Telex: 6808 VILAG FM, or through Continental Airlines.

All hotels have restaurants that serve a variety of dishes, including local vegetables such as breadfruit and taro, although in general we did not find the food very exotic. The Hotel Pohnpei only serves breakfast unless they have special requests for dinner. The Joy Hotel has a more varied menu to cater to American and Japanese tastes, and the PCR restaurant is noted for its variety of good food; both these restaurants are a little more expensive.

Many people speak some English, and the people are generally curious and helpful. The Tourist Commission provides maps and historical data. They are located on the main street (PO Box 66; Tel: 421); there is a bank, laundry, and travel agent nearby. All transactions are in U.S. dollars, but don't expect to use credit cards. This is a small community and you can easily walk around the whole town in less than thirty minutes. Pohnpei has an average daily temperature of 80°F (27°C) with humidity around 80 percent. Take the usual tropical clothes: easy-care cottons (local women tend to wear dresses rather than shorts), hat, sun protection, and perhaps an umbrella for the sun as well as the sudden tropical rains which are quite refreshing. November through April is a bit cooler. Typhoons can occur, but are more common in Guam and the Marianas. No special immunizations or health needs apart from the usual preparations for the tropics are required.

Most visitors to Pohnpei come primarily to see Nan Madol, and some stay for diving and fishing. The Joy Hotel and Ocean Service (Tel: 336) is the primary agent for trips to Nan Madol, which can usually be seen in a day trip from Kolonia, depending on the tides, as this is the only way to access the site from Pohnpei. A more pleasant option is to stay on Joy Island, off the southeast coast of Pohnpei, 22 miles (35 km) from Kolonia, down a very bumpy road that you wouldn't want to travel if you have any back problems! "Taxis" are local trucks that travel intermittently; you flag them down and negotiate the price. Your stay on Joy Island *must* be arranged in Kolonia through the Joy Hotel and the boat will pick you up at high tide near the PATS agricultural school. We were slightly late for our appointed time and the boat didn't wait. Luckily our driver was able to arrange another boat by radio-telephone, but we then had to navigate through the coral bay in the dark.

Accommodation is a thatched cottage with a futon-style mattress and cover. We were the only guests there for a week, but sometimes they are completely booked with Japanese tourists or local Pohnpeians who come to picnic. Bring all your own food from the shops in Kolonia; canned and dried foods are best. Sometimes the locals share their fresh-cooked fish. Wood is provided for an open fire under a thatched-roof shelter. A flashlight and mosquito coils and repellent are handy, and bring your own towel and soap for your fresh rainwater shower. The Joy Hotel will also rent snorkelling equipment. Joy Island is simple and rustic, in a quiet tropical paradise. For us, it seemed aptly named, providing one of the most peaceful experiences in all of our travels. There is nothing to do except visit Nan Madol, cook basic foods, read a good book, and swim and snorkle in the warm turquoise waters with grainy sand that welcomes your toes and fingers like a plush white rug. If you're looking for entertainment or night life, this is not the place for you.

From Joy Island, Nan Madol is a thirty-minute trip by motorboat, or by outrigger canoe if the tide is low. Boat trips are usually arranged and paid for when you book at the Joy Hotel, but we were also able to arrange special times and extra trips so we could stay at Nan Madol longer for the photography. All travel is subject to the tides, as the water level in the bay can be so low that it is impractical to navigate a boat, especially in the canals with their tangle of mangrove roots. It is possible to swim over, or even walk, although you may want to watch for stingrays in the canals, and there are no sign posts in the myriad of channels so it is possible to get lost! You may meet the son of the nahnmwarki (local tribal chief) who oversees the site and collects the five-dollar entry fee from those who come in by private boat without prearrangement. Although the site is under ongoing investigation by a team of archaeologists from the University of Oregon, there is no attempt at restoration yet; the fee seems a small offering to help the local people care for it.

The Sacred Site

Nan Madol was originally called Soun Nal-leng, meaning Reef of Heaven. The tangle of jungle and ancient rock is best viewed at Nan Dauwas, the high-walled mortuary compound of the saudeleurs. Oriented to a true east-west axis, its 25-foot (8 m) entrance walls are particularly awesome at dawn as the sky ripens into a peachy sunrise silhouetting these curvilinear basalt structures that look like the prow of a ship becalmed by the lush green vegetation. At night the stone shapes became our starship, as the immense sky cluttered with brilliant stars seemed to rotate the galaxies for our pleasure. Perhaps the shapes we envisioned were purposeful, in this culture whose most important families of gods were related to canoe building and seafaring. Ancestor worship was conspicuous and is evidenced by at least one tomblike underground room covered with eight hexagonal volcanic basalt logs about 16 feet (5 m) long. Despite their enormous weight, when we stood on them we discovered they rocked back and forth, and like the pipes of a giant's xylophone, produced a mellow sound that reverberated into the tomb below and across the silent jungle, competing only with the roaring of waves against the distant coral reef. Local legends also suggest that Nan Madol was built in the mirror image of a lost continent—perhaps Lemuria?—and some archaeological findings suggest the presence of underground channels, perhaps supporting another legend that holy eels came in from the sea through a gateway to another world.

After communing with the spirits here, your return to Kolonia must be planned with the tides. The locals will help you to snag a taxi ride back, but try to fit in a trip to the Kepirohi Waterfalls—a five-minute walk up the road into a cool and colorful tropical garden which will help you endure the two-hour ride back to Kolonia.

Photo Tips   *Nan Madol*

At Nan Madol you will be drawn to the hexagonal basalt volcanic columns forming the stacked walls and terraces of Nan Dauwas, the best-preserved area on any of the islands. As impressive and enchanting as these are, Nan Madol is not easy to photograph. Most of the islets are overgrown with mangrove, making it almost impossible to land a boat to explore. Yet the potential for exciting images taunts and tugs at the photographer.

As Pohnpei lies only about five degrees north of the equator, the overhead sun produces harsh and contrasting light all year long. Move out from the central

Nan Dauwas and predawn sky, Nan Madol, Pohnpei, Micronesia, June 1989/ Sacred Earth, *p. 53*

enclosures and explore the surrounding foliage when the sun is hidden. At Nan Madol it is either pouring sun or rain—it is rarely dry and overcast, ideal conditions for good photography. Bring your umbrella and pray for rain rather than sun (and your rubber boots so that you can stand in the canals at low tide without fear of stingrays). The huge banana leaves turn luminous green in the rain, providing a sensuous contrast with the chiselled lichen-covered stonework. The islets are small and crowded and the huge walls are built close to the water's edge so be sure to take wide-angle and super wide-angle lenses that can encompass the height of a wall at close range. A 17mm or 18mm lens would be ideal. Some photography of the colorful rock walls must be done from a canoe or boat because the base of the canal is too muddy to stand in. Use large lens openings and fast shutter speeds to prevent blur due to camera movement or blowing leaves, and focus critically on the stones as the depth of field is likely to be shallow.

Few archaeological sites can boast of surroundings that feel so primitive, untamed, and lush. Use a tripod, give yourself ample time to explore, be open to the landscape as well as the archaeology, and let your heart be your tour guide. Nan Madol was one of my hardest photographic challenges, but I was rewarded with some of my best images.

Australia

The Sacred Land of the Australian Aboriginals

The heart of sacred Australia beats to the rhythm of the Aboriginal "songlines," the ancient pathways of the mythical Dreamtime ancestors who created the land and all its beings. These ancient verses are like a multivolume creation story where each feature of the land is read like a Braille character, containing an aspect of mythic history that continues to instruct new generations. There is no written Aboriginal history—it is recorded in the land. If the land is altered or destroyed, this is tantamount to erasing history and destroying ancestors, as surely as if their graves were desecrated.

To the Aboriginal people, the stories etched in the landscape provide a constant visual reminder of the laws of their world. The Dreamtime events tell succeeding generations how to live ethically, and how to live in harmony with the land and with each other. Defacing the land or putting up billboards changes these historical reminders that need to be kept alive by walking the paths of the creator beings, reliving their experiences, and "singing" the songlines of the ancestors. *All* the land is important to tell the story, and specially designated sacred sites are set aside for the rituals necessary to maintain it.

One of the great joys in exploring Australia is seeing these ancient philosophies brought to life. The belief in the land as a living entity is honored in the national parks at Kakadu and Uluru, which are co-administered by the Aboriginal people and the government's National Park Service. Many tracts of land have been repatriated to the Aboriginal people in the last twenty years, but, in fact, it is the nonAboriginal rangers, sometimes in conjunction with their Aboriginal colleagues, who are most visible in maintaining these beliefs that have been officially adopted in the day-to-day workings of the parks.

Unfortunately, we also met some Australians (mostly people in their 50s and 60s, and often travelling in huge recreational vehicles) who blatantly expressed resentment of Aboriginal land ownership, and constantly found fault with contemporary Aboriginal lifestyles, referring especially to alcohol use. This is a real problem in some communities, and is sometimes evident to tourists at places like Jabiru or Yulara where, for example, local Aboriginals asked us to buy alcohol for them (against the community wishes). Critics also target their seemingly casual attitude toward material possessions and maintaining a tidy house and community. Ironically it is these same people who, as tourists in their own country, benefit from the commercial value of the indigenous people's history, and yet contradict themselves by denigrating Aboriginal conservation of the land at the same time as they support things like uranium mines and forestry practices that are killing the land. These attitudes are found in other parts of the world, but somehow seem more strident in this milieu of honoring the land.

KAKADU AND THE DEVIL'S MARBLES

July 10 ... The billabongs were bursting with white water lilies, as ten thousand magpie geese took flight and left us grounded with even more mosquitoes! From the dangerous sacred site of Serpent Dreaming near Jabiru, we traced the ancient pathway of the escarpment toward the secret wetlands of Arnhem Land and the incredible rock art of Ubirr.

Kakadu National Park is the Northern Territory heartland of the Aboriginal Dreamtime, the origin of the creator beings who sanctified the earth with its landforms and people, and who are now immortalized in some of the most prolific rock art on the whole continent.

Travel Tips

We flew on Indonesia's Air Garuda from Denpasar, Bali, to Darwin, the closest major airport to Kakadu, one of dozens of national parks in Australia. It was here that we had the first inkling of both the intensity and the casual nature of life in Australia. Just before landing, the interior of our plane was sprayed with insecticide, presumably to diminish any four-legged foreign pests who may have hitched a ride from Indonesia to ravage this agricultural land; then airport officials dressed in tailored shorts and knee socks led dogs across the rows of incoming luggage in the not-so-casual search for drugs or other contraband. This official welcome was henceforward modified by the cheerful "g-days" and inate friendliness of the people "down under."

Ansett and Australian airlines both service this huge continent with special tourist air passes based on mileage—the farther you fly, the cheaper it is. This is worth investigating, because driving distances are often impractical for the average tourist. It is, for example, 868 miles (1,400 km) from Darwin to Alice Springs, and another 1,100 miles (1,800 km) to Sydney—not exactly a Sunday afternoon jaunt, especially in the scorching heat of summer—temperatures reach 100°F (40°C) or higher—on a flat barren road. Several national coach companies also offer unlimited mileage passes, and a multitude of travel companies offer guided tours by bus. Group camping tours are popular and can be arranged from Darwin or through travel agents in major cities in Australia or North America and Europe.

Local Resources

Remember that seasons are opposite to North America, Europe, and Asia. Australians travel a lot, and although they generally love the summer heat (November through January), Darwin is busiest during the school holidays in the still warm but dry months from June to August, when rain, poisonous box jellyfish, and crocodiles are at a minimum to interfere with ocean swimming. Hence budget accommodation is also at a minimum. We learned this on arrival at the Darwin airport so wasted no time and rushed into town to the budget hotels. On the second try, we got the last room available at the Larrakeyah Lodge, 50 Mitchell Street, Darwin, NT 5790; Tel: (089) 7550; Telex: 85680. The higher-priced and deluxe hotels did have rooms available.

Car rentals were also at a premium, but we begged, and two days later secured a jaunty red Toyota from Cheapa Rent-a-Car, GPO Box 4444, Darwin, NT 5794; Tel: (089) 81-8400; Fax (089) 81-5247. They also outfitted us with camping equipment, as well as a car at Ayers Rock, although there was not a 4-wheel drive to be had for weeks. There are many tour companies in Darwin offering two- to ten-day tours of the Kakadu and Katherine Gorge areas (popularized in the movie *Crocodile Dundee*), as well as extended tours to Alice Springs and further afield. Within Kakadu National Park there is also a ParkLink bus service to the major tourist areas around Nourlangie Rock, Ubirr, and Cooinda. There is only one hotel near the park headquarters, the Four Seasons Crocodile Hotel, Jabiru; Tel: (089) 792800, and the Cooinda Center beside the Alligator River, 31 miles (50 km) to the south, offers a restaurant and a Four Seasons Motel—Tel: (089) 790145—as well as a campground that rents a few simple sleeping rooms in trailers. There are numerous government campsites throughout the park, with good showers and some are wheelchair accessible; there is not much shade due to the nature of the land. Camping is also allowed with a permit in some backcountry areas. A 4-wheel drive vehicle is necessary other than on the main roads around Nourlangie and Ubirr. For further information, write Northern Territory Government Tourist Bureau, 31 Smith Street Mall, Darwin, NT 0800, or any Australian embassy. The park headquarters in Kakadu and Uluru are valuable resource centers for historical, scientific, and social information, as well as for local conditions and events (and the drinking water supply for tourists in Kakadu). Their head office is the Australian Parks and National Wildlife Service, PO Box 1260, Darwin, NT 5794; Tel: (089) 5299, located on the first floor of the Commercial Union Building on Smith Street in Darwin. The Jabiru Shopping

Center in Kakadu is the main area for supplies, local tours, and a travel agent, although Ubirr has a small shop (no unleaded or diesel fuel) and Cooinda has a restaurant. Always carry extra gas and water if you travel off the main road. A special Northern Territory government permit is required to travel into Arnhem Land, although some tours are available.

The Devil's Marbles are on the Stuart Highway, 60 miles (97 km) south of Tennant Creek, an hour and a half flight from Darwin en route to Alice Springs. We rented a car from Barkley Car Rentals, Box 1114, Tennant Creek NT; Tel: (089) 62–2358. There is a small camping area that also rents sleeping accommodation in trailers, 6 miles (9 km) south of the Marbles, at Wauchope—population five—with a good restaurant and gas station!

If you plan to use your photography for commercial purposes you will require a permit from Australian Parks and National Wildlife Service, GPO Box 636, Canberra, ACT 2601; Tel: (062) 46–6211. Contact them at least three months ahead of your arrival as the number of permits at any one time is limited.

Both Kakadu and Uluru national parks are protected by UNESCO as World Heritage sites and unique biosphere reserves.

Sacred Landscape of the Northern Territory

Travelling through the 4,680-square-mile (12,000 km²) **Kakadu National Park** has a dreamlike quality. The three-hour drive from Darwin seems unending, past flat landscape interrupted by multishaped termite mounds up to 15 feet (5 m) tall, nestled like sand castles against the ghostly white gum trees emerging from the dark crinkly shapes of burned undergrowth. Their blackened trunks are softened by bronze and blond grasses interspersed with the occasional brightness of the candy-pink haze of turkey bushes. The effect is like a magical forest, where a child would expect spirits to be lurking behind every nook and cranny. Suddenly, after three hours of driving, the real spirits appear, in the form of the rocky outcroppings of Nourlangie Rock and its accompanying remnants of ancient cliffs along the escarpment. At Nourlangie it is easy to see why the ancients were inspired by the land; the contorted rocky shapes are fantastical, constantly stimulating the imagination to name them. The local Gagadju tell stories that explain every aspect of life as it is recorded in this landscape.

But that is not all that is recorded. In the cavernous overhangs of **Nourlangie Rock** and **Ubirr**, the ancient Gagadju and other indigenous groups have created galleries of paintings on the bare rock, using the ancient technique of painting with red ocher pigments to record a long-extinct Tasmanian tiger, or the red, gold, and white paint of the X-ray style displaying the internal organs or skeletal outlines of the barramundi fish, goanna (lizard), and magpie geese that graced their tables. The white handprints of initiation rituals are still used today in recording the rare ceremony of new elders; here, the simple technique of spraying mouthfuls of white pigment is used to outline the hand on the rock. The Dreamtime story of Namarrkun is clearly visible at the Anbangbang Gallery; here this Lightning Man with stone axes on his knees, elbows, and head is seen running through the country just before the wet season, striking his axes to create the lightning that will bring the rain to renew the dry ground and make it fertile again. In a small overhang at Ubirr, the rainbow serpent is depicted with her colorful halo which heralded the coming of the wet season.

But before she and Namarrkun produce the Gudjewg (wet season), the Gagadju take advantage of the Gunumeleng pre-monsoon season with their traditional land management of "fire-stick" farming. Aboriginal elders supervise park rangers in the burning of select patches which not only removes underbrush, thus minimizing the spread of wild fires, but also maintains the eucalyptus and other tree species with fire-resistant bark. In addition, this mosaic pattern of burning promotes the green tendrils of new growth that attract a diversity of animals and birds, and provide the livelihood of the people.

The same escarpment that extends into the wetlands and rain forests of Arnhem Land also harbors the spirits of two dangerous sacred places. The cliff face of Mount Brockman, which can be seen from the road west of Jabiru, marks the place where the serpent creator beings fought, the rock still displaying the dark marks of their blood stains. They still live here in the pools of **Serpent Dreaming**, which must not be disturbed lest they rise up and split the mountain. The same caution applies to **Lightning Dreaming** on the escarpment seen from Nourlangie Rock; both of these creator beings maintain the balance of the seasons, the lightning being and the serpent in his waterhole bringing the rain to placate the burning sun. These sites are approached only by initiated elders, appeasing these spirits who nourish the earth and humankind, thereby preserving the harmony of the Gagadju universe.

Far from Kakadu, but still in this immense Northern Territory, the drive to the **Devil's Marbles** from the old mining town of Tennant Creek was rather nondescript through the flat desert broken only by the occasional tuft of blond grasses, until we suddenly came upon the hundreds of huge red rocks sitting on red sandy soil out in the middle of nowhere. They looked like the beads from a giant's necklace, spilled haphazardly from the broken string. These are the eggs of Serpent Dreaming, the great rainbow serpent who created the natural features of the world and the first Aboriginal people. Serpent paintings in other areas have been dated to 10,000 years ago.

The Devil's Marbles lie in a 4,515-acre (1,828 ha) reserve on both sides of the Stuart Highway, about 250 miles (400 km) north of Alice Springs. The flat surrounding terrain with golden spinifex and green scrub enhances this dramatic collection of rock balls, some as large as 8 yards square (7 m²), which are thought to have originated from a solid block of 1,500-million-year-old granite. The drama is enhanced by the ongoing expanding and contracting of the rock which results in huge slices shearing off like a peeling onion. The shapes are most dramatic in the golden and red light of dawn and dusk, and at night when the gnarled shapes of shiny gum (eucalyptus) trees are silhouetted like white phantoms against a brilliant star-filled sky.

Photo Tips   *The Devil's Marbles*

An exciting and challenging opportunity awaits photographers at the Devil's Marbles. The rocks are big and bold, unlike any other landscape I know of in the world and at sunrise and sunset these gigantic boulders glow with a brilliance I have seen at only one other place—Ayers Rock. The rocks lend themselves to texture studies or as a dramatic backdrop for portraiture. They also serve as material for abstractions of positive and negative shapes; or, if you are interested in the portrayal of Aboriginal mythology, here, still hatching perhaps, are the eggs of Serpent Dreaming. But I think the most thrilling aspect of these rocks is the colors—for three or four minutes as the unshielded sun hovers near the horizon, the golden hues and ruddy reds are unbelievable. Try underexposing by a half- or a full-exposure setting. This simple adjustment (allowing less light than the meter indicates) intensifies and saturates the color to an even greater degree. A polarizing filter is also in order here to darken the blue sky relative to the tones of the rocks.

It is a good idea to scout your locations beforehand. When the magic time comes, you need to be front-row center, with all the faculties and resources that you can muster!

Sunset on Devil's Marbles, near Tennant Creek, Australia, July 1989/ Sacred Earth, *p. 213*

Photo Tips   *Kakadu Fires*

Photographing the ritualistic burning of the Kakadu forest was much easier than one might anticipate. I was never close enough for the heat to become a problem; my 80–200mm zoom lens was ideal for the job. For most of the exposures I stayed on the gravel road that ran beside the area in flames. This vantage point was ideal because the wind was pushing the fire in a line parallel with the road, allowing me to move along safely, yet in clear view of the spectacle.

To assure an adequate depth of field, I photographed most of my exposures at f11. I set the camera on automatic exposure and used the manual override to reduce the exposure by one setting, to keep the background dark and the flames a rich accent of color against the darkened tones.

To reduce the camera shaking in the wind for the relatively long shutter speeds of 1/4 sec and 1/2 sec, I secured the camera to my tripod and used a cable release.

I also tried to time my exposures to when there was a lull in the wind, and stood with my back to it to protect the tripod and camera from gusts. When the wind is relentless and strong, I will sometimes remove my camera vest, heavily laden with equipment, and hang it from the tripod as a stabilizer.

Forest fire, Kakadu National Park, Northern Territory, Australia, July 1989/ Sacred Earth, p. 144

ULURU AND KATA TJUTA

July 20 . . . The intensity of public response to this big rock is not underestimated in the tourist brochures. Its magnitude is only part of its presence . . . the panorama of ever-changing colors from brown, orange, gold, pink, purple, silver, and brilliant red was sufficient to entertain us for days, as we basked in its powerful essence.

Both Uluru (Ayers Rock) and Kata Tjuta (the Olga Mountains) contain some of the most sacred places of the local Mutitjulu people. The stories of the Dreamtime ancestors continue to be the main force in shaping the laws of their daily life, thereby maintaining the ability of these people to live in harmony with their land.

Travel Tips

Uluru is 200 miles (320 km) on a good road southwest of Alice Springs, or a half-hour air flight.

Local Resources

At Uluru, the new Yulara Tourist Complex, located 11 miles (18 km) from the park headquarters near the rock, offers all services including deluxe (the Sheraton; Tel: [089] 56–2200) and budget accommodation (Ayers Rock Lodge; Tel: [089] 56–2170) as well as a campsite which also rents trailer accommodation and has a swimming pool. There are no longer any facilities near the rock, and no camping allowed in the park. For information, contact Yulara Corporation, Uluru National Park; Tel: (089) 56–2144; Fax: (089) 56–2222. The Visitor Center offers excellent videos and a reading room, open from 8:00 AM to 10:00 PM, and is particularly cozy on cool July evenings. The park headquarters and interpretive center are within view of Uluru, offering a variety of programs including guided walks and talks by the Mutitjulu people who live in a private complex behind the monolith. Kata Tjuta is 12 miles (20 km) from Yulara on an unsealed (gravel) road, accessible by car or coach bus tours which go to view the sunset, but a car is convenient to allow time to stay and hike through the Valley of the Winds.

Uluru National Park is jointly administered by the Mutitjulu people and the government park service. Although climbing Uluru is a tourist attraction, the Aboriginal people do not, and this is honored by many park personnel. The climb is arduous, especially at the beginning where it looks deceptively easier than it is, as only one-third of the steep part can be seen from the bottom; loose shale and high winds at the top are also dangerous at times. There are clear signs warning of the heat and other pitfalls and a number of tourists have died in the attempt, so take these warnings seriously. The climb may not be made at night as the park is closed at sunset. The sacred sites around the base are clearly marked and strictly maintained—please honor them and do not enter or take photographs. There are so many beautiful vistas here that it is not necessary to take these.

The Dreamtime Map

Experiencing **Uluru** is like stepping back to primordial time—600 million years of geological recycling of a mountain range has left this 1.3 square mile (3.3 km²) sandstone monolith and the thirty-six hooded granite domes of **Kata Tjuta**. In fact Uluru is even larger, with an estimated 3-mile (5 km) underground depth. The immensity of these structures is enhanced by their surrounding desertlike environment, the flat dry land with sparse green vegetation suddenly broken by this gigantic rock which at times looks rather ominous. The quartz and feldspar of this sandstone composition continue to flake off in pieces as large as two-story buildings, creating a scene like a giant's playground strewn with toys. The 7-mile (12 km) pathway around the base is riddled with caves and ridges of the ancient beds of compressed conglomerate rock. The water holes around Maggie Springs (Mutitjulu) still provide a permanent source of ground water as they did for the Anangu (Aboriginal people) who lived here before the Europeans arrived in the late nineteenth century.

A common misunderstanding of the Dreamtime is to consider it a metaphor or an allegory of a mythical time. To the Aboriginal people, the patterns or tracks of the Dreamtime beings are true history, created as they wandered through the formless world, endowing the land with geographical features and all living species. The landscape is therefore not just a representation, but a manifestation of the creator beings; Uluru and Kata Tjuta are their transformation into the tangible world. Consequently it is a sacred duty of the Anangu (peoples of this western desert region), as direct descendents of these beings, to preserve this history as it has been given since the beginning of time in the Tjukurpa, a complex system of thought which incorporates Aboriginal religion and law and is often recorded through images on special sacred boards. It is a religious responsibility to impart this information only to certain people in the appropriate ceremony; hence sacred information is not talked about, even between men and women, who each have their own sacred places and rituals. The Anangu say it is important to learn how to think about the Tjukurpa, not just learn about it.

A further consequence of this belief system is the difficulty the Mutitjulu people have in accepting other spiritual beliefs, especially those of contemporary New Age mystics who see Uluru as a powerful center of earth energy and wish to practise their own rituals here. The Mutitjulu feel this is tantamount to sacrilege; perhaps it could be compared to Moslem or Hindu pilgrims wanting to perform ceremonies at St. Peter's Basilica in the Vatican or at the Church of the Holy Sepulchre in Jerusalem. It is unfortunate that disputes such as this arise, and if we have learned anything from our pilgrimage, it is the possibility for all of us to benefit from being in sacred places. Dogma or private belief systems do not necessarily enhance the experience of the numinous; it is the opening of the heart that allows us to take nourishment from the spiritual essence imbued in these holy places. As the Anangu say, "If you take it home in your heart, you remember."

BYRON BAY AND FRASER ISLAND

August 5 . . . The extremes of the central desert and the northern wetlands were even more profound when compared to the temperate eastern coastline at Byron Bay, where the first rays of sun greet the Australian continent as dolphins lark about in the crashing waves . . . and at Fraser Island, where sea and fresh-water lakes coexist side by side, separated only by the shifting margins of the largest sand island in the world.

The coastline of eastern Australia is defined by its waters. This symbol of the flow of life, which nourishes the northern rain forests and the Great Barrier Reef, offers silky sands to the sun worshippers of the Gold Coast, and provides a haven of islands and bays for the fruits of the sea.

Travel Tips

The coast road stretches 1,360 miles (2,200 km) from Sydney harbor to the northern rain forests and reefs near Cairns. Fly-and-drive combinations are sensible to cover these distances, and 4-wheel-drive safaris and cruise ships abound in most major towns along the way. The Great Barrier Reef extends for hundreds of miles north of Brisbane; one of the seven wonders of the world, it is protected by UNESCO's World Heritage Site designation. This coastline is a favorite holiday spot for Australians, so reserve early during the summer season (November to March) for the exotic resorts on the mainland and the islands.

Local Resources

In Brisbane, there is no airport tourist center; the Queen Street Mall office in the heart of the city is open daily, or Queensland Government Travel Center, 196 Adelaide Street, Brisbane, QLD 4000 provides excellent brochures on all aspects of travel. If you're looking for opals, go to Endor's Jewelry, Rowes Arcade, 235 Edward Street, Brisbane, QLD 4000; Tel: (07) 833–5255 for excellent selection and service.

Byron Bay is a three-hour drive south of Brisbane, in northern New South Wales. We were comfortable at the Lord Byron Resort, 120–130 Jonson Street, Byron Bay, NSW 2481; Tel: (066) 85–7444 with swimming pool, spa, and tennis court, a five-minute drive from the beach. Fraser Island is 99 miles (160 km) north of Brisbane; a 4-wheel drive is mandatory for Fraser Island. Book through All Terrain Vehicles, Anna and James Street, Fortitude Valley, Brisbane, QLD 4006; Tel: (07) 257–1101, Fax: (07) 257–1477. Some basic camping gear can be rented but not sleeping bags, so bring your own, as well as all your food and water for the duration of your stay. A camping permit can be bought at ferry locations. Ferries can be heavily booked so make reservations: from Rainbow Beach, call Inskip Point barge at (071) 86–3120 or –3154; from Hervey Bay, call Urangen Point at (071) 25–1906 or 27–9122; or from River Heads, call (071) 24–1900. Be sure to buy a good map of the island as tracks can be confusing, it is easy to get lost, and some 4-wheel drives are very light and can get stuck in the loose sand. Watch for the well-travelled areas. There is open camping in most areas, as well as in a few resort areas frequented by tours; these tours can be arranged from Brisbane, Hervey Bay, or Rainbow Beach. Hopefully the impact of increasing tourism will not spoil this wonderful wilderness; unfortunately the threat of logging companies is a very real and imminent problem that could irreversibly damage this unique ecosystem.

The East Coast

The delightful small but fast growing resort town of **Byron Bay** was a haven for us, providing the rejuvenation of bracing salty sea air and brilliant sun on sparkling water. The lighthouse, the most powerful in the southern hemisphere, marks this as the most easterly point of the continent, the land that receives the first morning light and the reassurance of a new day. Although it was named by Captain Cook in 1770, the Aboriginal people knew it as Cavanbah, meaning "meeting place." However, it was not only the meeting place of people, but also of dolphins, considered friends by the Aboriginals. Early reports by Europeans describe Aboriginal people using dolphins to shepherd shoals of mullet and tailer (indigenous fish) to the beach where they could be speared. While some Aboriginals claimed to own their own dolphins, dolphin protection was further ensured because of a common belief of the transmigration of souls of the departed into the dolphins. It is unfortunate that contemporary civilization still has difficulty in recognizing the spiritual essence of the dolphin; its playfulness is a wonderful reminder of the childlike experience of life that most of us have lost touch with. Byron Bay is also a place to feel the awe of schools of humpback whales on their way to and from Antarctica.

Byron Bay sits in the shadow of Mount Warnung, the largest shield (flat-topped) volcano in the southern hemisphere. Known to the Aboriginals as Wollumbin, meaning "cloud catcher," it was believed to provide the nourishing rain that maintained the surrounding ancient subtropical rain forest. Today Mount Warnung is considered by some to be a powerful center of electromagnetic earth energies, and communities have been established here in an ecological movement exemplifying living in harmony with nature. The 137,200-acre (56,000 ha) area is divided into a series of national parks with a UNESCO World Heritage Site designation, as a remnant and legacy of the ancient rain forest that broke away from the supercontinent of Gondwana perhaps 125 million years ago.

The combination of primordial rain forest and boundless ocean with the opportunity to renew each day with the blessing of the first light of dawn put Byron Bay high on our list of places where we felt we could still experience the world in a pristine form.

Located off Australia's east coast, **Fraser Island** is the largest sand island in the world, the result of eons of weathering of mountain ranges. Hundreds of miles of pure white sandy beaches line its Pacific Ocean side, bordered by cliffs of nonporous colored sands. These teewah sands produce incredible formations called "The Cathedrals" and "The Pinnacles" which look like impressionistic paintings with their palette of colors flowing into each other, and their shapes constantly changed by wind and water erosion. Inland trails lead through rain forests with 230-foot (70 m) stands of satinay surrounded by palms, pines, and eucalyptus, and mosaic burning of the undergrowth as seen in Kakadu is also practised here. Forty "perched lakes," some of the highest in the world sitting on teewah sands, provided fresh water and fishing for the indigenous Butchalla people who numbered several hundred thousand at the time of Captain Cook's landing in 1770. Wild horses (brumbies) and dingoes can still be found around the huge shifting sand blow that forms Lake Wabby. Platypus Bay in the northwest of the island is a procreation area for humpback whales, and their songs can be heard in August and September before they return to Antarctica.

Fraser Island provides a unique experience and is a delightful place to spend several days in relative isolation, walking on unspoiled beaches and under verdant canopies of ancient greenery beside trickling fresh-water streams. The proximity of sea and fresh water, separated only by shifting sands subject to the whims of weather, was another reminder of the intensity of experience offered by the interface of totally different aspects of the natural world. It left us with a great feeling of peace and spiritual renewal.

New Zealand

Sacred New Zealand of the Maori

The Maori relationship to the land is very special, not unlike other indigenous cultures in Australia and North America. Tribal history is written all over the natural features of the land which is seen as a living force; separation from the tribal land is felt as a spiritual and physical dislocation. This connection with the earth is beautifully expressed in Kiri Hulme's *the bone people*, by a character who carries a handful of home earth in her pocket " . . . for memory. And should I die in a strange land, there is little more than just my flesh to make a friend and sanctuary of alien ground." The landscape is seen to have the power to heal, educate, and unite those who are responsive to it (McNaughton, p. 3).

Not surprisingly, the Maori world is animated with spirits called atua, who keep the land alive, and with sacred places that are tapu, restricted to religious use. Maori poetry and myth speak of the earth and sky as the first parents, Rangitane and Paputuanuki, who came from the tapu land of Hawaiki, the mythical paradise to the east which is the source of all fertility. The creation of the world began with the separation of these earth and sky parents, who lay close together in darkness. Their sons, laying between them, resisted their parting until Tane, the greatest son, rested on his shoulders and pushed father sky and mother earth apart with his legs. The children of one angry brother became the winds, which still fight to this day; the sun, moon, and stars are the other offspring. Daylight and the rising sun signify life, while darkness and the setting sun are death—both were honored with songs at the appropriate time, and fires were always burned at night to appease the spirits. The seasons and varied weather patterns were considered prophetic and often in sympathy with human joys and sorrows. The rainbow, for instance, if seen from the right was a sign of good, but if it was pale and came from the left, it was an omen of death for someone.

The inseparability of the people and the land is further exemplified in the honoring of the ancestors who were seen as the continuity between past and present. The dead were always buried in tapu places to facilitate the journey of the soul back to Hawaiki, but if the tribe migrated, the ancestral bones were often taken with them so the living and the dead would not be parted and their descendents would be protected.

NEW ZEALAND

February 20 . . . The essence of this country is its primordial feeling . . . a unique vitality that I felt from the lonely peaks of Tongariro where the sun glitters over a fantasia of colors on the volcanic mineral pools of Red Crater . . . to the mist-shrouded thermals of the witches' cauldron at Rotorua, which, except for the spluttering mud and the gurgling sulfur streams, could be another Avalon, where the veil between earth and spirit seems very thin.

The New Zealand landscape is imbued with all the gods of the indigenous Maori people, who honor the land as though it is part of themselves.

Travel Tips

The North Island capital city of Auckland is serviced by major airlines from Southeast Asia, Australia, North America, South America, and Europe, many of which allow stopovers in Singapore, Hawaii, or Tahiti.

Local Resources

All the sites described are on the North Island and are linked by good highways that can be covered in a circular route from Auckland. Car and camper rentals are popular, so reserve ahead. Courtney had excellent service from Maui Campas, 100 New North Road, Auckland; PO Box 30020, Takapuna North; Tel: 793277; Telex: N260109 'Mauigrp.' A wonderful B&B in Auckland is Aachen House, 39 Market Road, Remuera, Auckland; Tel: 502329. Dozens of tour companies offer guided tours ranging from a few days to weeks, with the option to include many beautiful places on the South Island.

Sacred Sites

Tongariro, a massive mountain in the center of New Zealand's North Island, has two sacred peaks, Tongariro and Ngauruhoe, said to be the home of fairies and spirits who frolic in the mists. Higher up the mountain live evil spirits who sometimes rain fire on the land, a signal to the local tribes to prepare for war on their neighbors. The peaks of Tongariro are tapu and must never be disturbed by climbers; if anyone tries, the mountain grows taller so as to be perpetually out of reach. In 1868, an English adventurer named Richard Taylor described the barren lower grasslands as "a world blasted by sin" because of the failure of the local tribe to revere God, and he incurred the tribe's wrath for ascending the holy mountain, although no dire consequences were reported (McNaughton, p. 233).

Tongariro is the sacred mountain of a local tribe that believes it to be their ancestor. The mists and clouds are read as omens, while the direction of lightning carries great portent, and thunder is the voice of high-ranking ancestral spirits buried here. Tongariro was the most dreaded and venerated of all tribal mountains, and peace between tribes was often achieved by marrying their sacred mountains. The fairies, called patupaiarehe, took part in humanlike activities but had white skins and only came out at night or in the shelter of daytime mist. They were also capable of exciting women, and erotic dreams were the result of a visiting spirit. Their presence on a tapu mountain increased the sacredness of the peak.

Tongariro National Park encloses twelve volcanic cones, of which the third major peak called Ruapehu is still active. The area has a wild and solitary beauty, with brilliant red scoria plants surrounding the **Emerald Lakes** set in the red earth of **Red Crater**. Hiking in this area is exhilarating and lonely, with few people around to disturb the dramatic landscape. It can also be dangerous unless you are well prepared for the elements.

To the north, Tongariro overlooks **Lake Taupo**, the largest volcanic lake of the area, with white pumice beaches and thermal parks such as the silica encrustations of Golden Fleece Terrace and the barren Craters of the Moon. Continuing north in this bed of thermals is **Orakei Korako**, with the Ruatapu Cave (also known as Aladdin's Cave), sacred to the Maori women who bathed and birthed their children here.

Finally one comes to **Rotorua**, the caldera formed 150,000 years ago with domes and craters producing a fairyland of colors and shapes. Legend says Lake Rotorua was made with a digging stick by Rakuihaitu, the first man from Hawaiki. Rotorua sits on a huge bed of steam and hot water which bubbles out of five hundred hot springs in an area measuring 1,640 feet by 0.6 mile (500 m by 1 km). Local **Maori** still heat their homes and cook in the hot pools where their ancestors bathed for ritual purification before any religious or social ceremony. In Maori mythology, water was the primal element that was the basis of all life and capable of insulating the spirit from evil influences. Today the pools of silica still build terraces up to 60 feet (20 m) high, regularly watered by geysers of chloride gas. Nearby muddy pools of sulfate and kaolin produce hissing acid gases that swirl over the exotic colors of the mineral-laden waters. Here also is the magnificent Artist's Palette, which is not an understatement with its incredible beauty and changing landscape in the sulfur mists. We felt a special sense of vitality here, as we witnessed the evidence of a living earth generating an endless bounty from her internal laboratory.

Leaving the thermals, we continued north on our circular route to the 98-foot (30 m) white cliffs of **Cape Kidnappers**, named by Captain Cook after the local Maori tried to abduct a Tahitian boy from his ship. These cliffs are now a sanctuary for twelve thousand Australasian gannets who nest here between July and September (when the sanctuary is closed to the public) and produce their babies between October and January. The white feathers of the gannet were important to the Maori chiefs who wore them in their hair and used them as ear adornments.

This forlorn rocky headland is a place for true solitude and contemplation of nature. Experiencing this place felt like a completion—a perfect example of Maori integration with the natural world.

Photo Tips   *Mount Tongariro*

To reach the Emerald Lakes and Red Crater required a three-day trek up and over the saddle between Tongariro and Ruapehu on New Zealand's North Island. Though huts complete with bunks, mattresses, and cooking gear are provided, a diligent

Red Crater, Mount Tongariro, New Zealand, October 1984/ Sacred Earth, *p. 193*

photographer will need to pack warm clothes, food, emergency provisions, first aid kit, tripod, film, camera, and lenses. To photograph Red Crater, a sturdy and durable backpack is a must. You need to be able to swing it on and off quickly when events along route require your attention with the camera.

By leaving my camera on the tripod virtually all the time, it was quick and easy to set down and my 80–200mm zoom was always ready for action. If the exposure requires an 80mm format, the tripod is less essential. If you find yourself zooming in to the 200mm focal length, then the tripod becomes quickly indispensible. Many of my favorite views in this area were made at the 180mm or 200mm mark on my zoom. Telephoto lenses help to frame specific well-defined vignettes, drawing particularly exciting facets of the landscape into tangible view. Also, you will find that the mountain passes are often tremendously windy and you will need all the help you can get. Though this scene of Red Crater and its environs looks peaceful enough, I was photographing in a wind that almost swept me off the mountain. In order to make the exposure without camera movement, I used the tripod, employed the fastest shutter speed possible, and shielded the camera by standing with my back to the wind, while waiting for a momentary lull to release the shutter.

On trips where I am hiking a distance and photographing en route, I try to allow extra time so that physically and emotionally I remain strong while working in less than ideal conditions, and be sure I have ample resources to back me up. Even the Maori gods smile more favorably on those who arrive prepared.

Photo Tips   *"Artist's Palette"*

The "Artist's Palette" at the Waiotapu thermal area on the North Island of New Zealand contains an unsurpassed mix of pastel hues. So exquisite are the shadings and textures of this thermal landscape that a reproduction in monotones cannot do justice to the beauty of the scene. I highly recommend that the reader refer to the color rendition on page 148 of *The Sacred Earth* while exploring the following notes.

The colors in the minerals at the Artist's Palette are unbelievable and harmonize with each other, while the textures are subtle, delicate, and suggest an unearthly place. Slight overexposure (set the manual override to plus one-half, then meter normally) helps to maintain the delicate pastel coloring on film. The surface steam creates an ethereal veil that shrouds the rare colors in a misty white, and as the wind blows gently across the pond, the steam occasionally dissipates enough to allow glimpses of the distant shoreline—a hint of the deep greens of the distant trees.

Don't be in a hurry. Every second—every split second—the panorama is changing with a different balance of tones as the steam continuously rises to form new and different patterns. I set up my tripod on the adjacent walkway and framed the exact composition to set off the delicacy of the hues. Then, over the course of an hour, I made thirty or forty exposures, striving each time to execute the precise delicate balance of shading revealed by the steam. When I examined my results, only one frame had caught exactly what I had hoped to portray: a suggestion of deeper tones in the upper-left area to act as a visual foil for the dark textures in the lower right. To have come so far, and to have made fewer exposures would have been folly. The extra roll of film cost me little, and has provided me with more enjoyment than all the rest of my thermal area photography put together.

*"Artist's Palette," Waiotapu thermal area, Rotorua, New Zealand, October 1984/*Sacred Earth, p. 148

Chile

EASTER ISLAND

May 10 . . . Secluded white sandy beaches, palm trees, tropical breezes—this is much more exotic than the travel video showed it. It would be a perfect honeymoon spot! Hardly any tourists come to see these elegant stone statues lined up in their "Easter Parade."

Easter Island, the setting for hundreds of giant stone heads, is the most remote island in the world. Still one of archaeology's greatest mysteries, the heads are thought to personify the ancestors of the five Easter Island clans, carved for use in political and religious rituals of power.

Travel Tips

Easter Island lies in the South Pacific near the Tropic of Capricorn, 2,350 miles (3,790 km) west of South America, a five-hour flight from Santiago, Chile. Lan Chile Airlines has a thrice-weekly flight from December through February, and twice weekly for the rest of the year. An insular air tour ticket is available that allows travel anywhere within Chile or to Easter Island but it must be purchased outside of Chile. A regular one-way tourist class ticket is about a third cheaper than North American prices if it's bought in Chile, so it is very worthwhile if you can be flexible in your travel.

On flights to Tahiti, Lan Chile stops for two hours at Easter Island, which allows time for a brief glimpse, but the Tahiti-Santiago flight facilitates a two-day stopover, ample time to visit the important sites. From Tahiti, direct connections can be made to Lima (Peru), Japan, the U.S., Australia, New Zealand, and other South Pacific points. Santiago is easily accessible from North America (via Vancouver, Los Angeles, New York, Toronto, or Miami), and from all major cities in South America.

Local Resources

As in many small airports, accommodation can be booked on arrival, and hotel representatives meet flights to hustle business for their establishments. In addition to the Hanga Roa, the large (expensive) tourist hotel (Isle de Pascua, Chile; Tel: 55), there are at least fifteen smaller hotels or private home "residencias" which provide B&B. Staying in these smaller facilities is a great way to get to know the local people. Courtney had a wonderful private room with home-style service from Mrs. Anna Tepario Paoa at the Hosteria Taheta Oné Oné B&B, plus a packed lunch and delicious dinner (address: Tuu Koiho S/N, Isle de Pascua, Chile). Some people will even allow tenting in their gardens, or you can camp for free at Anakena Beach, but there is a lack of fresh water. A superb local tour guide is Peter Edmunds, who was born here, studied abroad, and returned to his beloved island. His English is good and he has a wealth of information on the history and the spiritual nature of Easter Island. Write to him care of Isle de Pascua, Chile; Tel: 274.

There are several restaurants and street-side cafes. Supermarkets are expensive and selection is limited because almost everything is imported. Alcohol is expensive in the shops and in the two discotheques in the Hanga Roa.

A valid passport is required; check with your embassy about visas and normal health regulations for travel in other South Pacific and South American countries. Currency is the Chilean peso, but U.S. dollars are used everywhere. Traveller's checks and the American Express card are accepted in some places and there is a bank on the island. The tourist office at the Hanga Roa Hotel (Tel: 282) will arrange tours of the island (as will many locals), and cars, motorbikes, or horses can be rented there as well. The only viable transportation for getting around on your own is a Honda 125 motorbike which is ideal on the poor roads and dirt trails to remote locations. The only pavement on the island is the airport runway.

The average daily temperature is 75°F (24°C), with a constant cooling breeze off the ocean, and the rainy season is February through August. The population is about twenty-five hundred; there are no true Easter Islanders left due to intermarriage with Chilean mainlanders and other Polynesians. English is spoken, as well as Spanish and the indigenous language. People love to barter for North American goods such as clothing and running shoes.

The Moai

For most of us, the **Easter Island** statues—known as moai—were immortalized in the books of the Norwegian archaeologist, Thor Heyerdahl. There are more than six hundred moai, many up to 30 feet (9 m) high. The most complete figures show only the upper body—none were carved with legs. Most are now broken and partially covered by a blanket of earth. Everywhere you walk, giant faces with elongated ears drape the countryside; some with intact torsos protrude from the rubble and the grass. Other partly finished moai are still trapped in beds of stone near the quarry. Several intact statues can be viewed standing on ahu (ceremonial platforms) at Vinapu, Pitikura, Vaihu, Tahai, and at Anakena Beach where Heyerdahl landed and later returned with a team of archaeologists to study and restore the statues. Although there is still much dispute among academics, the most common belief is that the statues were carved from the living rock at the Rano Raraku volcanic quarry. They were then transported on wooden rollers to other locations (although some islanders said they walked there), where they were erected on the ahus, between 1000 and 1400 AD. The red topknots known as pukao were sculpted at another inland quarry and were later mounted atop the heads, along with coral insets in the eyes that lend an air of vitality to the stern facial features. The precise fitting of the ahu stones is often compared to the best stonework of the Incas, believed by Heyerdahl to be the ancestors of these people, although most contemporary archaeologists believe Easter Islanders are of Polynesian origin.

Nearly one-third of Easter Island is preserved as a Chilean national park, and UNESCO is currently investigating these relics that are in danger of continued disintegration through neglect and the forces of nature. This would be a tremendous loss of a World Heritage Site that is unique in history and as an art form. The sense of dignity and glory felt here is unlike any other sacred site in the world.

Photo Tips   *Easter Island*

My most useful piece of photographic equipment on Easter Island was my tripod bag which I wore as a back pack. I left on my motorbike before dawn to catch the spectacular sunrises, slept through the midday heat, and then packed a lunch for a sunset trip. The low angle of light at these times of day gives a spectacular glow to the stonework and the landscape, and enhances the mystical feeling created by these enigmatic statues. My evening trips usually extended into the night to record the stone carvings with flash photography. For best results put your camera on the tripod, leave the shutter open (such as on "B" with the cable release locked in position) and walk along with your strobe in hand, flashing each carving in turn. Be sure to avoid being in direct line with the camera as your body will be silhouetted against the stone. However, if you stand close to the line of action, the stone faces will better reflect the strobe light for the camera.

Stone carvings at Rano Raraku, Easter Island, Chile, May 1990/ Sacred Earth, *p. 28*

VALLEY OF THE MOON

*May 18 . . . This land is profound—the extreme changes in temperature
between night and day heightened my response to these dramatic earthscapes,
the abruptness shocking me into a transcendent state of consciousness which
led me to wander for hours over this unearthly part of our planet.*

This Chilean Valley of the Moon, like so many other world landscapes dubbed
with the same name, provides a surreal experience that jogs one into some very
primal feelings. This deep psychological response feels like a pure sense of the
spiritual.

Travel Tips

The Valley of the Moon is in the Atacama Desert of northern Chile. Local airlines
fly from Santiago to Calama, the closest major town, or to Antofagasta and Arica
on the coast, where bus and train service is available. Buses and trains also connect
to these cities from Santiago or from La Paz, Bolivia.

Local Resources

Calama is a mining town of eighty thousand, with decent hotels, but not much
English is spoken. The Hosteria Calama-Hotel Edificio Alfa is clean and offers good
service, at Casa Matriz: Latorre 1521; Tel: (082) 211511 or 212817. Travel assistance

in English can be found through Cecilia de Valle D at Copper Tours, Sotomayor 2016-L.18, Calama, Chile; Tel: (056) 082–212414; Fax: (056) 082–210107. The Valley of the Moon is 63 miles (102 km) to the southeast on a good road to San Pedro de Atacama. This town is also noted for its archaeological museum with nearly four hundred thousand artifacts including desert-preserved mummies, paleolithic tools, and thousand-year-old Indian ponchos. A return day trip can be made by taxi or bus from Calama; the local bus stops 3 miles (5 km) from Pedro de Atacama—a nice evening walk watching the spectacular sunset after spending a day exploring the moonscapes. There are hotels and a campsite in Pedro de Atacama, but since it is at an elevation of 8,500 feet (2,600 m), be prepared for cold nights and early mornings if you explore the valley before dawn, followed by very hot daytime temperatures.

The Moonscape

The **Valley of the Moon** is part of the Atacama Desert which covers much of northern Chile and is an important source of mining (sulfur, borax, salt, and copper) in the area of Calama and San Pedro de Atacama. The real treasure for the pilgrim, however, is not the products of the earth, but the landscape itself, carved from salt mountains for thousands of years, leaving a legacy of surreal shapes. Evidence of inhabitation of this area dates from 10,000 years ago, but the vista of today is one of the loneliest and most desolate in this country. The incongruous shapes of sand tug at the subconscious, stimulating unconscious and unpolished feelings from some unknown time, engendering a tremendous sense of solitude (enhanced by the lack of tourism). This is the real strength of this land. The sense of peace here was yet another reminder of how the landscape can touch the inner spirit and mirror the soul.

Photo Tips   *Valley of the Moon*

I scouted the territory near Calama in the midday light to prepare myself for a predawn arrival the following day. The most exotic feature was a group of volcanic forms about 10 or 12 feet (3 to 4 m) in height that looked like people emerging from a prehistoric sleep and reaching for the dawn of a new age.

I arrived at 5:30 AM, just in time to witness the first glimmer of light and to see a crescent moon quickly erased by the light of a brightening eastern sky. In its place the sky displayed a band of soft gentle pastels expanding upward and melting into the blackness of night. My main thought was to record the undulating flow of tones with the humanlike shapes accented as silhouettes. To do so, I chose a wide-angle 35mm lens and moved up to the forms until they were dispersed across the frame. Over the course of ten or fifteen minutes the sky gradually changed, not only brightening but also changing colors. There was little to do but record the succession of hues, camera on tripod and exposure mode on automatic. I set the manual override for about two-thirds of a setting underexposed and used a cable release for each exposure. Since the success of the image rested almost completely on the subtle blend of color, I also bracketed slightly, making several exposures at the minus one-third and minus one exposure settings. When employing automatic exposure, it is important that the center of the frame represents the tone you desire. Because the black shapes in the lower portion would not appreciably affect the meter, I felt justified in using the automatic.

Saltstone formations, Valley of the Moon, Chile, May 1990/ Sacred Earth, *p. 153*

PAINE NATIONAL PARK

January 25 . . . The peaks of the Cuernos echoed the jagged sandy protrusions of the Atacama Desert in northern Chile, but this setting is profoundly different. The vicious katabatic winds sweep over this rocky land whipping at these "towers of pain," leaving me with an adrenalin rush that provokes not the tranquility of the desert, but a sense of exhilaration, awe, and enchantment.

These spiny tips of the Andes Mountains rest in Paine National Park in Patagonia, the southernmost part of the long thin country of Chile. Classified as a UNESCO World Heritage Biospheric Reserve, the extreme weather and this austere landscape are reminders of the spiritual strength needed to live off this land.

Travel Tips

Punta Arenas is the southernmost city in Chile. It sits across the Strait of Magellan from Tierra del Fuego, the "fire island" discovered in 1520 by the Portugese explorer Magellan, the surrounding waters still bearing his name. This is the last refuge of land from the angry seas of Cape Horn and the frozen land of Antarctica. Air service to Punta Arenas is by Lan Chile Airlines via Santiago, and is almost equidistant from New York or Los Angeles.

Local Resources

Cars can be rented in Punta Arenas for the day-long drive northwest to Paine National Park via the town of Puerto Natales. In the park, the Lake Pehoe Hotel (reserve at Turismo Pehoe, 21 de Mayo 1460, Punta Arenas) sits on a picturesque island overlooking the Cuernos; it is worth spending a day or two here to explore the peaks and take a boat to Grey Glacier. English is minimal in most of these areas but it is not difficult to get around. Climbing expeditions here and into the glaciers of Argentina can be arranged through the American Alpine Institute, 1212 24th Street, Bellingham, Washington, USA 98225; Tel: (206) 671–1505.

A Last Frontier

The impenetrable glaciers, jagged mountains, and windswept pampas of the 450,000 acres (180,000 ha) of **Paine National Park** have been described as a place of exile, and this certainly feels like one of the most remote places in the world. As one of the greatest physically challenging last frontiers of mountaineering, climbers come here to ascend the 7,000-foot (2,300 m) summits of the Cuernos, the sharply twisted, sheer-walled, and ice-capped peaks that look like chocolate-swirl ice cream cones ascending into layers of overhanging cloud. The very name of the katabatic winds, formed over the ice caps nestling under the Andes, is enough to chill one's spine— the prefix "kata" means "down," "back," or "against," which is exactly what they can do to suspended climbers, pulling them away from the peaks and throwing them back against the jagged spurs of rock. Even in summer the vicious winds can drive climber and pilgrim far back into the minimal protection of the pampas, which also harbors the circling condors, the legendary messengers of the gods, and the land-bound guanaco (llamas) serenely chewing their cuds.

This land of the Indians that the Spanish called patagones, or "big feet," is further chilled by the Antarctic ice floes from Grey Glacier, its terminus dipping into the 12-mile-long (20 km) Lago Grey, in the center of the park. Mammoth icebergs are hatched here, their vivid blue color a result of a millennia of tremendous pressure from the perpetual ice field above. Although the coldness of water and land is not welcoming, it stimulates the heart to pump faster to nourish the body and mind which are invigorated by this exciting landscape.

Antarctica

January 30 . . . The hell of crossing the vicious waters of the Drake Passage was quickly removed from my consciousness as I beheld the icy cap of Antarctica. It was not pristine—but powerful in its emotional appeal—this last bastion of wilderness, the southernmost point of nature on our planet.

Until recently, Antarctica was a pure land, relatively untouched by human hands, and a worthy example of a spiritual as well as a natural wilderness. Today it is fast losing that purity, the desecration a result of human thoughtlessness driven by economic and political desire.

Travel Tips

See the section for Punta Arenas, Chile.

Local Resources

Antarctica is only accessible by guided tours that can be arranged from North America or Australia. Adventure Network International, #200, 1676 Duranleau Street, Vancouver, B.C. Canada V6H 3S5; Tel: (604) 683–8033 offers professional guides under the leadership of Martyn Williams, an active mountaineer and conservationist. Tours are expensive, and take place in the summer months of December and January; travel to the South Pole is thankfully still limited, but is available if you are willing to pay the exorbitant costs.

The Last Wilderness

Antarctica's indigenous population is its wildlife, and until recently was the bastion primarily of gentoo and chinstrap penguins, krill, sea lions, and a few scientists trying to understand the icy nature of our world. In the past five years the scientific teams have multiplied, and Antarctica has been inundated by tourists who now number up to five thousand annually, despite the excessive costs of travelling to this land of permanent snow. Perhaps these costs really do reflect the uniqueness of this part of the world, available as it is only to the well-to-do, who unfortunately do not seem to have a higher level of consciousness about environmental protection to match their pocketbooks. One wonders if all these tourist dollars could not be better spent in protecting this valuable environment for all the world to share.

Antarctica is littered with garbage left behind by scientific teams and travellers too thoughtless to take it with them. Rusty barrels lie beside wooden hulls frozen in time, as new refuse washes onto the shores, dumped by Chilean boats carrying tourists as their primary cargo. We were incensed with this practice, chastised our crew, and even hid our garbage, but they found it and added it to the sea. They also clubbed the seals and raided the abandoned whaling stations for souvenirs; our only consolation was that the foul whaling practices are now eliminated here, but the desolate bones one sees still evoke a feeling of despair at the horror of this past.

Tragically, the potential for the continuing destruction of this vast land escalates every year. It threatens the world's most southern greenery, a small slope of mosses fed by underlying volcanic steam vents neighbored by the white edges of a glacier that feeds **Paradise Bay**. Though still a paradise, with pink snow, green water, blue ice, orange penguin feet, and turquoise icebergs, the waters full of krill that feed the penguin rookeries of King George and Deception islands are also threatened with decimation by overfishing.

This land of contrasts is a symbol of power, endurance, and resilience. Its vulnerability is to humankind, who may negate its eternal history in a few short years. Having endured since before the beginning of charted time, is it to perish under the reign of twentieth-century humanity? This space and desolation cries out for preservation, so that the world might always have one place to measure a true wilderness, untainted and able to maintain the natural purity of its ecosystem. The future of Antarctica is currently under review by the most powerful nations of the world. We hope they have the sense and sensibility to protect this land as a park for the heritage of the world, and allow only the inherent vicissitudes of nature to rule here.

Photo Tips   *Antarctic Penguins*

Of all the locations portrayed in The Sacred Earth Collection, probably the one you are least likely to visit is Antarctica. If, however, the rare chance of a trip presents itself, here are some pointers. As exotic as it is to cruise among the icebergs of the Antarctic Peninsula, many of them will be seen at a considerable distance, partly because it is unsafe to pass too closely. Consequently, I recommend 200mm and 300mm lenses for shooting from the boat. I dispensed with using a tripod on board because the waters were usually choppy, and the boat rocked and rolled. For practically all the hand-held work, I set the camera on automatic exposure and chose the fastest shutter speed that the existing light would allow with a wide-open f2.8 lens. Generally, that meant shooting at shutter speeds of 1/1,000 or 1/500 sec with ISO 100 film, barely fast enough for hand-holding the 300mm lens. Some high-speed film such as ISO 200 or ISO 400 would be a good idea for shooting from the boat on somber days.

Gentoo penguin and chick, Paradise Bay, Antarctica, January 1988/ Sacred Earth, *p. 130*

Once ashore, the equation is quite different. Though the penguins are generally not as tame as the animals in the Galapagos Islands, you can photograph them from close distances by approaching slowly and being nonchalant; the best angle is at their own level. Mature Gentoo penguins are only about 10 to 12 inches (25 to 30 cm) in height (although they often appear larger in photographs) which means getting down on your stomach with arms propped on your elbows. Be sure to avoid any fresh white areas on the rocks—it's not necessarily snow. After an exhausting five-hour blitz of photographing Paradise Bay, I collapsed at the edge of a penguin rookery for a few moments of rest, but when I looked up I saw this mother and small one standing above me. I slowly reached for my camera and clicked off a series, but only one frame showed the baby touching its tiny wings together. Because their nest was on high ground I was actually able to get in position on lower ground and could use the sky as a neutral background.

Peru

THE SACRED CITIES OF THE INCAS

January 10 . . . This is the closest I have felt to heaven . . . round the last bend of the steep narrow path suddenly reveals a sight more glorious than I was prepared to see . . . this amazing labyrinth of terraces, temples, courtyards, and ceremonial places, perched high on the precipitous slope between two jagged peaks of the Peruvian Andes . . . a perfect natural fortress, and a perfect earthly sanctuary.

Machu Picchu, the most glorified city of the Incas, is a vision of coherence and symmetry that continues to mystify scientist and pilgrim alike. It is thought to have been their most important ceremonial city, a place to worship the sun, moon, and stars that embodied the ancient gods who ruled all aspects of their life.

Travel Tips

The only reasonable way to access these sacred areas of the Incas is to fly into Cuzco from Lima, Peru, as land travel entails entering areas controlled by the Shining Path, the rebel movement whose political activities have been increasingly successful in recent years. It is wise to check with a reliable travel agent regarding local conditions, as several tourists have been injured or killed recently.

Local Resources

The daily train from Cuzco is the most common route to Machu Picchu, 70 miles (112 km) to the northwest. It leaves at 7:00 AM and arrives at 10:30 AM, returning to Cuzco at 3:00 PM. A day trip can be made, but Machu Picchu really deserves longer than that. There is a good hotel with a fabulous view of the ruins; Hotel Turista is government run and can be reserved in Lima through Entur Peru; Tel: 72–8227. In Cuzco, the Hostal Viracocha is charming, inexpensive, and has the best cappuccino in town, at the Plaza de Armas; Tel: 22–2128. The original Incan Trail, the footpath through the Andes, is heavily travelled by tourists and requires up to five days trekking in high altitude conditions which does take some acclimatization. Treks can be arranged in Cuzco. Sacsayhuaman is a half-hour walk from central Cuzco; the usual tours are available from a multitude of companies, many of which overcharge, so investigate the options. It is probably just as cheap and much more interesting to hire a taxi and driver who will go on your timetable, and English-speaking guides like Edwin Florez Zevallos, Residencine Belen D–29, Santiago-Cuzco, Peru, SA; Tel: 239721 have a wealth of information and enthusiasm to impart. Pisac is 20 miles (32 km) from Cuzco, and the Sacred Valley is 48 miles (78 km), on the route to Machu Picchu. Both of these areas are fascinating and worthy of at least a half day of exploration. Be aware that Cuzco is a popular tourist town in a very poor country, and many people will try to part you from your money. A wide range of hotels and banks are available to change pesos.

The Sacred Cities

So much has been written about **Machu Picchu**, but so little is really known about this famous Incan city thought to have been built in the 1400s by the ninth Incan emperor, Pachacuti, and abandoned in 1534 when the Inca Empire fell to the Spanish. The precision of the architecture and the building of multilevel structures adhering to the steep contours of the land between the peaks of Machu Picchu and Huayna Picchu still take one's breath away with their magnificence. How they could carve huge granite stones without the use of known tools, and flawlessly place them together on this hilltop, is a mystery. The sheer size of this city and its spectacular location hidden 2,300 feet (700 m) above the Urubamba River is awesome, but the complexity and diversity still reveal few cues to the true nature of the people who lived here.

The divine ancestor of the Incas was the sun, symbolically anchored by the sacred Intihuatana stone known as the "hitching post of the sun," designed to ensure his return and allow his subjects to plot the solstices, equinoxes, and movements of the moon. This authority of knowledge would have given the Incan priests power over all aspects of this agrarian-based culture, which is evidenced by the terraced retaining walls filled with fertile earth from the valley below, and fed by a sophisticated irrigation system built into the steep slopes. The importance of harmony between the earth and the cosmos is evidenced in the Incan legend of the rainbow, which is said to appear as a climax to the fertility ensured by the rainstorm, the sign that mother earth was satisfied in her mating with father sky. This self-contained and ethereal site would have been perfect for religious ceremonies and secret initiation rituals, and perhaps to secrete the highly trained Incan shamanic women known as the "Virgins of the Sun."

Modern mysticism considers Machu Picchu to be one of the eighteen mystery schools of the ancient world. Our local guide, Edwin Florez, and others, talk of a community of Incas hidden in the remote Andes who still practise the old rituals. He talks of his meditations at Machu Picchu, in which he sees the universe as a communion of the three worlds of the Incas: the under/inner world (acupacha) of the earth, this world (cuypacha) of water, and the upper world (caypacha) of the sun. He says the hitching post of the sun is the most sacred spot, imbued with powerful earth energies that he has often seen at night, like electromagnetic fluctuations in the atmosphere, around Machu Picchu. There have also been many reports of UFO (Unidentified Flying Objects) sightings in this area.

The enigma remains, and perhaps it really doesn't matter if we have more answers. This ethereal temple is sufficient in itself to inspire the contemporary pilgrim to appreciate this natural sanctuary and to feel a communion with the world.

Cuzco, in the indigenous Quechua language, translates to "sacred place," and was indeed known as the sacred royal city of the Incas. The Incan culture was based on a theocratic system, steeped in daily worship as evidenced by the 328 shrines found in a circular pattern around Cuzco and thought to represent the days of the Incan calendar. The shape of land pattern of Cuzco is symbolic of a crouching puma, with the nearby hill of **Sacsayhuaman** thought to represent his head, crowned with a Temple of the Sun. This 7,400-acre (3,000 ha) site is in the form of a serpent; twenty-two zigzagged terraces are formed by huge and irregular—but precisely interlocking—blocks of stone, the largest weighing 361 tons. Whether this represents the teeth of the puma, the god of lightning, or an outstanding defense system is unknown, but the beauty of the engineering is said to surpass that of Machu Picchu. The maze of internal chambers was largely dismantled by the Spanish conquerors, who used the stones to build their dwellings. Across the courtyard is the Rodadero, with a series of symmetrical sacred steps leading to the Throne of the Inca, which overlooks the parade ground and is still the site of the annual reenactment of the Festival of the Sun. The feast of Inti Raymi, the most important in modern-day Peru, takes place each June to commemorate the winter solstice with a symbolic sacrifice to the sun.

An even more splendid site is located at **Pisac**, 20 miles (32 km) from Cuzco, in dramatic countryside with no sign of contemporary civilization. The glory of this sacred site is enhanced by the sense of pilgrimage in getting there, hiking in from the isolated road, perhaps with no other tourists around (unlike Machu Picchu). The Incan masonry is even more spectacular, with three artificial terraces, baths, walls, gates, and the inevitable Intihuatanas or hitching posts of the sun. This amazing site is not mentioned in Incan chronicles, but is thought to be a solar observatory honoring the creator sun god Viracocha, from whom the Inca emperors were believed to descend, not unlike the Egyptian pharaohs. Here there is evidence of religious fertility ceremonies, and animal and human sacrifice to accompany the emperor on his journey through the underworld. A hill to the west is full of tombs, and may have been an execution cliff. Pisac probably played a major military role with its fortifications and towers, perhaps as a frontier outpost, with its magnificent agricultural terraces supplying the courts at Cuzco.

The bountiful **Sacred Valley** also supplied the royal courts at Cuzco. This key Incan settlement, 48 miles (78 km) northwest of Cuzco, is approached through an impressive gorge of red sandstone cliffs with long beards of Spanish moss. The fertile plain created by the Urubamba River produces fruits and vegetables that still supply Cuzco, and probably provided the cocoa leaf which was important to Incan ritual and festivities. The valley may also have been an important buffer zone against an invasion of Cuzco by jungle tribes from the north. Today, one mountain site is the focus of an annual pilgrimage to El Senor Huanca, a rock with a miraculous picture of Christ. It is easy to spend a whole day here, experiencing the spectacular light and the spirit of the culture in villages that echo the traditions of their sacred past.

Photo Tips   *Machu Picchu*

Stay at the Turista Hotel on site and obtain a night pass so that you can gain access to these captivating ruins at the first sign of dawn light. Praise the mists; don't curse them. Look for esoteric images through the mist, framed by the clouds as they drift over the wondrous city. When the mists are particularly thick, photograph the ruins closeup using the mist effect as a backdrop. Look for windows and doorways of the stone walls to frame vignettes of mountain landscapes beyond, as I have done here. Use a tripod and expose at f22 to assure that both foreground and background are sharp. Try lining up the background with a window so that what shows through is perfectly framed to look like a picture hanging on the stone wall. Then use a wide-angle lens to portray a good part of the wall so that it feels like the interior of a room. After all, these sacred places were quite possibly the homes of the Inca nobility and priests. Make sure you climb to the Funerary Hut at the highest point of Machu Picchu; the view down onto the ruins is superb and well worth preserving on film in any light.

   The site is enormous and many nooks and crannies have special significance

Detail of wall, fig tree in window, Machu Picchu, Peru, January 1988/ Sacred Earth, *p. 33*

so try to familiarize yourself with the layout before you arrive to photograph. Allow yourself time to adjust to the altitude. Many people find themselves short of breath as they attempt the hundreds of stone steps throughout the site. Finally, try to intersperse your photography with times without the camera—just for the sheer joy of being there.

Photo Tips *The Ruins of Pisac*

Like Machu Picchu, the Pisac ruins near Cuzco display the fine craftsmanship of the Incan stonemasons and I made many exposures closeup, concentrating on the rock work and ancient architecture. But it wasn't until I climbed above the ruins that real excitement gripped me for I now could photograph the site in context with its remarkable surroundings. Not only do the photographs from this vantage point show the beauty of the region, but also give a feeling for why the Incas would choose to call Pisac a sacred place. More than anything, I delighted in finding the symmetry and pattern in the erosion lines on the side of the hill. By placing the ruins low in the frame and including a large portion of the hillside, the resulting image portrays

Ruins at Pisac,
Peru, January 1988/
Sacred Earth, *p. 31*

the vertical lines of the hillside ending at the ruins, as though pointing to the sacred spot.

When you visit ruins that are couched in an area of natural beauty, pay as much attention to the natural geography as to the archaeological features. Look at the landscape in terms of its graphic qualities and how these natural features can be used in a visual portrayal. Valleys, rivers, and gorges often follow the ley lines of the earth, the areas of high electromagnetic energy that may have attracted the original builders to specific sites. Use your intuition and sensitivity to the natural contours to make images that portray the mystique and the mystery.

Bolivia

LAKE TITICACA

January 20 . . . This birthplace of the Incan world is truly a watery womb, the highest navigable lake in the world. Like Vilcabamba to the north, the shores of Lake Titicaca are said to offer longevity, as close to eternal life as one might hope to achieve on this earthly plane.

The creation myth of the Incas has left the legacy of a gold-plated rock on the Island of the Sun, dedicated to the sun god Inti. It was here on this island in Lake Titicaca that the founders of the Inca Empire emerged, and then travelled to Cuzco to fulfill their royal destiny in the sacred city.

Travel Tips

Lake Titicaca is split in two longitudinally by the border between Peru and Bolivia. It lies southeast of Cuzco, requiring a ten-hour bus or train trip to Puno in Bolivia. The high altitude of 12,500 feet (3,800 m) combined with the stark vegetation of the altiplano and the generally bleak, cold atmosphere is relieved by colorful ponchos and the dazzling blue of the lake when the sun shines. Copacabana is on a peninsula, a five-hour bus trip from Puno following the lake around the south and then east.

Local Resources

Puno is popular for boat excursions to the floating islands, which are held together by totora reeds. Copacabana, the best place to access the sacred islands, offers many boat excursions, but shop around for the best price, and be aware that this sealike lake can be very rough and dangerous, and guides may cut trips short in bad weather. This city is a major beach resort, so it is not as cheap as might be expected. Be sure to change enough money at the border as it cannot be done easily (if at all) in Copa; traveller's checks and credit cards are useless, and it is wise to avoid the black market. In general, Bolivia lacks tourist services—travel can be difficult in this military state, with its lack of information, basic services, travel tickets, and unrepaired roads.

Land of Mythical Beginnings

As in many other colonial cities, Copacabana is a blend of the old animistic traditions overlaid with Catholicism. Ancient deities who inhabited mountain peaks and other spectacular natural settings are now honored with Christian symbols, such as the famous **Stations of the Cross** leading to the highest point of land around Copacabana. Even the **Island of the Sun** in **Lake Titicaca** has a small chapel, but it has maintained the Incan legacy of ruins of temples and lodgings which suggest it was an important place of pilgrimage and religious ceremony. It is here that Manco Capac and Mama Occlo were born of the Incan legend, the creation story following a flood comparable to the Old Testament torrent, after which the creator god ordered the sun, moon, and stars to emerge. Their brilliance shone on a great rock projection on the tip of this island, the chosen place of creation of the Incas. The rock was once plated with gold and covered with a sacred cloth under a sun temple with windows and niches for the gods. Pilgrims came and offered penance, honoring the sacred spot from a distance. Contemporary pilgrims can see ruins dotted over the island including the so-called palace or Pilco Caima with its two-storied chambers and courtyards.

The nearby **Island of the Moon** with its Palace of Vestal Virgins and Temple to the Moon Mother is closed. Like so many ancient sacred places, the natural beauty of the setting and the journey entailed to get there is the real reward, rather than the ruins themselves. After all, it was this segment of mother earth that first inspired the Incas to revere their sacred history here, and it is this same earth that is here today to stimulate our imagination and inspire us with the same awe and honoring of the spirit in the land.

Photo Tips   *Island of the Sun*

Armed with the story of the Island of the Sun, I sought to capture something in my photographs that would relate to this epic legend.

Instead of taking a tourist boat from Copacabana, which lands you on the island in the uninspiring midday light, I chose to walk 12 miles (20 km) to a point of land where a local fisherman took me across the channel to the island in the late afternoon. I photographed clouds that looked like the legendary umbilical rope and made other exposures relating island and sun, but nothing seemed as ethereal as when I made a double exposure in the camera. I zoomed in on the island from the rowboat when I was about halfway across. Then I flipped the multiple-exposure lever to prevent the film from advancing when I cocked the camera for the second exposure. Zooming out to the wide-angle end of my zoom, I made the second exposure on the same frame that I had recorded the island on, thus placing the sun directly over the island and superimposing the cloud effect on top of it. The result looks somewhat like an apparition, an island in the sun from the land of impossible dreams. When my imagination is rich with the mythology of the relevant culture, then things just seem to unfold with the photography.

Rope-like cloud, Island of the Sun, Lake Titicaca, Bolivia, December 1987/ Sacred Earth, *p. 214*

Ecuador

March 5 . . . This country is amazing in the diversity of its natural heritage . . . even the name, Galapagos, conjures up visions of the most unique ecosystem of our planet . . . to the primordial jungles of the Amazon basin . . . the Andes' highest mountain resting on the waistline of the earth . . . a legendary valley of eternal life . . .

The sacred sites of Ecuador are places of nature, where the legacy of some of the world's most unique fauna and flora still display their primal beginnings, and the animistic deities of the natural world find haven in some of the most splendid settings of divine creation.

Travel Tips

Quito is serviced by airlines from all major South American cities and some in North America. Boats, trains, and buses also connect with other South American points.

Local Resources

The Galapagos Islands, 600 miles (1,000 km) west of South America, can only be reached by Ecuadorian Airlines, which flies to the island of Santa Cruz; a ferry and bus combination then connect to the tourist center at Puerto Ayora, where hotels, simple rooms, or a campground are available. The prime tourist season is December through May, when flights and tour boats may be completely booked by guided tours, although some independent island boats may be available. Contact the National Tourist Office, Reina Victoria 514 and Roca, Quito; Tel: 527–002 for up-to-date information as tourism is increasing here and changes are likely. Because of this, it is necessary to have a local guide on many of the islands, so most tourists choose tours to see as much as possible of the thirteen major islands and more than fifty small islets which are scattered over 155 miles (250 km) east to west, and 217 miles (350 km) north to south in this remote Pacific Ocean location. This is a marine reserve which was declared a national park in 1986, and is also a UNESCO World Heritage Site. Please don't buy coral souvenirs—the reef is being destroyed to provide trinkets for tourists. Back on the mainland, if you don't have your own car to explore the Panamerican Highway, local buses, trains, and taxis will ferry you anywhere. Mount Chimborazo is south of Quito and Ambato, but can be seen (if you're lucky with the mists) for hundreds of miles along the road; Ingapirca, in the southern highlands, is accessible from Cuenca by train (leaves 4:00 AM!) or buses leave every hour (drop you 8 miles [13 km] away but there is lots of local traffic); Vilcabamba is 18 miles (30 km) south of Loja; local buses travel there via the market town of Malacatos. There are several hotels available. Excursions on the Rio Napa tributary of the Amazon River leave from Misahualli; local buses travel from Puyo and Tena. Trips can be arranged for from two to ten days—inquire in Quito or go directly to Misahualli.

Eternal Islands to Eternal Life

The volcanic chain of islands that make up the **Galapagos** is like a symphony, but with more than four movements, rather like Mozart gone wild with endless variations on a theme. The main theme is endurance with diversity, overlaid with a sense of our primal beginnings that feels like the commencement of time—in fact, that is why Darwin was so fascinated with it. This prehistoric biology laboratory contains some of the most ancient species on earth, 23 percent of which are endemic. Five-hundred-pound (227 kg) tortoises, land and marine iguanas, blue-footed boobies, finches, penguins, sea lions, and fur seals all live their separate tranquil existences in a variety of marine and land environments that are almost lacking in predators—except for those we have inadvertently introduced, the primary one being ourselves. For millions of years these creatures have lived within their own ecosystems in a kind of time warp; the tourist comes face to face with monsters more fearful than the best reptilian fantasies that Hollywood could conjure up. Here we must also face the worst fear: what nature has taken millions of years to create and maintain, we are fast disrupting, and could destroy, leaving only a mirage on the ocean and an illusion of the past.

Ecuador lies not only on the equator, but also on the avenue of volcanoes that follows the spine of the Andes Mountains from Colombia to Cape Horn. This backbone of South America is often disrupted with fires from the bowels of Mother Earth that still send smoke and ash through the cones of Cotopaxi and Sangay. **Mount Chimborazo** no longer steams, but sits on the throne as the King of the Cordillera, the highest mountain in the Andes. This "mountain of snow" is actually the highest mountain in the world if measured from the center of the earth whose equatorial bulge pushes the mountain to 20,571 feet (6,300 m). This diffident monarch is often hidden in clouds described as eyebrows of the mountain, which start at about 6,500 feet (2,000 m), not far above the highest terracing of fertile soil.

Nature animism abounds at Chimborazo in the legends of the Quechua tribes; shamanic elders call upon mountain spirits to provide sacred waters to irrigate the land, or prevail upon the healing powers of electromagnetic forces in volcanic rock and chickens' eggs, or invoke the cosmic symbols of the "ghosts of granite" in the rock art. The Purnhua Indians believe Chimborazo is their ancestor, while, to the east, where mountain meets jungle, it is said that souls turn into clouds after death. This may be the only time I wished to see a waistline bulge! as the clouds miraculously dispersed during our visit, revealing this mountain which is "only to be revered, never seen," and the "king" floated like a phantasm above the sandy desert, draped with a cape of snow and mist.

From this natural mountain glory we then explored a man-made remnant of royalty—the ruins of **Ingapirca**. This isolated temple complex, the only major Incan monument in Ecuador, is thought to have been a palace for important personages travelling from Cuzco to Quito over the extensive network of Incan roads. The huge engraved stones positioned without bonding material are impressive in this sanctuary and ceremonial site with its trapezoidal windows and niches for the gods. Some also think it was a lunar observatory, with its perfect east-west alignment that could track the sun as well as the moon, still venerated as the primary deity of the contemporary local Canari Indians.

Back to nature again, we followed the trail to **Vilcabamba**, the Valley of the Whelca Tree named from the Ecuadorian word, Whelcapampa, and local songs speak of this Valle Sagrado (sacred valley) as eterna de vide (eternal life). This valley is noted as one of three worldwide centers of longevity, the others being the Abkhazians in Soviet Georgia and the Hunzas of Pakistan's Karakoram. But the inhabitants of this valley don't need the validation of modern-day science; they know their neighbors live to well over a hundred years. Our guide was 112-year-old Samuel Chengo, who still climbed up to his fields every day with a load of wood on his back without breathing heavily as I gasped for air and straggled behind him. Whether it is the high-fiber diet, the extra oxygen produced by the whelca tree, the lifestyle of constant physical exertion, and the feeling of usefulness in the community—or the high level of potassium and minerals in the water flowing from the sacred spring on the hill—it doesn't matter. Pilgrims come here for healing, feel rejuvenated, and experience that sense of the eternal and the spiritual peace radiating throughout this Valley of Longevity.

The contrast of the southern highlands and the jungles of the **Amazon River** is almost beyond description. We photographed the **Rio Napa**, one of eleven hundred tributaries of this great river system which starts as a brook 16,000 feet (5,000 m) high in the Peruvian Andes, and flows 4,000 miles (6,400 km) over 2.5 million square miles (6.5 million km²) of land to reach the Atlantic Ocean. One-quarter of all the fresh water on our planet is here, driving back the Atlantic salt water for 100 miles (160 km) at its 200-mile-wide (320 km) mouth, which still yawns 7 miles (11 km) wide when it is 1,000 miles (1,600 km) upstream. The Amazon contains 2,000 species of fish, 14,000 of mammals, 15,000 of insects, and 3,500 of birds. The jungle breathes 30 percent of the world's oxygen.

But the experience of this biological hothouse is much more exciting than its statistics. The feeling of catapulting down raging tributaries in a 60-foot (20 m) dugout canoe is one of the most fundamental experiences of the flow of nature that one could comprehend. Hurtling through primordial vegetation and past aboriginal villages is like a journey back in time, a trip into prehistory that even the most fertile imagination could not summon. The place is alive with ancient spirits, but the feeling of exhilaration comes from deep within one's being, accessing a mysterious primal response that nourishes a poignant sense of the spiritual.

Photo Tips   *The Galapagos Islands*

I have made four trips to the Galapagos Islands, each unique because there are so many habitats to visit, with each island rich in its own balance of nature. But all the islands have a common feature: they all offer an amazing assortment of wildlife within easy reach of the photographer's lens. Some wildlife—like the famous blue-footed booby and the land iguana—are so tame and accessible that one must take care not to step on them while walking along the trail.

Leaping porpoise and boat reflection, Galapagos Islands, Ecuador, February 1985/ Sacred Earth, *p. 89*

An umbrella is an ideal accessory, partly to shade oneself from the relentless sun, and partly to shade whatever you are photographing, thus resulting in a more even tonality for closeup photography. Wide-angle lenses are also more useful here because of the tremendous perspective that can be produced by getting up close to wildlife with the horizon also in sharp focus—being in among sea lions as they sprawled out lazily on the warm sand beaches was particularly enjoyable.

One of the greatest thrills, however, was photographing the dolphins that come five or ten at a time to leap and play in the wake of the bow of the boat. The best way to see them and to photograph them is to lean over the bow sprit as I did in this picture (previous page)—the glassy surface of the ocean allowed us to see our own reflections among the dolphins. No polarizing filter is needed in these situations; in fact, to use one would obliterate the reflections from the scene. When the call comes that dolphins are nearby, run for your camera, grab extra film, and be sure to have at least one wide-angle lens within reach. Put the camera strap around your neck, and shoot at 1/1000 sec or 1/500 sec to catch the peak of the action.

Photo Tips   *Mount Chimborazo*

For days I drove around the country that flanks Mount Chimborazo in search of views that would reveal its sacredness. For much of the time the elusive mountain remained hidden in the mists, but suddenly one morning as I drove through an alpine desert, the mountain revealed itself in brief glimpses. I leaped from the jeep and quickly sized up the possibilities for foregrounds. I made a number of exposures as I followed the gravel bottom of a dry river bed, but it wasn't until I found these small eroded cliffs that the ideal image began to emerge for me. I still had the problem, however, of getting a clear view of the mountain peak; the mists seemed to be closing

Alpine desert and Mount Chimborazo, Ecuador, February 1985/ Sacred Earth, *p. 201*

in and only occasionally uncovering the snowy summit. I put the camera on the tripod, set the lens opening at f22 for maximum depth of field—and waited. Several times I tripped the shutter when Chimborazo came into view, but only once did the mists perfectly frame the peak with equal portions shrouding each side. Once is all that it takes and I was ready and willing for the grand split second.

Venezuela

ANGEL FALLS

May 25 . . . There aren't enough superlatives to describe this preeminent vista of water plunging in an unbroken fall for 3,212 feet (988 m), and then springing up again into the rain-laden air to paint the most brilliant double rainbow I have ever seen. The Incas would have said that mother earth was very happy in her mating with father sky!

Although Angel Falls is best known as the highest waterfall in the world, this paramount creation of nature is also the making of a legend, a secret sacred place frequented by the Incas and honored by the local Indian tribes of the Venezuelan jungle.

Travel Tips

Angel Falls is located in Canaima National Park, a two-hour flight south of Caracas, Venezuela, which is connected to all major South American cities and on direct routes to North American cities such as Miami, New York, Los Angeles, and Toronto. Access by a complicated land and river route is also possible.

Local Resources

Avensa (Venezuela Airlines) flies daily into Canaima over the spectacular falls; these are package tours with one or two nights accommodation at Canaima camp, where most tourists stay to enjoy the swimming in the red lagoon fed by seven waterfalls of the Carrao River. It is wise to book ahead as accommodation is limited, especially during the holiday seasons. Contact your local travel agent or Avensa booking agent—in Caracas, Tel: (815) 2515–59. Travel agents can also book into another camp, Jungle Rudy's, a few miles upstream. We received excellent service from Escursiones Canaima S.R.L., A.V. Tachira, Qta Isnorga, C.S. Electoral, Ciudad Bolivar, Edo Bolivar,

Venezuela; Tel: (085) 28956 or 22965. They provided cheaper accommodation and a variety of boat tours as well as flights over the falls. Flights will be preferable for those not prepared for the arduous hiking which is often a part of the boat trips. The owners, Alberto and Ramon Jimenez, have been in operation since the beginning of tourism here, and guarantee their native guides "will bring you through troubled waters!" And they did, managing to get us there through hazardous conditions during the highest rainfall in years. Boat trips to the falls usually go for three or four days between June and November when the river is high enough. Overnight accommodation is in hammocks under open shelters with thatched roofs. We were also warned by several locals that the crime rate in Caracas is one of the highest in South America, including the trade in human body parts (horror stories of people waking up minus a kidney), so it may not be the best place to spend much time.

The Waters

The local Kamara Cota Indians speak of **Angel Falls** as Tulume Bena in Spanish, or Churún Merú in their language. For them, this is a dangerous sacred place; the falls are angry, and the Indians avoid speaking the name of the nearby mountain as this could cause harmful rains and thunderstorms. One elderly man reported that the Inca gods are still present here, as evidenced by the sounds of night in the jungle.

The sheer height of Angel Falls is unrivalled, and the transcendent feeling of being here in the rainy season when the flow of water is at its peak is almost beyond description. It was definitely worth the pain and severe danger endured to get here, although this would not be recommended for everyone. Many people in our group wisely refused to walk over slippery logs across raging torrents, or through dripping jungle vines threatening to snag or permanently soak our equipment, to half a mile from the base of the deluge where the spray inundating us from all sides made it almost impossible to see. It was purely amazing that Courtney was able to take photographs with a dry lens!

The glory of this jungle labyrinth is further exalted in the downstream waters of the Carrao and the Charun rivers. Seven cascades converge into a lagoon of an incredible sherry-red color, produced by the interaction of minerals with the decomposition of plant roots along the shore. These unique sites are certainly some of the most beautiful of nature's creations in South America.

Photo Tips   *Angel Falls*

There are two ways to photograph Angel Falls. One is to photograph from the air; the other is to make a trip by river and then a steep hike through jungle to a lookout about 3,280 feet (1,000 m) from the falls. I did both, and found the approach on foot more dangerous and adventurous, but also more rewarding. The major problem with photographing from a small plane is that unless the door is taken off, the plane's plexiglass window can interfere appreciably with the sharpness and clarity of the view. I got good results with the door off by exposing at fast shutter speeds but the falls seemed quite far away and did not appear as spectacular or imposing as when seen from the ground.

The trip through Canaima National Park by dugout canoe can be dangerous if the river level is too high or too low. I was on the first expedition to the falls after three days of unceasing torrential rains; the water level was up, the current extremely fast, and the trail to the falls treacherously slippery. When I finally made it to the lookout, gusts of wind were blowing the water directly at me, making it impossible to carry anything but one camera and lens which I kept dry under a raincoat. Fortunately I chose the right lens, my 17mm, which was the only one that could have encompassed both the falls and the double rainbow below. After every exposure, I hid the camera under cover and dried both it and the lens with tissue. Ironically, it was when the wind sprayed the strongest that I got the best pictures, because it was the sun shining on the increased volume of water that produced the brightest rainbows. To reduce the blur caused by droplets on the lens, expose wide open. Even with a wide-angle lens, the wide-open aperture reduces the depth of field, making any spots on the lens less noticeable. And come prepared for a thorough and joyous soaking!

Angel Falls after heavy rain,
Canaima National Park,
Venezuela, May 1990/
Sacred Earth, p. 103

Mexico

PALENQUE AND THE MAYAN TREASURES

March 5 . . . The Temple of the Foliated Cross is like a fairy-tale cottage tucked up on the hillside under a canopy of green jungle interspersed with brilliant pink bougainvillea. The corridor mazes of the Royal Palace dominate the courtyard which is flanked by the Temple of the Sun with its decorative roof combs, and the Temple of Inscriptions with its 220 stairs, which for centuries quietly harbored the treasures of Lord Pacal in its underground tomb.

Palenque, called "Palisade" by the Spanish, was the ceremonial center of the Yucatan during the classical Mayan period which flourished between 600 and 800 AD. The religious ritual, riches, and splendor honored Quetzalcoatl, the great plumed serpent god of the Mayans.

Travel Tips

Cancun, the tourist mecca on the eastern tip of the Yucatan Peninsula on Mexico's Caribbean coast is the easiest entry point to the Mayan treasures. A two-hour flight from the U.S. (Miami, Florida) makes this an easy jaunt for weekenders, with the resultant building boom of luxury hotels and resorts. West coast flights come via Los Angeles and Mexico City, and there are even direct flights from northern U.S. and Canadian cities to allow cold bodies to quickly escape icy winters. Palenque is the farthest point from Cancun, at the bend where the peninsula meets the isthmus of Mexico, and is also serviced by local flights from Cancun and Villahermosa, or via Mexico City. Coach buses travel from Mexico City, and there is a thirteen-hour overnight train from Merida, on the west coast of the Yucatan, or Cancun.

Local Resources

Local buses travel around the Yucatan but are slow and irregular even though cheap. The easiest way to see a lot is by renting a car from one of the many competitive local and international companies at the Cancun airport. Hotels in Cancun are always busy, so it is wise to book ahead; we paid dearly for what seemed to be the last decent room during the popular U.S. college spring break, when this place is inundated with young people lathered in tanning oil. We made a quick break down the road on a two-hour drive past Cozumel and Isla Mujeres to Tulum, and stayed at the nearby resort of Chac Mool, which can be booked through Apartada 403,

146

Cancun, Quintana Roo, Mexico. This is a delightful small village with thatched-roof cabanas and beds swinging from ropes to the accompaniment of crashing waves and sometimes ferocious winds. These winds also threaten the flicker rate of candles lighting the dinner tables that are draped with delicious vegetarian dishes and seafood. The drive to Palenque is long—608 miles (980 km) from Cancun—but roads are good and we tended to drive into the cool of the night although we were later warned this is not safe due to banditos (we never saw any). Kohunlich is on Hwy 186, 44 miles (70 km) west of Chetumal, the last Mexican city before the border with Belize. Palenque has a number of budget to moderately priced hotels (La Canada on Calle Merle Green 14 as you enter town—write Apartado 91, Palenque, Chiapas, Mexico), a campsite and several resort-style complexes (Hotel de las Ruinas with swimming pool, 5 miles [8 km] on the road to the ruins; write Apartado 49, Palenque, Chiapas, Mexico) on the outskirts; the archaeological site is a ten-minute drive out of town and is serviced by taxis and a local bus. To see the Mayan villages of Chamula and Zinacantan in the Chiapas highlands, we stayed in the old colonial city of San Cristobal at Posada Diego de Mazariegos, Ma Adelina Flores No. 2, San Cristobal de las Casas, Chiapas, Mexico C.P. 29200; Tel: 8-16-25. Local flights go from here to Tikal (Guatemala) and Yaxchilan and Bonampak, two Mayan pyramid complexes in the jungle that are noted for their colorful frescoes. Outside of the main cities of the Yucatan, accommodation can be very rustic and infrequent, so you may want to plan your itinerary accordingly.

Sacred Sites of the Yucatan

The Yucatan Peninsula is replete with the glory of the Mayan civilization which flourished here as early as 2000 BC. The Mayans created impressive ceremonial cities with terraced pyramids, religious ballcourts, and temples and palaces like Palenque, which was at its height of influence between 600 and 800 AD. Important structures were elevated on pyramids or other platforms, their tops decorated with roof combs to create the illusion of height. The highly ornate wall friezes of stucco and sculptured stone were probably also painted with bright colors to enhance their effect.

The eastern tip of the peninsula is dominated by **Uxmal** and **Chichen Itza**, the home of the plumed serpent who symbolized the Mayan god-king Quetzalcoatl. Mayan skill in astronomy is evidenced here in the observatory and the castillo, covered with fifty-two frieze panels corresponding to the Mayan calendric cycle, and eighteen terraces that represent the religious year. The castillo is actually an astronomical clock that casts an equinox shadow resembling an undulating serpent. The rain god Chac is seen in his typical reclining position holding a bowl above his naval to catch the freshly sacrificed hearts dedicated to keep him happy and ensure regeneration. Chichen Itza is built around a 197-foot-wide (60 m) cenote or fresh-water pool, the now-murky waters having yielded treasures of sacrificial objects and human bones from its 148-foot (45 m) bottom. Other cenotes on the peninsula are popular for swimming and exploring the underwater caves that were thought to be places of sacred ritual and ceremony to honor the gods who brought precious fresh water to these underground cisterns. If you're fit and adventurous for a climb into the earth, try the cave of Balankanche near Valladolid. It contains the Throne of the Jaguar and a stalactite/stalagmite formation of the sacred ceiba tree amidst hundreds of ceremonial bowls positioned as the Mayan priests left them around a crystalline cenote with its altar to Tlaloc, the Toltec rain god.

Past Merida on the northeast coast is Uxmal, the old capital of the northern Yucatan, noted for its simplicity and uncluttered facades. This is the setting for the unusual oval-shaped pyramid that is the base of the Temple of the Magician, honoring the legendary dwarf king who attained his status through magical means. The steep staircase lined with masks of the rain god Chac leads to the doorway which is actually the mouth of a monster whose face shapes the temple facade. Uxmal is connected to another pyramid complex at Kabah via the sacbe, a network of sacred roads stretching over the Yucatan.

From the grandeur of Uxmal, we travelled to the spectacular seacoast setting of **Tulum**, the Mayan "Place of the Dawn," to find a group of rather uninspiring ruins overlooking a windswept turquoise sea stretching for miles around a coastline indented with white sand beaches. The location is breathtaking, and the swimming and snorkeling at nearby Xel-Ha is rated among the best in the Yucatan. Continuing south and east, we came upon the simple elegance of **Kohunlich**, a lesser-known Mayan site that is built over a huge underground reservoir, and is expected to reveal two hundred buildings when excavation is completed. Of the five structures found, the Pyramid of the Masks is the most interesting, its broad stairway lined with six huge faces portraying the sun god, Kinich Ahau, whose wide eyes are carved with the Mayan glyph "Chuen," which represents the 260-day Zolkin ritual celebration of the sacred Mayan calendar. The thatched roof has been reconstructed in the thousand-year-old Mayan tradition of palm leaves cut at the full moon, then woven and placed to the correct pitch during the right conditions of sunlight to ensure its long endurance.

But for us, the crowning glory of the Mayan sacred places was the jungle city of **Palenque**, the westernmost site in the province of Chiapas. Hidden deep in the folds of dense tropical rain forest at the foot of the Sierra Madre mountains (locally known as Mother of Mountains), it is like a Garden of Eden, a majestic haven from the sun and the tourists. Palenque belongs to the night; as twilight descended, turning the cold gray stone of day to pink and purple softness, Venus arose over the steps of the Temple of Inscriptions, glowing white under a full moon. As the heat of the day melted into the dew-touched grass, the air filled with raspy breathing sounds from the jungle just steps away. The effect was haunting and entrancing, but we discovered later that the sounds were made by male monkeys moaning in romantic fervor under the full moon! This primordial experience was the highlight of our time here, but required some quiet negotiation at the gate to allow us to remain after dusk.

Palenque is the elegant queen of the Yucatan. The Royal Palace with its unique four-story tower has astronomical symbols of Venus and an altar stone at the top along with a glorious labyrinth of ornately decorated passages that lead to living rooms and steam baths used for ritual purification. The baths drained into the stream running through a corbel-vaulted aqueduct under the structure, an interesting example of the geomantic principle of siting sacred places over natural water sources, thus increasing the surrounding electromagnetic energy. The palace can be explored for many hours but is best at dawn as the low-angle light turns rock to gold.

Near the Royal Palace is the relatively small Temple of the Sun, a typical five-stepped pyramid graced with lacy stonework in the symbol of the underworld jaguar god, and considered a masterpiece of Mayan workmanship. Other than the remnants of decorative roof combs there are no ornate carvings or stelae to see here; consequently many tourists pass it by, ascending the steps to call back, "nothing to see here," while we spent hours exploring the cool dark rooms and found flashes of brilliant color creating surrealist landscapes where water and minerals have seeped down the walls from corbel-arched ceilings.

The Temple of Inscriptions is also worth the long climb up 220 steep stairs, providing a view of the whole complex and the contemporary city in the distance, as well as the plain stretching to the ocean. Herein lies the recently discovered (1952) tomb of Lord Pacal, his jade mask with obsidian and shell eyes and his bejewelled sarcophagus carved with the nine lords of the underworld awash with red cinnabar. This color is associated with rebirth from the east, signifying the completion of his journey as he followed the setting sun through the underworld. The passage above his deeply embowelled tomb is believed to be symbolic of this journey, as he was guided into the light by the plumed serpent carved on its walls.

From the sumptuous glory of Palenque, we drove northwest to **Agua Azul**, a series of waterfalls produced by the convergence of streams fed by the hills of the Sierra Madre. These turquoise waters were a refreshing respite from the humid jungle, as we watched local boys grab tentative footholds and climb through the rushing waters to the top of the falls, where they would dive to the deep pools below, delighting us with their daring. We wondered if this was just a display for the tourists, but we later discovered Agua Azul is one of the nine holy waters of the world, on a list of mystical places known through antiquity.

Our research also revealed that the Mayans of Chiapas consider their mountains to be the home of the Earthlord who directs the clouds and rain to nourish the land. In May, shamans and religious elders bring fireworks and music to the sacred caves just below the summit of Moss Mountain near San Cristobal de las Casas, to celebrate the beginning of the rainy season, which these agricultural communities still depend on as they have for thousands of years. This importance of seasonal cycles is further reflected in the geometric designs worn by the Mayan women, whose weaving displays the course of the sun through thirteen layers of the sky and the underworld, and the creation of clouds by the Earthlord with the help of his servant toads and snakes. This harmony of the Mayan cosmos is monitored by the use of the ancient calendric system where the sun god is primary and directs all the rhythms of life. Many traditional ways are still practised by the Lacondon Indians in the jungle around Palenque, and in the small Mayan villages of Chamula and Zinacantan near San Cristobal. These are not just charming examples of traditional Mayan villages, but are important religious centers that are taken very seriously by the inhabitants who may not be very friendly to tourists. Please honor them (and protect yourself) by not taking photographs, especially of their church, either from the inside or the outside—a number of photographers have been attacked by the locals, and we heard that several tourists were killed for these indiscretions.

Photo Tips   *The Gold Brick of the Palace*

The major drawback to photographing at Palenque in the most desirable light is that the grounds don't open until well after sunup, and close before the sun drops low enough to bathe the grounds in a warm rich glow. There is considerable inconsistency in the rules regarding special entry—some sources will tell you it's not possible under any circumstances; others will say that at the right price (perhaps $20 U.S.) the guard will allow you to stay. The best approach is to have one of the English-speaking tour guides negotiate on your behalf. If the request falls on deaf ears, try again the next day, perhaps with a different guide who might approach a different guard (the shifts change and some guards are more open than others). You will be issued a pass that you should keep handy to avoid being evicted unceremoniously from the grounds.

Once permission is granted, you are home free. I made this image of the Royal Palace mere seconds after sunrise. Only for a few brief seconds did the slab of rock remain golden, the color that for me speaks of the sanctity and sacredness of Palenque. To be certain that I had the right exposure setting, I used my hand-held light meter and took a spot reading right off the golden area of the rock. I was then assured that the golden color, as well as the background opening of similar tone, would receive a normal exposure, showing it off to best advantage.

Morning light in hallway, Royal Palace, Palenque, Mexico, March 1988/ Sacred Earth, *p. 39*

Hawaii

February and March ... How can one say anything new and novel about Hawaii, probably the most familiar tourist destination in the world. Even the sacred hula has become a novelty ... but the diversity of the landscape is still sufficient to entice me back again and again ... there is always another small haven to explore, or the same one to see once more, with fresh eyes.

For many people, sacred Hawaii is her beaches. But to the early Hawaiians, as to so many indigenous cultures around the world, all the land was sacred, suffused with nature spirits and a pantheon of gods who ruled all events of the heavens and the earth.

Travel Tips

Hawaii is easily accessible, whether via hundreds of direct daily air charters from North America, or en route to Australia, New Zealand, or Southeast Asia; or by any seaworthy vessel from a luxury liner to a single-masted craft.

Local Resources

The best way to see the islands is by car. Competition for the tourist dollar is so great that many hotel packages are extremely reasonable and include a car literally for free. All the islands are so developed that local tours and guides are rampant. Camping is popular although there have been tensions between some native Hawaiians that in recent years have precipitated problems on some of the more remote beaches. To hike into Maui's Haleakala Crater, write the National Park Service, Haleakala National Park, Box 369, Makawao, Maui, HI 96768; Tel: 572–7749. They provide three cabins with beds that are distributed in a lottery system that you and your party can enter as many times as you wish til you get the dates requested. Take in all your equipment except cooking utensils. Two private companies also lead day excursions on horseback and there is a tent and trailer camp near the rim. Helicopter trips over Kilauea leave hourly from the Volcanoes National Park Golf Course. If there is significant volcanic activity (as there often is), you will need to book your flights a day or two in advance. The National Park Headquarters provides free information on all of these services. Whale watching is best around Lahaina between January and April.

Sacred Places

Aboriginal Hawaiians came from the Marquesas in 750 AD. The spiritual development of Hawaii continued until after 1200 AD, though, with the arrival of Polynesian kahuna priests who brought with them kahuna stones imbued with mana from four Tahitian priests. These stones can still be seen at the Surfrider Hotel, one of the many hotels in **Waikiki**, the primary action center for tourists on the island of Oahu. Waikiki, which means "spouting water," was the home of Hawaiian royalty for the thousand years before the Europeans arrived and imposed Christianity on this "Land of the Living Gods." On the south coast of Oahu, the kahuna established the most sacred heiau (temple) dedicated to Ahu'ula, the god of the chiefs, who were considered descendents of the creator god Kane. Kane formed the three worlds: the upper heaven of the gods, the lower heaven, a transitional place above the earth, and the earth itself, the garden for mankind. Every family altar had a Kane stone which was frequently annointed with sea water. Diamond Head, the "Brow of Ahi," the yellow-finned tuna, was a power spot marked by another important heiau, where the great chief Kamehameha offered human sacrifices to the war god Ku.

Hawaii is a chain of volcanic islands sitting on the Pacific Plate. This tectonic plate continues to creep northward and move new land over the "hot spot" in the earth's crust which then explodes into a new flow of molten lava from the belly of the earth. The **Big Island of Hawaii** is the most recent in this chain of volcanoes, and the home of the active ones, **Kilauea** and **Mauna Loa**. Both of these began on the ocean floor about 3 million years ago, but didn't emerge from the sea until 500,000 years ago. Mauna Loa is the most active volcano on earth, with a mass reaching 18,000 feet (5,500 m) below the sea, and 13,800 feet (4,200 m) above it. This is the stuff of creation—Mauna Loa has added more than 850 million cubic yards (646 million m³) of lava to this island since 1983, and for the Hawaiians, the fire goddess Pele is responsible.

Pele is probably the most revered (with good reason!) of the Hawaiian goddesses, with a home on every island. However, all her craters stopped burning, except on the Big Island where she lives in the boiling lake of **Kilauea**; temples were built on each side of the caldera, and sacrifices of all kinds were common. Today it is not unusual to see a bottle of gin, Pele's favorite, tucked behind a tree near Kilauea, and it is still often said "you don't want to mess with Pele." She produces the hottest lava in the world, which fountains up to 2,000 feet (600 m) in a curtain of fire that cools as it falls, forming pumice strands which are called Pele's hair or Pele's tears. These can drift for miles, or if her gases are hotter, ropes of pahoehoe lava will spread in sheets or form lava tubes. A helicopter flight over a raging lava tube is the closest experience one can imagine to being in Dante's Inferno, with 2000°F (1079°C) heat roaring in your ears and baiting you to get too close. It is not wise to mess with Pele above ground either, as one fellow reported the soles of his running shoes melted on his feet as he capriciously tripped over a lava flow.

Travelling away from the volcanic centers to the east coast, the tropical botanicals of **Hilo Gardens** give haven to the nature spirits of some Hawaiian gods, while the fossilizations of **Lava Tree Park** provide primeval landscapes of a vastly different sort. Here molten lava has engulfed living trees that then burn inside their dark graves; their debris flows away, leaving only their molded shape in the twisting grip of lava.

This ghostly black forest is a grim reminder of the wrath of Pele as well as a fascinating example of her creativity. The brilliant red blossoms of the ohia trees are a reminder of the story of Princess Lehua who fell in love with the commoner Ohia; the match was not permitted, and the lovers were turned into this tree with its colorful blossoms so they would not be parted. Legend directs that picking the blossoms brings Princess Lehua's tears of rain, but also warns that the sacred flowers must not be plucked on the way up the volcano, although it is permitted to take them on the way down. Nearby **Akaka Falls** provides a cool respite under the 420-foot (130 m) semicircular falls in a lush valley of torch-red and white ginger, fragrant orchids, and bamboo. It is here that the god Akaka fell to his death and was so mourned by his two mistresses that they were turned into the two smaller falls nearby to quench their tears.

Continuing north, the east coast road displays more of the incredible diversity of this island which harbors so many of the Hawaiian spirits. The west side with the Kailua-Kona coast is the place of tourist beaches and sun, while the east is lush with more rain and peaceful living. The dividing line at **Waimea** (Kamuela) is purely geographic, and this is the place to see the sacred rainbows, which myths report are indicative of the presence of divine chiefs. Rainbows are also considered a bridge to the other world, and, here in particular, the rope for gods to descend to earth. Other legends mark Waimea as a place of violent death due to the tricks of the god Maui who caused trouble here and his blood flow made a rainbow.

The nearby coastline at **Waipio Bay** also demands attention as the home of "arching waters" at the mouth of the **Valley of the Kings**, the largest political and cultural center in a prolific vale that sustained a population of one hundred thousand in earlier times. It is here that Chief Kamehameha was designated as king of the archipelago, and where, in 1791, he fought the first naval battle using cannons with the help of the war god Ku. According to legend, the god Wakea, progenitor of the island, favored this valley, as did the great gods Kane and Kaneloa; the Nenewe "shark man" is believed to live in a pool here which has a tunnel to the sea. It is also said that this valley has a sacred doorway to the land of the dead, but all its ruins were washed away in a 1946 tsunami (a tidal wave following an earthquake) that left 161 people dead.

The northernmost island of **Kauai**, the oldest and the most lush, is another Garden of Eden, and is small enough that one can drive to any point within an hour or two of base. The colorful **Waimea Canyon** is the Grand Canyon of Hawaii, with incredible colors that can be viewed from many places along its ridge. Over the next ridge to the east is the wettest spot on earth at Mount Waialeale which records over 500 inches (1,270 cm) of rain per year, often leaving the canyon shrouded in mist, the perfect place for the legendary meeting of the gods to plot the future of the island. Perhaps it is here that the mythical Menehune "little people" live in caves and hollow logs; the many stoneworks around the island are attributed to these dwarflike aborigines who are said to complete their superhuman building in the middle of the night.

But for us, the crowning glory of Kauai is the **Na Pali Coast**, the birthplace of the sacred hula dance in the Kaulu Heiau. This symbol of Hawaii was originally a form of worship performed by men in sacred rituals taught by the androgynous deity call Laka. Eventually the male Laka departed and left the female to establish the hula heiau at Haena Point, where girls as young as four years old came to learn the sacred dance. Novitiates were required to jump more than 2,700 feet (800 m) to the churning waters below and swim to Kee Beach to demonstrate their dedication. The crashing waves of Na Pali reminded us of these mermaids, as for hours we watched an endless display of water shapes reminiscent of the graceful motions of the hula— perhaps the spirits of those maidens still direct these waters to seduce our reverence of this holy place.

The final sacred place of Hawaii is a completely different world, a former home of Pele when it was an active volcano and now a moonscape like no other. This is **Haleakala**, the 60-mile-wide (100 km) crater on Maui that the kahunas say is a place of transformation. Thought to be a burial place for chiefs, food offerings are still left on the crater rim for Pele, who still owns the spirit of the crater. This is also the House of the Sun, where the god Maui used a rope of sacred coconut fibers to lasso the sun's rays and slow them down as they passed over the crater. It is a moot point whether he did this to have more sunlight for his fishing, or for his mother's laundry to dry, but he succeeded, and the sun shines more brightly here— when it shines. This huge crater is also filled with mist, fog, and rain of the most terrible sort, turning the moonscapes into an incredible array of purple, red, gray, and black which entice one to explore and can easily lead you astray down its 1,400-foot (425 m) depth into a labyrinth of cinder cones, lava tubes, and trails which can be confusing in one of Pele's wrathful storms. It is wise to plan your trips with lots of time, making day hikes from the visitors' center or longer treks when a bed is available at the cabins on the crater floor. Plan your energy, maintain your power, and don't be seduced by Pele, or you will miss the northwest coast of this island which provides haven for more whales per square inch than anywhere in the world.

The spirits of ancient Polynesia lived happily in Hawaii until the advent of the Europeans, who by 1819 banned public worship of the old gods. The last hurrah was said by Queen Kapiolani in 1824 when she defied the kahunas and walked into the Kilauea caldera to challenge Pele and affirm her new profession of faith in Christianity. But like so many indigenous cultures throughout the world, the ancient gods were not lost—only overlaid by Christian symbols and beliefs. Today Hawaii seems to be experiencing a spiritual renaissance, and although it may sometimes seem primarily for the benefit of tourism, the underlying message of peace resulting from living in harmony with each other and with the natural world is the essence of all life on earth, and a timely reminder.

Photo Tips   *Haleakala Mists*

Haleakala Crater is a panoramic spectacle of color in any light and any season, but it is the sun-lit mist that gives it a special visual quality. Predicting the best time to see it is difficult, as the mists, like the spirit of the goddess Pele, seem to materialize at will, and vanish as quickly. It is a two- or three-hour walk from the visitors' center into the crater, and if you are carrying an ample supply of photography and support equipment, it is not easy to hike quickly. Pack horse is one option although I prefer the flexibility of travelling on foot with my camera easily accessible at all times. Because the mists do come and go at will, the most esoteric effects are often fleeting and require reflexive action. The crater is enormous, one of the largest in the world, stretching for over 19 square miles (49 km²). If you want time to explore, then more

Mists on floor of Haleakala Crater, Maui, Hawaii, February 1987/ Sacred Earth, *p. 189*

than a one-day trip will be required and you should apply to stay in the cabins on the crater floor (see section on Local Resources). There is much to photograph, including the exotic nene bird and the mysterious silversword plant. Take a tripod, plenty of film, and plan extensive explorations using your cabin as a base.

Photo Tips   *The Volcano Dragon Shape*

Photographing volcanoes and lava lakes from a helicopter is a very specialized pursuit, but with attention to a few basic techniques, the payoff can be highly rewarding. If your trip is primarily for photography, they are willing to take the doors off the helicopter and will tilt the craft so that you can get an unimpeded view of the action (you are strapped in with a very secure seat belt!).

Just after dawn is the best time to go; the light is low and rakes across the lava flows, enhancing the texture, and there is often a lot of steam and smoke to add to the atmospheric quality of the landscape. As you hover over the hardened lava, (most of which will have turned black even if quite recently emitted), you will see the lava lakes, lava tubes, and rivers of lava accented in a brilliant orange. For these exposures consisting predominantly of black lava, it is imperative that you underexpose by two settings—if the meter says 1/125 sec at a given lens opening, you expose at 1/500 sec. I photographed some of my aerials at one setting underexposed and the results were surprisingly too light to look natural. The best way to proceed is to shoot on automatic and leave the manual override set at minus two. Then if you come upon scenes that are mostly orange and red molten lava, rather than black, (as was the case here) flip the override from minus two to minus one. This purposeful underexposure is to keep the blacks looking black, and to enhance the dramatic graphic effect by making the reds leap out in contrast to their darker backgrounds. Because I have a weak stomach to start with, I load all my cameras before boarding, so that I minimize the need to change film while bouncing around in the air.

Dragon pattern on lava lake, Kilauea volcano, Big Island, Hawaii, January 1987/Sacred Earth, p. 175

Continental U.S.A.

The Southwest

CHACO CANYON

September 5 . . . Suddenly after miles of driving across flat plain, one is enticed into a pale canyon, its 1-mile-wide (1.6 km) valley floor laced with thirteen ruins of golden bricks nestled like dollhouses against the creamy sandstone cliffs jutting more than 328 feet (100 m) high to meet azure blue sky speckled with powder-puff clouds.

This is Anasazi land, perhaps the most famous ceremonial site of the southwest Pueblo Indians. A trade route with a road network feeding from as far as Mexico, this epicenter of an advanced civilization was also the most important ritual center of the Anasazi world.

Travel Tips

Chaco National Park is a UNESCO World Heritage Site located in the northwest corner of New Mexico, a three-hour drive from the Albuquerque airport. If you're driving in from the north, turn off Highway 44 at Nageezi, follow local road 7800 for 12 miles (20 km) to NM 57, and the visitors' center is 17 miles (28 km) further at the end of the canyon. From the south, turn off I-40 at Thoreau and go 47 miles (75 km) on the paved road (#9) that turns to the right just after Crownpoint, then follow a 20-mile (32 km) stretch of unpaved road (#14) that leads to the visitor center. Park and road information can be obtained by telephone (505) 988–6767; this road may be difficult after rains, especially with trailers and campers. For general information on New Mexico, write Tourism and Travel Division, 1100 St. Francis Drive, Santa Fe, NM 87503; Tel: (800) 545–2040.

Local Resources

There is no food, gas, or lodging at the park. The last trading post is at Nageezi in the north, and at the junction of the unpaved road from the south. There is a sixty-three-site campground 1 mile (1.6 km) east of the headquarters, with flush toilets but no other water—don't expect showers or dish washing. There are no reservations, so arrive early during prime tourist season (May 24 to Labor Day), although there is also an overflow site. Drinking water is usually available at the visitors' center but they have been known to run out. There is no electricity or telephone (except in an emergency at the center). An 8-mile (12 km) paved ring road goes to all the sites in the canyon—it is not walking distance, but many people bring bikes. All except one of the ruins can be seen from the road, and there are several back country self-guided hikes with excellent park explanatory notes.

Chaco is closed between sunset and sunrise, and special permission is needed to photograph during these times. It is wise to inquire ahead of your arrival—contact Superintendent, Chaco Culture National Historic Park, Star Route 4, Box 6500, Bloomfield, NM 87413; Tel: (505) 988–6727.

A stop in Santa Fe is a delightful way to prepare for a unique southwest experience. Although very touristy, the pueblo theme is carried through in the architecture of this city, and the extensive art galleries and cultural events are reminiscent of its Anasazi history. The LaPosada de Santa Fe Hotel, 330 East Palace Avenue, Santa Fe, NM 87501; Tel: (800) 727-5276 (within the U.S.) or (505) 986–0000; Fax: (505) 982–6850, is a pleasureful haven with swimming pool, extensive grounds, and an excellent restaurant. Its adobe-style rooms are all built around an historic Victorian mansion, two blocks from the main city plaza. The nearby Planet Cafe, a half block west at 215 East Palace Avenue; Tel: 982–0280, serves excellent internationally styled natural foods cuisine, in a congenial atmosphere of indoor and outdoor dining.

Home of the Ancient Ones

If **Chaco Canyon** is high on your list of sacred sites, go soon. These "primitive" visiting conditions (which to us was one of the best parts of being there) are a concern to the park authorities and to the outlying communities that want to capitalize on the economies of tourism. There is serious talk of paving the southern access road which will bring in more tourists (they have nearly 100,000 per year now), and they may close the ruins to the general public and have access only on guided tours by the busload. Their concern for the fragility of the ruins and the environment is well taken, but the real joy of Chaco would be lost if this occurs. Some areas are cordoned off, but it is still possible to walk among the ancient bricks, peer into the kivas, and walk through low doorways that have stood for more than a thousand years.

Walking the trails beside petroglyphs (and unfortunately grafitti) and above the canyon overlooking Pueblo Bonito gives one an incredible feeling of walking in the footsteps of these Ancient Ones, as the Anasazi are called. It was a mysterious culture, technologically advanced with masonry techniques perfected to create multistoried buildings with rubble cores and shaped stones, a water storage and agricultural system sufficient to support up to five thousand people in the valley, and a network of roads connecting more than seventy-five villages over 400 miles (644 km). Artifacts indicate they traded widely in the southwest and probably into Mexico, as evidenced by the remains of exotic birds, similar artistic and decorative styles such as Mayanlike ear pendants, precious turquoise not mined in this area, and thousands of seashell beads used in decor and ritual. Although the Anasazi probably lived here from 300 AD, the culture flowered between 900 and 1180, when they mysteriously disappeared, perhaps due to climate changes, an overtaxed environment, or religious or social decrees.

All of the large pueblos were probably shared community living spaces and all had round kivas, the underground communal and ceremonial rooms derived from pit houses used by the earlier Anasazi. The kiva is still used in the Navajo and Hopi villages, its womb symbol embodying the four underworlds of the Anasazi cosmology. The Great Kiva at Chaco Canyon is called Casa Rinconada; the underground pit was entered by ladder through a hole in the roof of Ponderosa pine logs. Here the initiated gather to receive the spirits who have their own entrance through a sipapu or opening in the floor; wall niches hold ceremonial objects such as turquoise and shell necklaces that gleam in the firelight as the dancers wildly jump on their foot drums which echo throughout the kiva, increasing the excitement of the ceremony. The kiva at Casa Rinconada is unique in its alignment to celestial north where all the stars in the heavenly sky can be seen to revolve around Polaris. Priests may also have studied the heavens from Fajada Butte at the south entrance of the canyon, where a recently discovered cleftlike opening in the rock forms an arrow marking the shadow of the sun's passage overhead.

The ruins are fascinating and a joy to explore in almost quiet isolation after the summer visitors have gone and the heat is somewhat diminished. The splendor of the man-made legacies integrated with such a beautiful natural setting allows the spiritual energy of Chaco Canyon to flow, almost as though one can inhale it and take a bit home to remember the solitude and the feeling of connecting with the past. The Hopi suggest that their Anasazi ancestors knew continuity more than change, and in their constant quest for balance and harmony, they say: "interrogate the landscape—the earth reveals their story . . . everything is alive."

Photo Tips   *Casa Rinconada with Star Trails*

The many sites at Chaco Canyon are open to explore between sunrise and sunset, provided you stay on the paths away from the fragile and tipsy walls. When I realized that the two main entrances to the kiva at Casa Rinconada lined up with Polaris, the pole star, I became excited that the evidence suggested that the Anasazi were sky watchers. I wanted to make an image that portrayed the relationship of sacred site and sacred sky. After dark (with special permission), I lined up my camera on the steps of the south doorway, pointing it at the north entrance with Polaris directly above. By using a fisheye lens with a 120-degree angle of view, I was able to include the woodwork of the threshold above me and portray a significant area of the sky. Then by leaving the shutter open for one hour with the aperture set at f8 for ISO 50, I recorded the movement of the stars around Polaris. During the exposure I walked around the kiva flashing my strobe at the walls, and brightly flashing the wall niches by setting the flash inside each one. Here I feel I have come as close as I have anywhere to portraying the significance of a sacred monument as it may have been seen and revered by its makers.

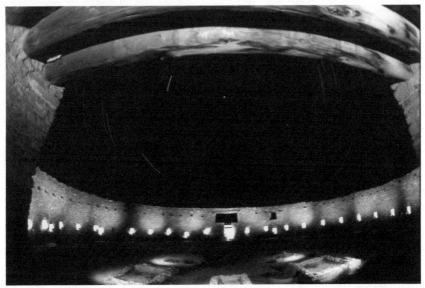

Casa Rinconada and star traces around Polaris, Chaco Canyon, New Mexico, September 1990/ Sacred Earth, *p. 59*

NAVAJO COUNTRY

September 18 ... The overhangs of peachy-apricot-colored sandstone patched with the black patina stains of desert varnish protect the minute ruins tucked under their ledges ... the houses look like dinky toys carelessly flung against the steep cliffs of the canyon nourished by the waters of Chinle Wash, which dribbles past grid patterns of corn greening the stream bed far below the 1,000-foot (308 m) stone walls.

Canyon de Chelly (pronounced Shay) is the Spanish corruption of the word tsegi, meaning rock canyon, the ancestral stronghold of the Navajo, from the early Basketmakers to the later Anasazi cliff dwellers in northeastern Arizona. Dating from as early as 300 AD, these ruins, like Chaco Canyon, display many subterranean kivas with their ritual sipapu entrances for the spirits to emerge from under the ground.

Travel Tips

Canyon de Chelly is a national monument and can be approached from all directions on good roads: from the north and west on highways 59 and 191, and from the south and east on 264 and 191 to Chinle and the Grand Canyon, 3 miles (5 km) from the canyon. All the surrounding lands between here and Flagstaff to the east and over the Utah border to the north are partitioned to the Hopi and Navajo nations, the descendents of the ancient Anasazi. The Navajo Nation Tribal Council is based in Window Rock, while the Hopi Nation is concentrated in communities on three mesas along Highway 264 east of Tuba City to Jeddito. This is a high-volume tourist area, and all the trading posts and national parks and monuments sell maps and books for all areas, or write to the state Tourist Information Office, 1100 West Washington Street, Phoenix, AZ 85007; Tel: (602) 542–TOUR.

Local Resources

Thunderbird Lodge, Box 548, Chinle, AZ 86503; Tel: (602) 674–5841, near the visitors' center, is the only accommodation other than in Chinle; there is also a cafeteria-style restaurant, gift shop, tour-booking center, and a large campsite (open year round, no reservations). The visitors' center (Tel: (602) 674–5436) provides driving maps and individual tour guides can be hired here or at the lodge; the only public access to the canyon floor is the trail to the White House ruins. Large open-air 4-wheel drive vehicles take tours down the valley, but a Navajo guide must be hired (and you must have your own 4-wheel drive vehicle—no rentals nearby) if you wish to explore further on a daily or overnight basis. A good road follows the canyon rim from the west to the north and south, but does not link up in the east so requires retracing your route.

Betatakin is one of the two sites at Navajo National Monument, 10 miles (16 km) north of Highway 160 at Kayenta. There is an excellent campsite (no reservations) and a visitors' center that provides guided hikes to Betatakin, a three- to four-hour return trip that is fairly demanding but not difficult although summer temperatures can be over 100°F (30°C plus). Trips leave once a day (sometimes twice in the summer) and you must register for it there—numbers are limited, but it is definitely worth the effort to see this beautiful canyon. Overnight hikes to Keet Seel are only possible between May 24 and Labor Day weekend. Call (602) 672–2236 for information.

Antelope Canyon is near Page, Arizona, a two-hour drive on Highway 89 north of Flagstaff, or from the east off Highway 160 onto Highway 98. Almost 4 miles (6 km) east of Page is a bridge, followed by a dirt road turning to the left, and immediately left again into a trailer camp. If you pass the power station you have gone too far. At the trailers you will find Floyd Bennet, a young Navajo man who will guide you into the canyons if you wish to photograph; this may entail being lowered by rope. We paid ten dollars per day to photograph, plus extra money for his help in accessing the canyon. An official photography permit can also be obtained from the Navajo Nation at LeChee Chapter House, 2.6 miles (4 km) down Coppermine Road which is 2 miles (3 km) on Highway 98, east of the Page junction. The Big Lake Trading Post at the junction of Highway 98 and Coppermine Road also sells permits. The upper canyon is about 3 miles (5 km) from the highway in a 4-wheel drive over sandy terrain. There is an excellent campsite on Highway 98, with a pool and jacuzzi—the Page-Lake Powell Campground, PO Box BB, Page, AZ 86040; Tel: (602) 645-3374. This Lake Powell Recreation Area offers a diverse range of activities; for information, contact the Page Visitor and Convention Bureau, Lake Powell Blvd., PO Box 727, Page, AZ 86040; Tel: (602) 645-2741.

The Anasazi Legacies

One of the most spectacular outlooks at **Canyon de Chelly** is at Spider Rock, the most easterly point on the south rim, 12 miles (20 km) from the visitors' center. Here, according to legend, at the meeting point of Canyon de Muerto and Canyon de Chelly, is the sacred spot where the Navajo emerged from the Underworld; Spider Woman sits high on her needlelike projection where she kidnaps and takes children who are bad—the white rocks at the top symbolize their bones. The adjacent Speaking Rock reports their names to her. The terror of Spider Woman is softened by the Navajo prayer on a nearby plaque: "Listen, smell the juniper. Feel the gentle power of beauty. Ancient Black Rock hunches on the distant horizon. A dark cloud above means the rain will soon be upon us."

The walk to the White House ruins is a joyful one, following a winding path down 700 feet (213 m) of geological time. On the valley floor, leafy cottonwoods provide the only shade and the Chinle Wash may cool your feet if the rains have come. The **White House**, so called because of its whitewashed exterior, is tucked behind a row of brick walls under a sandstone overhang. The creamy color of the sandstone is marred by jagged black streaks of desert varnish, caused by the extrusion of chemicals from the rock after years of water seepage, which produces an abstract art of its own. In front of the overhang, at the base of the valley floor, is another set of ruins which frames the upper level. The ceremonial kiva, thought to be the heart of village life, is in the upper portion. Turn to the high buttes on your right and look for a face shaped by the rock, as though one native spirit still watches over his ancient home.

We stayed til after sunset, watching the glow of low sun turning the stone to a warm pink. The rippling water in the stream became an impressionist painting of burnished gold, green, purple, pink, and blue. As we trudged back up the hill, we met two young Navajo children returning to their home on the canyon rim after escorting their old grandmother up the valley to where she lives alone. Many Navajo families live on the canyon floor where they cultivate their crops, but move up during the winter season partly to allow the children to go to school.

Canyon de Chelly has a different echo from Chaco Canyon. Here it is more alive, the spirit living on as the vitality of present-day life reflects the continuity of a lifestyle that has existed for more than a thousand years. On another nearby plaque, a Navajo prayer reads: "There is purity and strength here. And places sacred to the people. Places strong in the oneness of earth and sky and all things. I am indeed its child. Absolutely, I am earth's child."

Northeast of Canyon de Chelly the states of Arizona, New Mexico, Colorado, and Utah meet at the Four Corners, an area sacred to all Indian nations, considered the heart center of the living earth. West of this junction near the mouth of Monument Valley, is the **Navajo National Monument**, the site of a unique Anasazi ruin. Hidden deep in a slickrock canyon, even with a telescope viewer we had to strain our eyes to see this tiny settlement tucked in an overhang across the 700-foot (213 m) valley lookout. This is **Betatakin**, and it is worth the one-hour guided walk deep into the canyon to see the details of multistoried brick structures accessed by wooden ladders planted casually against their walls. Almost hidden in a perfect arch of peach-colored sandstone, this site evokes a feeling of delight in its perfection and mystery. From here it is surmised that the Ancient Ones travelled past the San Francisco Peaks (sacred to both Navajo and Hopi nations) to Tuwanasavi, the Center of the Universe, 60 miles (100 km) to the south on the Black Mesa, the move that was prophesied in their ancient legends.

The final stop in Navajo Country is the amazing **Antelope Canyon**, purported by some to have been a sacred place in the past. This is a slot canyon, a narrow fissure of soft homogenous sandstone formed by the solidification of ancient sand dunes pressurized by overlying sedimental layers that fold back on themselves, carved by wind and water and leaving only a narrow opening at the top. The pale adobe-colored rock is easily cracked and tempered by the elements, as well as by the spirits the Navajo say live here. The "chundi" are the miserable ones who can't be seen but take on shapes and make noises. The crevice monster called tse do nahu nti and the crushing rock monster called tse aheeniditii have obviously been hard at work in this grotto which is more like an underground cathedral. It is best to walk above the lower canyons and jump across the narrow crevices that spill down several hundred feet to the bottom, but the upper Corkscrew Canyon is easily accessible and safe to explore. The only monsters we came across were the film-eating type, which devoured far too many rolls, transforming the amazing shapes of creamy sandstone to every color of the rainbow as the sun bounced its golden light deep into the crevices of stone.

CATHEDRAL ROCK

September 25 . . . This valley is bathed in pink light reflecting from its cradle of red rock. The striated spires are the most incredible color of bronzed scarlet twisted into amazing contortions—a Gothic cathedral with praying hands, a luminous Christmas tree bell, a coffee pot cum eagle, a group of wise elders . . . The effect is both exciting and dreamlike—a set from a Hollywood cowboy movie, and a magnificent meditation chamber.

Sedona, Arizona, has long been an artists' colony and a mecca for desert retirement living and spiritual renewal. More recently its power spots have attracted many New Age pilgrims whose incorporation of Native American spirituality and ancient mysticism have embodied the sacred paths of many religious beliefs.

Travel Tips

Sedona is a two-hour drive north of Phoenix, and less than an hour south of Flagstaff on a scenic route through Oak Creek Canyon. Elevation is 4,000 feet (1,219 m); days are hot and dry, with summer thunderstorms providing a sound and light show of sheet and fork lightning and torrential rains that can wash out back-country dirt roads. The view from Schnebly Hill Drive is spectacular and accessible without a 4-wheel drive if you are careful.

Local Resources

The Chamber of Commerce on Highway 89A, Sedona, AZ 86336; Tel: (602) 282–7722 will provide information on accommodation from budget to super-luxury resorts. Tent and trailer camping is popular with several sites to choose from. Jeep tours abound to see the main sites and back-country roads via 4-wheel drive: Red Rock Jeep Tours offers six options including a Sacred Earth Tour; 260 N. Highway 89A, Sedona, AZ 86336; Tel: (602) 282–2826. Hot air ballooning is a fun way to see the desert nestled in the red rock canyons: Northern Light Balloon Expeditions, PO Box 1695, Sedona, AZ 86336; Tel: (602) 282–2274. For an interesting private guide who offers a blend of mysticism and esoteric ideas from a variety of traditions, contact Rahelio, 10 Traumeri Lane, Sedona, AZ 86336; Tel: (602) 282–6735.

The Sacred Red Road

The Native American history in Sedona is not well documented although evidence of dwellings, pictographs, petroglyphs, and medicine wheels indicate habitation by the Sinagua peoples from 500 to 1400 AD; other remains have been dated as old as 10,000 years. Myths of the Yavapai and Apache who inhabited the region after 1500 AD talk of Red Rock country, as do Hopi legends that speak of migration on the Good Red Road. This red road symbol is found in many North American indigenous groups, signifying the path of righteousness that leads to the spirit. The color red was also primal with many early tribal peoples throughout the world, and was often the only color named and used in ceremonials and art work. In Sedona, one is surrounded by red—the earth, mountains, and even the waters run red. It is an awesome and majestic experience, although some people report feeling overstimulated and irritable when they are here.

Sedona is named after Sedona Schnebly, who moved here with her husband in 1901 to establish a postal station. Her name comes from the Greek, meaning "way up," and is also an anagram for "anodes" or positive electrodes. It is interesting how these interpretations fit in with contemporary ideas of psychic vortexes or concentrations of earth energies that can affect one's consciousness. The ancient art of geomancy or Feng Shui (see section on China) is being studied here by Nicholas Mann who has found many earth formations that fit into a geomantic perspective that identifies energy places and strong electromagnetic forces. The presence of more than one hundred springs in Oak Creek Canyon could be another major source of earth energy. No one really knows what a vortex is but strong emotional experiences are reported by many visitors, especially at Airport Mesa, Boynton Canyon, Bell Rock, and Cathedral Rock. **Cathedral Rock** is a well-known backdrop for cowboy movies, but the shape of its central spires also suggests a male and female figure linked harmoniously; from the symbolic and earth-energy point of view, the jagged hard rock can be interpreted as the male energy, balanced by the female essence of the creek flowing below.

From the New Age philosophy perspective, Sedona is a ruby of the earth, connecting to the heart center and working on the emotions. Even people who are unaware of these ideas experience a powerful attraction and feeling of well being in Sedona. Despite the tremendous increase in tourism and construction that is fast changing the natural feeling in this valley, it is still a place of harmony and its incredible earthscapes feel like they could be part of that spiritual red road. As Rahelio says, "The land is the teacher—I'm just the spokesperson."

The Plains

BIGHORN MEDICINE WHEEL

September 1 . . . This is a real "you can see forever" view, as nearby hills drop off in layers to the distant plain. What a journey it must have been on foot—the sun beat down on our car which constantly overheated as it labored up 10,000 feet (3,000 m) on a 10 percent grade. This is a powerful place, as close as one can get to the sky.

Of the more than eighty known medicine wheels in North America, Bighorn is the best known and preserved, as well as the largest. Thought to be a place of cosmological significance and ritual for the indigenous Americans, it is now honored by the local Arapaho tribes of the Shoshone Nation.

Travel Tips

The Bighorn Mountains stretch from southern Montana through north-central Wyoming, and are now part of a national park with a wide variety of attractions including hundreds of miles of hiking, 4-wheel-drive trails, fishing, boating, and seasonal hunting. The high elevation can entail road closures for snow except from June to August. The medicine wheel lies halfway between Lovell and Sheridan, Wyoming, near the Montana border. The ascent is more gradual from the east side (Sheridan) via a paved switchback road rising through evergreens growing out of slabs of ancient striated rock. Continue west on Highway 14A, after it turns south as #14 at Bear Creek Crossing, where there is a lodge, shop, restaurant, and gas. The right-hand turnoff to the medicine wheel is well marked 44 miles (70 km) later with a Historic Monument sign—the site can also be seen for several miles as the hill is topped with a white radar tower. The 3-mile (5 km) dirt track is well maintained but steep and not wide, so trailers might be best left at the bottom. There is a small parking area and pit toilets. Park regulations allow parking more than .5 mile (.8 km) off the highway, and there are three campsites with water nearby. The ranger's station is 3 miles (5 km) away, and park headquarters is at Lovell (Tel: [307] 548–2251) where accommodation and shopping are available. Tour boats travel down the waters of Bighorn Canyon near Lovell. The forest service has proposed putting an interpretation center and more services at the medicine wheel but this is opposed by local Native American groups and others; considering the unique location and natural setting, we felt happy that finances would probably not allow that to happen. The purpose seems to be to increase tourism and the local economy, and although there may be a small argument for better maintenance of the area, it is a weak one.

The Wheel

All our anticipation did not prepare us for the powerful experience of being at Bighorn. The location is spectacularly high above the flat plain, and the vista is awesome, perhaps enhanced by the isolation. Very few people visited during the three days we spent there and the solitude magnified the energy we felt. Even the ugly barbed-wire fence enclosing the wheel took on a spiritual dimension, draped in pieces of colorful cloth, bits of leather, feathers, and the occasional sock, remnants of a recent ceremonial occasion that reminded us of Buddhist prayer flags fluttering in the breeze in Nepal.

This medicine wheel has been studied extensively by astronomers and archaeologists who date parts of it to 300 years ago, but speculate the site could have been used for thousands of years (see Moose Mountain Medicine Wheel, Canada). Most agree its markers are cosmological; the 80-foot (25 m) diameter is in the shape of a turtle that may signify the Turtle Island of Indian legends. The turtle is the life-force image for the local Arapaho Indians, whose legends suggest that the twenty-eight spokes of the wheel indicate the seats of medicine men who were granted special powers from the Great Spirit. The most significant markers include the one pointing to the summer solstice as well as three other alignments that define the rising points of three bright stars: Aldebaran, Rigel, and Sirius, which rise consecutively at sunrise twenty-eight days after each other.

Despite all of these studies, it is surprising how little is really known about the medicine wheel. The most important common concept shared by Native Americans (as well as by other cultures) is the circle, the symbol of completion and of eternity. The circle honors the four sacred directions; the north, the place of wisdom and intellect; the south, the place of the heart and emotions; the east, the place of rebirth, illumination, and renewal; and the west, the place of death, transformation, and darkness. The circle is repeatedly used in the medicine wheel, the round tepee home, the fire circle, the Anasazi kiva—these are the sacred gathering places of the community. Local Crow Indian legends say the medicine wheel is sacred, and stay away; the Shoshone talk of the Sheepeaters, the "Little People" who live beneath the wheel; the Arapaho legends tell of the wheel for ceremony on Medicine Mountain; and elders today say there are spirits there that should not be disturbed.

Nobody knows why the nomadic plains people built these medicine wheels when they built little else. The hundreds of tepee rings nearby suggest a place of ceremony, and other cairns on distant hills may have given directions to people coming from afar. A unique stone arrow, 65 feet (20 m) long with a 9-foot (3 m) arrowhead has been found 80 air miles (130 km) to the southwest, pointing directly to this wheel, as well as other rock formations such as a 10-foot-diameter (3 m) circle with a 2.5-foot (.75 m) stone wall found on an 11,000-foot (3,350 m) plateau to the south.

Explanations are useful for the left side of the brain, but the Bighorn Medicine Wheel is for the right side—the emotional part of the self that seeks to experience the world with the heart. The squeal of honey-colored prairie dogs playing in the sun, the sometimes fierce winds whipping around the eroded peaks jutting up from verdant slopes below, and the distant desert-pink plains were sufficient to convince me that this place is alive with a very special sort of spiritual energy.

Photo Tips   *Bighorn*

For many medicine wheels, including the Bighorn, there are only two practical options to photographing them from above: from a plane, or from a giraffe (the mechanical kind!). As I get nauseated easily with the banking and rolling of light aircraft, I opted for the latter choice. The power company in Lovell gave us a lead on one of their private contractors who was stringing cable for them near Bighorn and after a lengthy search we found him. His truck was equipped with a hydraulic arm at the end of which were two buckets—one equipped with controls, the other just large enough for me with a vest full of lenses.

Bighorn Medicine Wheel, aerial view, Bighorn Mountains, Wyoming, September 1990/ Sacred Earth, *p. 57*

The high barbed-wire fence around the medicine wheel all but disappears at a height of 45 feet (14 m), providing a spectacular vantage point for viewing the wheel and relating to its panoramic surroundings. A wide-angle zoom is the ideal lens here because at any given height one can zoom to find the desired angle, the ideal being to include the entire shape of the wheel without the surrounding fence line. It was an added bonus to have the giraffe operator immediately beside me so I could easily communicate directions. I am convinced that to remain stable and have the luxury of making a number of exposures from the same viewpoint is far superior to attempting the photography from a plane.

I recommend photographing at sunrise or sunset because the light is low, providing a textural effect that helps to accent the design of the stonework. When the sun was hitting across the area, it was easier to position the giraffe truck so that its shadow and my shadow were clear of the medicine wheel. In this way I could also avoid being directly over the wheel, which some elders suggest might agitate the spirits.

The West Coast

CALIFORNIA AND OREGON

August 18 . . . We felt very mellow under the bright sun beaming on this sleepy little town nestled in the Cascade Mountains. The two peaks of the sacred volcanic mountain dominate our vision, hanging over the town in an almost protective way. High on the hillside beside a gurgling stream, a local Native American group performed a private ritual of water purification.

Mount Shasta has always been sacred to the Siskiyou tribes of northern California. They called it Wyeka, meaning "white and pure," although its anglicized name may have been derived from the Russian community who called it "shastal," or perhaps from the English word "chaste." This area has become a meeting place of contemporary mystical groups who identify Mount Shasta as a center of the ancient Lemurians, the White Brotherhood, and one of the nine sacred mountains of an ancient mystery school.

Travel Tips

Mount Shasta looms on the horizon near the Oregon border, a three-hour drive north of San Francisco on Interstate 5.

Local Resources

This is a popular spot for hiking in the summer and skiing in the winter. There are motels—we used The Evergreen on Mt. Shasta Blvd. (Box 65); Tel: (916) 926-2143—B&Bs, camping, good restaurants, and an excellent bookstore, the Golden Bough on the main street. For details, write Chamber of Commerce, 300 Pine Street, Mount Shasta, CA 96067; Tel: (916) 926-4865. Weather on the mountain can be very changeable and dangerous; hikers are warned to check local conditions and be prepared for emergency situations. Guides and maps are available from the recreational outfitting stores in town. Mountain excursions by llama are also available.

The Mountain and the Sea

Mount Shasta is part of the volcanic Cascade Range that includes Mount St. Helen's which erupted suddenly and unexpectedly in 1980. This range is the backbone of North America, and Mount Shasta is sometimes called the base or navel chakra that channels powerful energy to the rest of this continental earth-body known to Native Americans as Turtle Island. Local indigenous groups called Shasta the "Great White," and their creation stories say she was created by the Great Spirit because the land was so flat (not unlike the creation stories of the Australian Dreamtime). This was no small task, as Shasta rises 14,156 feet (4,316 m) above sea level, and more than 10,000 feet (3,077 m) from the plain. Most Native Americans respect her sacred power and do not climb the mountain, although seasonal rituals are enacted here, and non-natives are asked to leave during the ceremonials.

Many contemporary mystical groups believe that Mount Shasta is the vestige of the lost continent of Mu, and that a secret priesthood is hidden within the mountain, with powerful crystals that allow them to change their physical bodies into the etheric realm. Many citings of Unidentified Flying Objects have been reported here, often in conjunction with lenticular cloud formations that are unique to the area.

Whatever your spiritual leanings, Mount Shasta is a place of harmony and powerful psychic and emotional energy—some call it a doorway to the fifth dimension, beyond time and place as we know it. It is definitely a place to commune with nature and with gentle people who seem to flow with life as though they really are in tune with the nearby bubbling streams.

Bodega Bay lies on the coast north of Point Reyes, a one-hour drive north of San Francisco, but several more hours south from Mount Shasta if you take your time wandering down the picturesque roads meandering through the ridges leading to the Sonoma Valley. This coastline is rugged and exciting, not meant so much for sun worshippers, but for outdoor lovers who like to breathe the sea air and peer through morning mists which can last all day. Bodega Bay is a fishing village, a haven from the jagged offshore rocks and crashing waves that bring in sea lions by the thousands. Although it lies on the San Andreas fault line which may someday send it crumbling into the sea, Bodega Bay is a great place to watch the setting sun produce a rainbow of colors and variegated shapes through the off-shore mists, and to catch a glimpse of the green flash, the last color of the spectrum, seen as the sun sinks below the horizon, reflecting the mystique of the end of the day.

Continuing north of Mount Shasta, one can follow the backbone of the Cascades on Interstate 5 all the way to the Canadian border, but a detour to the seacoast is much more interesting. Here are ancient redwood trees towering as high as one can see, and long sandy beaches punctuated with rocky outcrops topped with sea lions and seals baptized by the ocean spray. Hundreds of miles of beach provide sand dunes to explore, and small villages to enjoy clam chowder in. Here nature is at her best again, giving one an opportunity to tune into the land and feel a sense of the continuity that this ocean symbolizes.

The East

THE GREAT MOUNDS OF OHIO

October 30 . . . The low-angle sun cast purple shadows over the huge beast coiling in this earth tinged with autumnal bronze and gold. These royal colors seemed fitting for this emblem of eternity, a universal symbol of both good and evil, seemingly poised here, ready to release its kinetic energy to join the flow of the kundalini of the earth.

The Ohio Serpent Mound is the largest prehistoric effigy earthwork in the world, and is considered sacred because of its ancient and universal symbolism.

Travel Tips

Take a bus or car from Columbus, Ohio, forty-eight miles (77 km) south on Highway 23 to Chillicothe, then 10 miles (16 km) west on Highway 35 to the Mound City Group of earthenworks. The Great Serpent Mound is southwest, via Highway 50 to Hillsboro, then #73 to the site—a one-hour drive. Both are government-protected monuments; for information, contact Serpent Mound State Memorial, 3850 State Route 73, Peebles, OH 45660; Tel: (513) 587–2796 (restricted opening), and Mound City Group National Monument, 16062 Ohio Route 104, Chillicothe, OH 45601; Tel: (614) 774–1124 (open year round).

Local Resources

There are good motels, hotels, camping, and restaurants near both sites; the Holiday Inn, on Route 23N, is recommended. Reserve through 1250 N. Bridge Road, Chillicothe, OH 45601; Tel: (614) 775–7000.

The Mound Builders

The origin of prehistoric cultures of North America is still a mystery. The **Ohio Serpent Mound** is attributed to the Adena culture, thought to have developed as early as 1000 BC during the beginning of the hunting and gathering stage of history; the great effigy figures such as the Serpent Mound were built sometime later, probably in the first century BC. This is one of the more than one hundred thousand earth mounds concentrated in the Ohio and Mississippi River valleys. Although many were grave mounds, the Serpent Mound was not, and is thought to have been a place of sacred ritual. The serpent motif is common in world mythology: it symbolized enlightenment in the divine cosmic life energy of the Hindu philosophy of the kundalini, lying dormant at the base of the spine until stimulated to rise through the chakra energy centers in the body to the crown chakra, where it unites with the soul, achieving a sense of oneness with the universe; the Mayan and Aztec plumed serpent, Kukulcan, was symbolic of the sun god as well as the rain or storm gods that fertilized the earth; the Australian Dreamtime being laid the eggs of Serpent Dreaming in an analogous creation myth about fertilization of the earth; the Hopi incorporate the power of the snake in dances to produce the rain necessary to fertilize the earth, while the concept of eternity is portrayed in the snake's life-renewing habit of annually shedding its skin.

Whatever its function might have been, this serpent is impressive, with a total uncoiled length of 1,348 feet (411 m), 20 feet (6 m) wide, and 3 to 5 feet (1 to 2 m) high. The shape incorporates seven curves, with a coiled tail at one end and an egg-shaped oval nestled within 17-foot-diameter (5 m) jaws at the other. Some have suggested that this is symbolic of a solar eclipse where the dragon eats the sun, a common theme in Iroquois and Cherokee myths, or it may be the wall of the snake's open mouth. The placement of the serpent also suggests a geomantic perspective; the body rises above a stream, providing an increase in electromagnetic energy to the area. One wonders, in fact, if these huge effigies that can only be completely visualized from the air were meant not to be seen, but simply to be experienced through feeling the ambience of the site.

In contrast, the **Mound City Group** to the north was a burial place, with twenty-three restored mounds of the more than 2000 on 13 acres (5 ha) along the Scioto River. Lined with sycamores, cottonwoods, and maples and surrounded by a low earthen embankment, this is thought to be the work of the Hopewell people whose culture honored an elaborate cult of the dead between 100 BC and 300 AD. Some scholars believe the mounds signified a concept of the respect for nature, where burial meant rebirth, and a reaffirmation of the life cycle of the Earth Mother—in other words, a celebration of life. Artifacts found in these graves are evidence of influence extending as far as Lake Superior on the northern border with Canada, the Gulf of Mexico in the south, and Yellowstone to the west. Petrified remains of wood also suggest wooden ceremonial houses were in use. Many of the mounds are barely raised, and some are overgrown, but the Mica Mound has been restored, with a window inserted to show the placement of a grave laden with copper artifacts. After 900 AD, evidence of a later culture centered in the southwestern U.S., called the Mississippian Tradition, can be seen in the temple mounds at Cahokia, Illinois, with the 100-foot-high (60 m) ceremonial center of the Monks Mound, sometimes compared to the early Israelite temple mounds in Canaan. This 14-acre (5 ha) site is the largest mound in the world, bigger than the Great Pyramid of Egypt, and built in terraced stages looking not unlike the ziggurat temples of the east, suggestive of the cosmic mountain uniting earth and sky. This planned city has a central place of ritual oriented to the four cardinal directions, and a sun circle of wooden poles suggesting an astronomical calendar.

These earthworks are fascinating and thought provoking. Many visitors report a feeling of high energy, while others feel tranquil and serene. The Ohio Serpent Mound has become a symbol of New Age mysticism and unfortunately it was severely damaged by a large group gathered for the 1987 harmonic convergence celebrations, and required major reconstruction. The fascination of this structure is more than just the curiosity of tourism—one wonders what primal knowledge or experience is invoked here.

THE EAST COAST PILGRIMS

November 24 ... The traditional harvest dinner was being prepared but I had difficulty leaving the natural bounty seen all around us ... the autumnal bronze colors were like a halo leaving a golden haze over the land, a fitting mantle for such prolific earth.

North American Thanksgiving Day is a relatively recent addition to a long tradition seen in many cultures throughout the world. This celebration of the harvest is not only to thank the earth spirits for producing such munificence, but to ensure the fertility of the next harvest.

Travel Tips

The American traditional thanksgiving is identified with Plymouth, Massachusetts, 35 miles (56 km) southeast of Boston. Rockport, Maine, is 100 miles (160 km) north of the capital city of Rockland, on the Atlantic seaboard. Both are urban areas, highly travelled by car and local bus transportation.

Harvest Celebrations

The legacy of harvest rituals can be seen the world over. The transition from hunting and gathering to cultivation resulted in a dependence on the seasons, and in aboriginal cultures, a series of ceremonies to please the gods who ruled these cosmic events. Harvest celebrations frequently involved ceremonial practices with the last sheaf to be reaped—sometimes it was even left standing as an offering to those under the earth. The cutting of the last sheaf was often compared to the cutting of the umbilical cord at birth. When cut, the sheaf was sometimes swaddled like a child (like the Malaysian Baby Rice Soul); in Indonesia, two sheaves were ritually married to ensure an increased yield next year. Many European cultures made harvest knots or plaits of straw that were worn in the hair or on the coat as a fertility charm, and corn dolls were given to protect against witchcraft—a practice similar to contemporary decorative straw braiding hanging over a door to protect the household in many rural communities. The joyful Dionysian feasts of ancient Greece celebrating the grape crop are still popular, as is the Polish Wienjec parade where a virgin female wearing a harvest crown leads a parade through the village and is drenched with a bucket of water symbolizing the rain that brings fertility. Special sacrificial rituals were also historically related to the harvest: biblical accounts speak of men put to death in times of famine, and sixteenth-century English reports link executions to the success of the harvest. Tribal groups in Bengal practised sacrifice as recently as the midnineteenth century, where parts of the victim's body were buried in the fields surrounding the village, and Tibetan harvest feasts involve a special Dance of the Sacrificers to propitiate the Zidah, the local mountain spirits, to ensure they send enough sun and rain, not frost or hail. The practice of ringing church bells in England was said to ensure the safety of the crop, and Scottish islanders celebrated the harvest of the sea at the end of the fishing season.

Some of these practices were brought to the New World by the *Mayflower* Pilgrims who landed at Plymouth Rock in **Plymouth**, Massachusetts, in 1620. These separatists from the Church of England came to seek religious freedom, as well as to bring the gospel to the Indians. The hardships of the first year were many, including diseases that wiped out the majority of the adult females and half of the men. The new settlers had to rely on two local Indians to show them how to grow and plant their first crop of corn. In the fall of 1621, Governor William Bradford invited the indigenous peoples to share their harvest, in celebration of what has become the traditional Thanksgiving Day, officially proclaimed by President Washington in 1789.

Unfortunately the prolific natural harvest of the east coast forests such as those near **Rockport**, Maine, was not so honored by the early settlers, who cut down nearly all the stands of hardwood for their own use. These acts, based on human materialism, combined with the failure to renew the decimated forests, continue to cause ecological disasters nearly four hundred years later. It seems we really are on the slow-learner's planet, still believing that we can use the earth and her fruits in any way we see fit, rather than recognizing that we only have a short-term lease with an obligation to leave things in better condition than we found them. Perhaps the real message of Thanksgiving will be heard again, as cultures the world over reacquaint themselves with their environment and seek to live in harmony rather than in competition with nature.

THE FLORIDA EVERGLADES

February 10 . . . The nights are like a step back in time—a faint memory of our primordial beginnings. After sunset the marshes come alive with the sounds of night herons, owls, limkins, and the constant chatter of frogs breaking the stillness that is like no other.

Everglades National Park is a 1.4-million-acre (.5 million ha) swamp that covers only about one-seventh of the surrounding largest saw-grass marsh in the world. It is home to a wide variety of flora and fauna sharing an ecosystem that displays a profound interrelationship of the workings of nature.

Travel Tips

The Everglades cover almost the entire land area of southern Florida, stretching from Lake Okeechobee in the north to Florida Bay and the Gulf of Mexico in the south, and is accessed by a network of roads directly west of the east coast cities of Palm Beach, Fort Lauderdale, and Miami.

Local Resources

The National Park Service manages all activities; for information, contact PO Box 279, Homestead, Florida 33030; Tel: (305) 247–6211. Accommodation is available in the park at Homestead and at Flamingo in the south. Backcountry canoeing and camping on raised platforms is popular; permits are required and free, but in limited quantities and available only in person twenty-four hours in advance from the Park Center.

The Glades

The Everglades were originally called by the Indian name Pahayokee, meaning "river of grass." This huge flat area is composed of six-million-year-old porous limestone covered with several inches of water in the wet season (June to November), and transformed to a vast expanse of stalagmites in the dry season, the white pinnacles baking in the hot sun. Fresh-water peat and marl (organic mud laced with lime deposits) provide a fertile bed for a wide range of tropical and temperate flora. In the south, hammocks (from the Indian word meaning "garden place") of land a few feet high support a variety of species with many hardwoods interspersed with ferns, orchids, and bromeliads in a forestlike atmosphere. These islands vary in size from a few square feet to a few hundred acres. In the distant Ice Age past, the Glades were home to mammoths, wolves, bison, bears, and saber-toothed tigers driven south from the cold northern glaciers.

Unfortunately the workings of nature have been modified by the hand of humankind; most areas are now controlled by dikes and pumping stations to serve the human need for water. The Okeechobee River no longer overflows as it did at the turn of the century, covering 8 million acres (3 million ha) of land with a few feet of water many miles wide, still capable of flowing a little every day toward the sea. Consequently, today there are fewer living things here—a few thousand instead of more than a million alligators, and a few hundred thousand birds rather than several million. Bald eagles, ospreys, roseate spoonbills, wood storks, sacred white ibis, and red, white, and snowy egrets with their angel wings can still be seen, however. The king of the beasts, the alligator, portrays the balance of life here in the Glades as he uses his broad snout and powerful tail to dig "gator holes" in the bedrock, producing fresh water for all his neighbors. Then, once or twice a week he satisfies his need for sustenance by eating any animal that comes his way. Although well populated with twenty-six species of snakes, visitors are relieved to know that only four are venomous.

In the three areas where the Glades drain to the sea, pink shrimp and oysters can be found with the great white herons who collect in droves to feed in this juncture of fresh and salt water. These transition points are clearly visible with the proliferation of the salt-resistant umbrellalike red mangrove trees that act as a barrier and as a land builder, while the dense roots of the black and white mangrove grow further upstream in the fresh water.

The famous Anhinga Trail is probably the best place to view a wide variety of animals and birds including the anhinga, the snake bird who dives into the water to feed, and preens as he spreads his wide wings to dry his shiny black feathers. This path is easy to walk and is a photographer's paradise, perhaps even better than some of the more remote backcountry. The Flamingo Inn on Florida Bay is a great place to see these elegant pink birds perform their daily rituals. West of the Glades, separated by a hammock- and cypress-covered ridge, the Big Cypress Swamp harbors some of the oldest trees in North America including several cypress varieties that are cousin to the majestic Redwood and Sequoia of California. Black bears, Florida panthers (cougar), wild turkeys, and deer populate this forest which is bordered on the east by the Seminole Indian Reserve.

This is irreplaceable wilderness—a naturalist's paradise, and a fragile world balancing man and nature, providing us with a profound experience of a unique blend of primeval life.

The Bahamas

January 5 . . . The culture shock on arrival here is pure delight. The air resounds with the rhythms of reggae, instilling a joyfulness in every bone of our bodies. The inate friendliness of these people is infectious, coming alive particularly at night, negating the slower formality of the day echoed in the British architecture gracing the old colonial towns.

The Bahama Islands are more than just a series of beach resorts, offering a joie de vivre unlike anywhere in North America. On this almost treeless island, Preacher's Cave is surrounded by lush greenery, offering a tranquil haven from the midday sun.

Travel Tips

Frequent flights link the U.S. mainland and the West Indies. Miami or Fort Lauderdale, Florida, are the main gateways to Eleuthera. The latter is recommended, to avoid the hassles of Miami airport, which often entails huge lineups in customs and immigration. Although several airlines offer island services, Bahamas Air is best because of its larger propeller planes rather than the frequently used small "puddle-jumpers" of other airlines. The airport is on the northern tip of the island, near the ferry terminal that services Harbour Island as well as the thrice-weekly mail boat from Nassau.

Local Resources

Eleuthera is a long narrow island 200 miles (320 km) southeast of Miami on the Atlantic side of the Bahamian chain. The east coast is frequently buffeted by storms while the Carribean coast is cradled by the warm gulf waters. Life appears quite carefree here, with tourism as a main industry; tiny Harbour Island is popular as a Club Med resort but also has large colorful colonial-style hotels adorning miles of pink sand beaches. Other options include Governor's Harbour, located half-way down the west coast, or Gregory Town and Alice Town, not quite so far away, where you can experience contemporary Bahamian small-town life. The Cambridge Villas, Box 5148, Gregory Town, Eleuthera, Bahamas (Tel: (809) 332–2269) are comfortable, and a fifteen-minute taxi ride to Preacher's Cave on the north shore of the island, facing the Atlantic. The cave is a twenty-minute journey from Harbour Island (of which ten minutes is the ferry ride). Small private villas or cottages can be rented through Diane Thompson, Tel: (809) 028–121; anyone in Eleuthera can be contacted through the operator at the grand trunk exchange, Tel: 332–2269.

An Island Haven

The islands of the Bahamas rest on the Grand Bahamian Bank, a limestone ridge similar to the geology of the Atlantic Coastal Ridge which protects Florida and the Everglades. Retained by the Gulf stream, the Bahamas ridge continues to pile up grains of sand surrounded by calcium carbonate. This protective low ridge is further reinforced from the other side by marine invertebrates that build rocklike colonies.

The Bahamas is a magical group of islands in a vast warm sea. The discovery of huge blocks of ruins off the coast of North Bimini links it to the mysterious disappearance of Atlantis, which has been prophesized to arise here. This is also within the "Bermuda Triangle" where many strange events have been reported over the years. Despite massive tourism, Eleuthera is still a fitting symbol of its name which means "freedom" in Greek. It has been home to many—the aboriginal Arawak Indians came here from South America, and in 1492 Columbus made slave raids to Arawak from his base in San Salvador. In 1629 King Charles I of England gave the island to one of his ministers.

In 1647, English Puritans fleeing religious persecution in Massachusetts went first to Bermuda and then to Cigantoo (the Arawak name for Eleuthera); here their ship floundered on a reef and they were forced to take shelter in a cave where they held a church service in front of a natural stone altar. They were able to salvage a small boat and send it back to Massachusetts for supplies to start a colony, and later repaid their benefactors by sending a shipload of Braziletto wood to Boston, with instructions for it to be sold and the proceeds donated to Harvard College "to avoid the foul sin of ingratitude."

Preacher's Cave is a short distance from the narrow road that skirts the northwest side of the island not far from Governor's Harbour; locals will direct you through palm trees and scrub brush to a secluded area ringed with greenery. Pushing the overgrowth aside, one enters the dark volcanic grotto that gave refuge to the pilgrims so long ago. The rough stone altar where the Puritans worshipped can still be seen, lit by filtered light from a natural opening above. From here they went on to set up the first democracy in the new world, and were finally free of the religious persecution that had followed them to so many places on their long journey.

Canada

The West Coast

NINSTINTS, ANTHONY ISLAND

May 25 ... The smoke from the burning underbrush wafted across the cove, blurring the already hazy outline of the totems, their wooden bodies devoured by the constant dampness and softened by the winds which constantly blow off the straits.

Ninstints on Anthony Island is Haida land, the burial place of chiefs for hundreds of years, whose spirits live in the memory even longer than in the symbols carved on these mortuary poles.

Travel Tips

The Queen Charlotte Islands are off the west coast of northern British Columbia. Prince Rupert, 960 miles (1,550 km) from Vancouver, is a three-day drive on a good highway, a two-hour flight, or a seventeen-hour year-round car ferry trip from Port Hardy on the northern tip of Vancouver Island. The latter route can be very busy in the summer and reservations can be made through the B.C. Ferry Corporation, 1112 Fort Street, Victoria, B.C. V8V 4V2; Tel: (604) 386–3431 (Victoria) or (604) 669–1211 (Vancouver). From Prince Rupert another ferry travels regularly to Queen Charlotte City, and then to South Moresby Island, but Anthony Island, where Ninstints is located, is accessed from there only by rental of a zodiac boat or a private floatplane. Guided tours are offered by a variety of companies including Ecosummer Expeditions, 1516 Duranleau Street, Vancouver, B.C. V6H 3S4; Tel: (604) 669–7741. Individual travellers must obtain permission to visit Haida reserves or unoccupied village sites; contact the Masset Band Council, Tel: (604) 626–3337, or the Skidegate Band Council at (604) 559–4496. For other information about the area, call the Queen Charlotte Islands Chamber of Commerce at (604) 626–5211, or write Ministry of Tourism, Parliament Building, Victoria, B.C. V8V 1X4.

Local Resources

There is no accommodation on Anthony Island—hotels are available in Queen Charlotte City and Prince Rupert, both famous for ocean fishing. The Khutzeymateen Valley is 40 miles (70 km) northeast of Prince Rupert, accessible only by boat. Tours may be organized through NorthSouth Tours, 1159 W. Broadway, Vancouver, B.C. V6H 1G1; Tel: (604) 736–7447. Pacific Rim National Park is on the west coast of

Vancouver Island, and is serviced by a good road from Nanaimo on the east coast of the island, where a frequent daily ferry links to Horseshoe Bay near Vancouver on the mainland. From Vancouver, the driving and ferry time is about five hours to Tofino, the small resort town at the most northerly point of the park. A number of small hotels and campsites are available, including the beachside Ocean Village Beach Resort, Tel: (604) 725-3755; and Crystal Cove, Tel: (604) 725-4213, which also offers campgrounds that supplement the government-operated campsites. This area is inundated with tourists in the summer, and can be busy all year round, despite the reports of heavy rainfall! Don't miss the Whale Song Gallery and the work of native artist Roy Vickers at his Longhouse Gallery.

West Coast Culture

The indigenous people of the northwest coast of British Columbia have lived here for at least five thousand years, probably originally crossing the land bridge over the Bering Strait. Their culture strongly identifies with the land and all aspects of nature; the search for a tutelary or guardian spirit is one of the primary elements of all the coastal tribes, including the Haida, Tsimshian, Coast Salish, Nootka, Kwakiutl, and Lummi. This spirit quest had significant cultural, social, and psychological meaning, providing the individual with the supernatural power of the animal guardian who chose to help him throughout his life. Vision quests involved fasting and arduous experiences of physical endurance in social isolation, and their success was often celebrated with winter ceremonials such as the spirit dancing of the Salish and the Nootka potlatch. These quests echo many other spiritual experiences sought out in other world cultures, as a way of accessing the Great Spirit or divine force within each seeker.

But the greatest symbol of the west coast is the totem, the symbol of the guardian spirit watching over the family or tribe. Unfortunately these totems are not recorded in stone, but in the local wood, and most disintegrate after several generations. The art and the impetus to create these were almost completely lost with the imposition in the mid-1800s of Christian ethics and Canadian government edicts to stop the spirit dancing and other "pagan" rituals that nourished the tribal spirit. The resulting cultural anomie has taken many years to heal, and a renaissance of northwest coast arts, including the carving of new totem poles, has emerged and grown strong over the past twenty years.

Ninstints is one of the oldest Haida settlements, an important place of ceremony nestled in a small bay on Anthony Island. Only the poles live here now, the largest stand of mortuary poles in the world, protected as a national park and a UNESCO World Heritage Site. But their decay continues, as the wood yields to the elements and falls to the damp ground, where deer nuzzle against it as they nibble for delicate greens. This is a haunting and mysterious place, little visited, and worth the effort.

Back on the mainland of British Columbia, our sail boat glides through calm waters to the **Khutzeymateen Valley**, where stands of old forest have endured for generations. This valley is a haven for about sixty grizzly bears, one of the few places left in the province where these magnificent beasts can find shelter and be well fed from the salmon-filled river. The soundlessness in this valley is awesome and evokes a sense of tranquility only disturbed by our guide who shifts his rifle and carefully watches the trees for telltale shaggy-brown shapes that he will fire at only in an emergency. The most dangerous time for humans is during the September salmon run when the bears eagerly approach the water to fill their bellies before their winter hibernation. Unfortunately the dangerous season for these bears is always present now, as this valley is threatened by logging, which will destroy this ecosystem and kill the bears who will likely be shot. Recently a one-year moratorium on logging was imposed, but the reprieve is only temporary, and an ongoing battle of politics and economics continues to rage.

The west coast of Vancouver Island faces similar problems. The Nootka and Kwakiutl people have lived for thousands of years in harmony with the sea and land at the present-day **Pacific Rim National Park**, of which 95 percent is primordial rain forest. The environmental fight to save the old rain forest has raged here for many years, and continues to threaten some of the largest trees in the world. This forest is animated with spirit legends of the Kwakiutl Thunderbird who creates thunder with his beating wings and lightning with the blink of his eyes, perhaps with the help of the mythical Hai-et-lik or Lightning Snake. In the nearby waters of **Wikaninnish Beach**, the salmon were believed to dwell in human form in a huge house under the sea. Here they would put on salmon robes and convert themselves to fish for the salmon run, sacrificing themselves for the benefit of humankind, who would honor their fish kin by eating their flesh and by washing their bones and returning them to the sea where they would be reassembled and come back to life.

The aboriginal here recognizes his total dependence on the powerful spirit of the universe, and integrates his lifestyle with the natural world around him. He lives within the mystical unity of nature, using only what he requires and giving thanks to the spirits who provide for him. The Pacific Rim coastline retains a sense of that wilderness and harmony, and provides the invigorating experience of the primal sea juxtaposed with the ancient forest.

The Yukon

July 28 . . . There is a clarity in the air here . . . and a vitality in the people that echoes the vibrancy of the landscape . . . from the crystal waters of glacial-fed lakes, to the majestic peaks of the highest mountains of the Canadian Cordillera, this land continues to inspire and rejuvenate.

The Yukon is a 78,000 square-mile (200,000 km²) territory of the Canadian northwest. Taking its name from the Indian word "diuke-on," meaning "clear water," it is a place of physical and spiritual rejuvenation. Fueled by the legends of indigenous peoples and tales of excitement from the Klondike gold rush, this land nourishes the inner spirit and the adventurous soul.

Travel Tips

Primary access is by air from Vancouver, B.C., or from Edmonton, Alberta, to Whitehorse, the capital city. It is also possible to drive from the south or east via the Alaska Highway which runs north of Fort Saint John, B.C., or take cruise boats through the Inside Passage along the B.C. coast to Skagway, Alaska; from here it is a three-hour drive to Whitehorse over the White Pass route, following the original narrow-gauge railway that delivered prospectors to Carcross where paddlewheelers took them north to Dawson City. Dawson was the boomtown center of the 1897–98 Klondike River gold rush that brought 250,000 adventurers in the first year. Yukon towns are not highly populated, and most try to capitalize on the Klondike theme: Dawson, once known as the "Paris of the North," has been completely restored to the 1898 period; Carcross sports an original paddlewheeler on Lake Bennett; Whitehorse boasts the high-kicking dancing girls of the follies; and sourdough bread is a staple on every restaurant menu.

The history of the gold rush provides one prime tourist attraction; the other is the spectacular scenery and outdoor activities. The chance to navigate the 400-mile (650 km) stretch of the Yukon River by canoe, shoot rapids by kayak on the Tutshi, go whitewater rafting, backpack and fish in bountiful lakes, or climb some of the world's most rugged mountains in Kluane National Park beckons tourists from afar. All of these activities are easily accessible by car, bus, boat, or bush plane from Whitehorse or Dawson.

Local Resources

We chose to rent a van in Whitehorse to travel some of the back roads and long distances up the Top of the World Highway to Dawson City and to the Pacific coast port of Skagway, Alaska. From Dawson, it is possible to continue north on the Dempster Highway to Inuvik, above the Arctic Circle and near the Beaufort Sea in the Northwest Territories. Rental vehicles should be reserved at least a month in advance. There are good hotels in all the major cities but reservations are advised in the summer season; information on tours, cruises, and whitewater experiences can be obtained from Yukon Tourism, PO Box 2703–FF, Whitehorse, Yukon Y1A 2C6. For climbing permits and information, write Superintendent, Kluane National Park, Haines Junction, Yukon, Canada Y0B 1L0; Tel: (403) 634–2251.

The Sacred North

The land of the north has the spiritual ambience of a great provider as well as a potential destroyer. Geography and climate rule here, producing the milder coastal rain and snow west of the Coast Mountains, and the dryer subarctic conditions to the east in Whitehorse and the remaining major mass of the Yukon territory. The St. Elias Mountains constitute the largest nonpolar glacial system in the world, forming part of the southwest border between Alaska and the Yukon; they include Mount Logan, the largest massif in the world and the highest point in Canada, at 19,849 feet (6,050 m). Mount St. Elias was named by the Danish explorer Vitus Bering who first saw the 18,008-foot (5,488 m) mountain in 1741 on the feast day of St. Elias, the Russian Orthodox saint identified with the mountain transfiguration of Christ.

These mountains provided spiritual nourishment to the ancestors of the seven indigenous language groups of the north. Alaska's Mount McKinley, the highest mountain in North America at 20,320 feet (6,193 m), was known as Denali, The High One, revered by local tribes who were humbled by this massive mountain. The coastal Tlinget people tell the story of the flood that covered all the land except two summits and Mount St. Elias, whose white peak, "like a seagull on the water," guided their ancestors from Alaska. This mountain is also a totem for one clan who sing of how Mount St. Elias "opened the world to sunshine" (Bernbaum, 1990, p. 145). Southern tribes also believe the mountains and glaciers harbor supernatural spirits who sometimes manifest themselves as frost. Careful not to offend these spirits, locals wear their best clothes, speak with humility, and avoid gazing at mountains and glaciers by covering their faces with pitch. Only the shamans will venture into the forest to seek supernatural powers. It is said that if mountaineers gaze on the mountains without wearing goggles, the spirits hide in the clouds and cause bad weather. Tlinget mythology also speaks of the marriage of Mount St. Elias and Mount Fairweather, who later separated, but left a legacy of children in the form of a string of peaks to the east. The indigenous tribes are seminomadic even today, still practising ancient traditions of living off the land in harmony with the spirits of nature. The southern Tutchone people knew Kluane as "Big Fish," which distinguished them from the northern tribes who were dependent on meat.

There must have been many active spirits when we viewed Mount St. Elias from the southwest corner of Kluane National Park. Here is Alsek Pass, the deep cleft cut by the only river to carve through an Ice Age environment in the highest mountain range in Canada. Legends say there are giant worms in the glacier and orange animals nearby; remnants of a raft found high on Mount Decoeli, and an axe-hewn oar in the rocks high above the present riverbed perhaps give some credence to the flood myth or the existence of an ancient lake. But we found only the dawn mists draped over Mount St. Elias, swirling like a golden halo, and backlighting the hoarfrost gleaming from the trees in this pristine wilderness. In Kluane Park we trekked around Lake Katherine as she mirrored the jagged peaks at the edge of the mountain range, and into the upper valleys where Dall sheep clung to the rocky slopes and grizzly bears were said to lurk in the shadows. At nearby Haines, Alaska, known as "the end of the trail," there is the world's largest gathering of bald eagles, from October to January.

Southwest of Whitehorse we explored the old town of Carcross where the *SS Tutshi* paddlewheeler on Lake Bennett stimulates the imagination of the glory following the Klondike days, reminiscent of elegantly dressed tourists and luxury dining in a private stateroom. Nearby, **Emerald Lake** suggests a different kind of riches, with its glacial waters gleaming a deep jade color, disturbed only by a paddling muskrat trailing a V-shaped wave that rippled to the far shore where it undulated into the purple colors of the silt-fed banks. The legends of large fish and huge monsters rising from the lake to eat moose and caribou seemed very far away from this tranquil lagoon.

Travelling north to Dawson at the junction of the Yukon and Klondike rivers, the Top of the World Highway revealed another display of the natural grandeur of this land, where we were reminded that all creatures are significant inhabitants of the indigenous world, as spirit helpers to humans. These encounters with nature were considered to be the peak experiences in a person's life. We felt the aura of this type of primal experience here, and were tempted to continue north on the Dempster Highway to Inuvik; it is this stretch of land called Old Crow where the porcupine caribou migrate in huge herds in the spring and late fall, thousands of Dall sheep enjoy the salt licks, and peregrine falcons, Canada geese, and golden eagles can be seen nesting. The long evenings of this Land of the Midnight Sun, with the northern lights flickering in colors reminiscent of Emerald Lake, bring to mind the poems of Robert Service, the transplanted Englishman who lived in Dawson City and wrote of the glory of the north—"the land that beckons."

The Prairies

MOOSE MOUNTAIN MEDICINE WHEEL

July 10 . . . The domelike hills are alive with the colors and warmth of summer, exuding a unique sense of solitude from this high point of ground marked with a circle of stones. The big sky melds into gentle slopes turned golden as blowing grasses ripple over them like an undulating sea. There are no sounds to break this magical stillness . . .

A series of hills suddenly rise 200 feet (61 m) above the flat prairie; the highest harbors one of the more than eighty medicine wheels in North America (see also Bighorn Medicine Wheel, U.S. Plains). Although Moose Mountain Medicine Wheel is thought to date as early as 300 AD, its spiritual significance to indigenous peoples is just beginning to be understood.

Travel Tips

The wheel is located on private land near Moose Mountain Provincial Park in southeastern Saskatchewan, a two-hour drive from the capital city of Regina. If you start from there, a visit to the Museum of Natural History is worthwhile. Then take Highway 33 southeast to Stoughton, continuing on Highway 13 to Kisbey where you turn north on #605 and go 9.5 miles (15 km) to the last hill before the radio beacon; there is an abandoned farm on the right and a road to the left that may be locked—if not, follow it for another .5 mile (.8 km) to the juncture of a small private road where you can park and walk (about forty minutes) up to the highest dome hill. If the first gate is locked, there is an alternate walking route following the fence from the main road about .25 mile (.4 km) further on.

Local Resources

The medicine wheel is located on the land of Elvin McArthur; he can be contacted through the Pheasant Rump Band Office, Tel: (306) 753-2926 for permission to enter. Although most people do not ask, the courtesy is suggested. Also be aware that some members of the McArthur family do not agree with outsiders entering their land and exploring the site; because of this dispute, access to the site may change, so it is wise to check ahead although it is not always easy to make contact with Elvin! The nearby Moose Mountain Provincial Park offers a wide range of outdoor activities and a large government campsite to stay in, although there is other accommodation nearby and in the town of Carlyle, a twenty-minute drive away. For park information, contact Box 100, Carlyle, SK S0C 0R0; Tel: (306) 577–2131. The best time to visit is late spring to early autumn. Other sites to explore in Saskatchewan include Wanuskewin and the Minichinas Hills, a few minutes drive northeast of Saskatoon in the central part of the province. The cool, forested uplands of the Cypress Hills are a unique feature in the surrounding plains, a three-hour drive southwest of Regina on the Trans-Canada Highway via Swift Current and Maple Creek. Cypress Hills Provincial Park offers summer camping, swimming, fishing, golf, and hiking as well as an historic park at Fort Walsh in the west block. The Four Seasons Resort (P.O. Box 1480, Maple Creek, Sask. Tel: (306) 662–4477, Fax: (306) 662–3238) offers year round accommodation with a conference center, swimming pool, and jacuzzi, and cross-country and downhill skiing in the winter. Public access to the Great Sand Hills is best from the village of Sceptre on Highway 32, 75 miles (122 km) northwest of Swift Current.

The Spirit of the Land

The **Moose Mountain Medicine Wheel** is part of the native spiritual path known as the Medicine Way. The circle is one of the primary symbols of native spirituality, encompassing the four directions (see Bighorn Medicine Wheel) which provide a sense of place in nature and in the cosmos. Many native groups are reactivating their traditional ceremonies in an attempt to overcome the sickness of spirit and sense of anomie they feel, particularly associated with alcoholism, loss of land (some of which is now being returned by the Canadian government), lack of work, and subsistence living conditions related to the depressed economy in most Indian communities.

Medicine wheels have been studied by anthropologists and astronomers for many years now, and the opinions about their purpose vary. The fact that the wheels are always on high points of land with unobstructed views of the horizon suggests their use as astronomical observatories—if the Moose Mountain Medicine Wheel does in fact date as early as 300 AD, then its spokes match alignments to the rising of the stars Rigel, Aldebaran, and Sirius. Some researchers compare the wheels to the astronomical functions of Stonehenge, although wheels such as Moose Mountain and Majorville (Alberta) may even predate it by one thousand to five thousand years. Other scientists suggest these were burial places, chosen because they were close to the sky where ancestors were said to rest, but the Moose Mountain site shows no evidence of burials, and other experts say there are no legends to support this theory. Some Blackfoot people, for instance, believe the spirits of their ancestors went instead to the Great Sand Hills in southwestern Saskatchewan. Local elders do not know the original purpose of the wheel, but suggest that it may have had a variety of purposes. The different shapes of the wheels may support this notion; some have cairns sheltering human or animal bones, others suggest ceremonial circles and have no remains, while those with spokes, such as Moose Mountain, are thought to be places of divination or fertility rites.

What is clear is that medicine wheels were highly utilized, as evidenced by the many tepee rings found nearby. It has been suggested that the wheel, like the concept of the Good Red Road (see Sedona, U.S. Southwest) cannot be understood on an intellectual level—it is a spiritual tool to help one reach the goal of the east, the experience of the eternal. It is interesting that a Hopi prophecy suggested that the deterioration of native pride would be healed when the new age came, with the eagle flying to the moon. On July 21, 1969, the space ship Apollo VI landed on the moon, with the message "the Eagle has landed." In subsequent years, the resurgence of interest in spirituality has grown not only in indigenous communities but in the nonnative world as well, as people search for an inner meaning to fill the void in their lives. Perhaps the balance and harmony of the circle will help us all to understand and heal that yearning.

The Prairies abound with other natural sites that exude a sense of spirit and harmony with the land. Some of these places have been identified by aboriginal peoples as traditional sacred sites, while others are honored for their sense of grandeur or solitude. On the edge of Saskatoon is a place known as **Wanuskewin**, meaning "seeking peace of mind," which has been used for as long as eight thousand years. A Heritage Site to open in 1992 will display a buffalo jump, buffalo pound, medicine wheel, sweat lodge, and numerous indigenous artifacts found on this ancient riverside gathering place. Further east is a series of low hills rising up to 1,000 feet (305 m) above the surrounding plain, stretching north and east of the South Saskatchewan River. These are the **Minichinas Hills**, covered with fescue grasses and stands of aspen in depressions sheltered from the sun. Little is known about them, but the Plains Cree who lived in this area often sought out high places as spirit quest sites where they might contact an animal or bird that would become their guardian spirit (see also B.C. coastal tribes). The hawks found here are reminders that in native medicine the hawk teaches one to be observant, and brings omens and messages from the spirit, not unlike Mercury, the Roman messenger of the gods. Perhaps this area was also a site of the Cree Thirst Dance, the "anpagwasimuk," also called the Rain Dance or Sun Dance by other Plains Indians; for this ceremony, a round lodge was constructed of branches gathered from the area and placed around a sacred center pole that housed the three-day ritual of singing, dancing, and praying during a fast and thirst that could only be quenched by rain.

In the southwest of the province, the **Cypress Hills** are located in a provincial park on an area of bedrock with strongly dissected escarpments whose geology dates them to be at least 135 million years old. These hills are the highest elevation of land in Canada between the Rockies and the Appalachians. In the west block there is a group of large cubelike rocks known as the Mystery Rocks; although little is known about them, this type of glacial erratic boulder has been significant to some indigenous tribes. Thirty-five miles (56 km) north of the Trans-Canada Highway is another unique geological feature, the **Great Sand Hills**, a range of active sand dunes stretching for 60 miles (100 km) to the north and constantly shifting with the winds. These dunes are like a dreamscape with huge towers of sand changing shape and texture against the backdrop of the static nearby hills covered with cedar, sage, and groves of poplar harboring mule deer, antelope, porcupine, and rabbits. Some

Blackfoot Indians say this is the home of their ancestral spirits, and for us, the peaceful ambience and sense of cosmic harmony felt here is consistent with a heavenly abode.

In the far reaches of Saskatchewan, beyond the prairie into the Precambrian Shield covering the north, lies a place Courtney calls "**Spirit Ridge**." For him this place illustrates the importance of having our own personal sacred place—an area in nature to gravitate to when we need to recharge our batteries. It may be under a favorite tree in our own backyard, or it may be a mountain, a stream, or a beach, but sharing these places with others diminishes the magic and personal inspiration. It is a place of harmony and balance, a place to discover a sense of true self and come away spiritually renewed and able to enter the real world of everyday life again.

The East

NIAGARA FALLS

April 10 . . . The roar of the water is intense as 12 million cubic feet per minute (340,000 m³) flow over the Horseshoe Falls. It is mesmerizing to watch the swift waters approach their demise, and produce mountains of mist that billow up from the river below where the Maid of the Mist lives forever with Hinum the Thunderer.

Niagara Falls is now best known as a popular honeymoon resort in southern Ontario, but the legend of a sacrificing Indian maiden, and an esoteric list of holy waters give credence to the meaning of this sacred place.

Travel Tips

Niagara Falls is a three-hour drive south of Toronto, and adjacent to the American city of Buffalo, New York, at the juncture of Lake Ontario and Lake Erie. Quetico Provincial Park extends over 1,800 square miles (4,660 km²) on the border of Minnesota, a few hours drive west of Thunder Bay on the western tip of Lake Superior, Ontario. Prince Edward Island lies in Eastern Canada, offshore from the provinces of Nova Scotia and New Brunswick in the Gulf of St. Lawrence.

Local Resources

Niagara Falls can be seen on a day trip by bus, train, or car from Toronto and has a wide range of accommodation if you choose to stay overnight in the company of hundreds of honeymooners and raucous night revelers. It is worthwhile staying into the evening to see the colored lights turn the falls into a magic wonderland of rainbows. Many people also like to walk over to the American side but identification is required and perhaps visas, depending on your passport. For information, contact Niagara Falls Convention Bureau, 4610 Ontario Ave., Niagara Falls, Ontario L2E 3P9; Tel: (416) 356–6061. Quetico, on the other hand, only requires a sense of adventure and strong muscles to explore the backwoods by canoe; this wilderness is highly protected and backcountry permits are required. For information, contact the Park Headquarters, Tel: (807) 929–2571 between May 16 and September 1, or the Dawson Trail Campground near the park entrance can be contacted at Atikokan, Ontario P0T 1C0, Tel: (807) 597–6971. On Prince Edward Island, stay at the elegant late nineteenth-century Dalvay House now operated by Environment Canada; reserve through Box 8, Little York, Prince Edward Island C0A 1P0; Tel: (902) 672–2546 (winter), 672–2048 (summer). Other travel information is available through Visitors Services, Box 940, Charlottetown, P.E.I. C1A 7M5; Tel: (902) 368–4444.

Sacred Places

Niagara Falls is thought to be named from "nia-gara," the word from a local tribe meaning The Mighty Thunderer. Several legends speak of Lewlawala, the lovely maiden who plunged over the falls, either to avoid having to marry her unloved betrothed, or at the urging of her father in the hope of ending a village plague. In any case she was rescued at the bottom by the god Hinum the Thunderer who lived behind the falls. She still lives there with him and can be seen in a rainbow arching through the billowing mists of the Horseshoe Falls, the perennial Maid of the Mist, after which the popular boat tour of the falls is named.

These legends are illustrative of the seemingly common phenomenon of other suicides which are said to occur regularly at the falls. Although statistics are hard to come by, estimates suggest more than thirty people per year kill themselves by plunging over the falls. Other people report being enticed by the power of the water which leaves them dizzy and powerless to resist; perhaps the high electromagnetic field force which is produced around a flow of water accounts for this. In any case, it seems that the majority of the million annual visitors to the falls have birth rather than death on their minds. This is the honeymoon capital of the world, where couples come from near and far to consecrate the birth of a new relationship; it is also known as "Baby City" due to the high rate of conception attributed to a visit here!

The contemporary pilgrim will also feel the enchantment of this water which has been flowing over the hard Niagaran dolomite for about twelve thousand years. The underlying soft layers keep the falls flowing vertically, although erosion occurs at the annual rate of 3 feet (1 m), which explains why the falls were at one time 7 miles (11 km) upstream. Only once in recorded history have they stopped flowing, in the late nineteenth century when ice backed up the water for two days, and the stillness and quiet were reported as an unearthly silence. Do not expect any silence in this tourist center, however, but perhaps the Maid of the Mist will appear, and the dazzling array of nighttime color is a splendid reward for enduring the hordes of people who congregate daily to honor this natural wonder of the world.

In complete contrast, a visit to **Quetico National Park** will be bathed in silence. This wilderness area is well protected, and backcountry canoers can experience total isolation in this huge wilderness of lakes and forest. The landscape is a gift of the ancient glaciers that gouged depressions in the Precambrian granite to leave a legacy of thousands of lakes populated with beaver, bear, moose, otter, and the haunting cry of the loon. Hundreds of paddle routes followed by the eighteenth- and nineteenth-century voyageurs of the fur-trading companies still meander through this land of solitude. Perhaps one will meet the Mishipizhiw (Missipeshu), Ojibway demi-god of water or see his serpentine image in the many pictographs preserved in the rock, consistent with the ancient pictorial tradition seen in so many parts of the world. The meaning of Quetico is uncertain; it may come from the French words "la quête de la côte," search for the shore, which seems appropriate in this watery landscape, or perhaps it is an alteration of the Cree word Windigo, the name of a horrific cannibalistic spirit. More likely, Quetico is associated with the benevolent spirit felt in beautiful places like this that nourish the soul and remind us of a primordial legacy.

Another soul-nourishing place is **Prince Edward Island**, known to the native Micmac Indians as Abegweit, meaning "cradle in the waves." Early explorers wrote of it as a luscious garden, which is still an apt description 450 years later. Only partly sheltered from Atlantic storms, the red sandstone cliffs are buffeted with wind and water which produce an unusual dune system and a shelter for many birds such as the great blue heron and the endangered piping plover. Gnarled white spruce and sweet wild roses blow in the wind with white-haloed brown-eyed Susans, a marked contrast to the rich red soil and fertile green crops. Cycling, beach-walking, and camping are popular in the national park, as is watching fishermen bring their bounty into small villages sporting the best clam chowder in the world. This is a real haven from a chaotic busy world.

Epilogue

The Final Journey

It seems fitting to conclude our pilgrimage in Canada, our home. We have come full circle, back to where we started with great enthusiasm and earnestness to search out the sacred. Our sacred circle is not only physically and geographically complete but emotionally and psychologically as well, with these aspects of our journey becoming more obvious as we progressed.

Our journey encompassed monuments built by humankind centuries ago to search out the spirit of the heavens on earth; waters that purify; havens that rejuvenate; summits that soar as close to divinity as life on earth will allow; and places where great spiritual figures are believed to have transcended the bounds of earthly existence. Many of these sacred places reflected a deep sense of shared consciousness and made us aware of our place in the continuity of our world. It was a spiritual experience—the feeling of attunement from within, and the yearning to be in harmony with the world outside our bodies. We also learned, however, that it wasn't necessary to go all those miles; the sacred valley is within ourselves and can be reached through almost any earthscape we choose. Here, in our own special place, we feel a connection not with the mind, but with the heart, secure in the knowledge of our place in the natural order. It is here that we finally feel authentic and blessed. Perhaps this is Shambhala, after the Tibetan myth of the sacred valley just beyond the next ridge of mountains, a place where we can feel safe and live in peace forever.

Appendix

Notes for the Travelling Photographer

by Courtney Milne

The majority of the photographs for The Sacred Earth Collection were taken on a ten-month global tour. I returned with 61,500 slides, now neatly stored on my bookshelf, each one numbered and catalogued. For anyone contemplating an extended photographic journey, here are a few insights into organizing and exposing a large quantity of film.

Preparation

I set out from Toronto with 1,350 rolls of film and had an additional 500 rolls delivered to me in Hong Kong six months later. I used a variety of 36-exposure slide films with speeds ranging from ISO 25 to 200, and also a minimal amount of print film for family snapshots that we could enjoy along the way and send back to family and friends. I stripped off all the cardboard cartons at home to reduce the bulk and weight, and added to each canister a strip of masking tape, on which I placed a number as the roll was exposed. Where film canisters looked identical (such as Kodachrome 25 and 64), I placed a code on the adhesive strip. With these labels I could then quickly identify the next roll of film I grabbed from the camera vest in the heat of the moment.

I know some photographers who remove the cassettes from their canisters in order to further reduce the volume of their pack. I tried this once during a trip to the Galapagos Islands and ended up with moisture damage, as well as several squashed cassettes. One enterprising soul packs his cassettes in plastic slide boxes—the ones designed to hold 36 mounted slides. Four cassettes fit perfectly in a box.

X-rays and Heat

Because the vast majority of my films were of low or medium speed, I took no precautions in shielding the rolls from X-rays, except, as a general procedure, to have the rolls that I carried onto a flight hand-checked when possible because of the horror stories I have heard of film being damaged in airports that advertise their machines as "film safe." I travelled on more than forty flights and had no way of knowing whether checked baggage was being X-rayed. I can't find any evidence of streaking or uneven processing that could be attributed to X-ray damage. I did, however, try to minimize the amount of X-ray exposure by stashing my film in several depots along the way and carrying only what I had budgeted for on each side trip.

A greater problem was heat. I had little opportunity to refrigerate my film, but more important was protecting it from intense heat and humidity. Several times in Bali I made long hikes back to the car to re-position it in the shade. As long as film isn't subjected to excessive heat, and is exposed and processed before the expiration date, there shouldn't be a problem.

Buying Film

When I am on long trips I don't scrimp on the film budget, because no matter how much is exposed, it represents only a minor amount of the overall trip expense, and it is the single most important item. When travelling for months, the temptation is to buy film abroad. Don't. When you buy film before leaving, you can negotiate quantity discounts, particularly if the supplier is also doing your slide processing. It is safer to buy at home because you know that companies stand behind their products. There is also the enormous saving in buying film with processing included. One never knows how long film sits on the shelf in other countries, whereas at home you can make sure it is fresh; buy your supply a month or two in advance, refrigerate it, and expose a few rolls before you leave.

How much film should you take? Take as much as you think you will shoot, and then half as much again. Think of the amount in 36-exposure rolls per day. It's no crime to return home with some unexposed film. Put it in your freezer and it will be preserved without any deterioration until you are ready to use it.

Exposing Film

Over the course of several months, film actually changes ISO. The ISO labelled on the cassette is only an average and is therefore not completely accurate. For this reason I sometimes bracket my exposures when I am faced with exotica in my viewfinder. I always rate the film according to its declared ISO, but will make small deviations in exposure from that indicated by my camera meter. A half to one f-stop each way is generally sufficient to be sure you are exposing the film as intended. I had a few rolls processed abroad to be sure of sharpness and exposure and to check for heat, humidity, or X-ray damage.

Equipment

About the only word I learned to pronounce in Chinese was for "crazy glue." I slipped on a steep muddy mountain trail in the middle of a rain storm in the Guilin Mountains, and my 80–200mm zoom lens cracked in two. Instant glue held the lens together and I was able to continue shooting throughout the student demonstrations in China.

While that incident prompted ingenuity on my part, a photographic expedition of any length must be meticulously planned for. I started out with two manual-exposure and two automatic-exposure cameras, none of which was autofocus. By the end of the second week both automatic cameras and the electronic spotmeter succumbed to the electromagnetic power of the standing stones of Callanish in the Outer Hebrides of Scotland. Fortunately, both antiquated manual cameras kept clicking away, unaffected. After repairing the automatics in London, I set out again. But in the King's Chamber of the Great Pyramid of Giza, claimed by some to be the most powerful energy vortex in the world, my expensive automatic cameras failed again, and the manual models saved the day.

Replacement batteries are essential, so take several sets as you may have difficulty finding them in small towns. Those you buy abroad are also not always reliable, since batteries, like film, deteriorate with prolonged shelf-life. To save batteries during time exposures, use a manual camera because the shutter is held open mechanically. Night skies sometimes require keeping the shutter open for two or three hours, causing severe battery drain in some automatic cameras. (Also be aware that some airlines do not allow batteries to be carried on in hand luggage and will confiscate them, so if you want to maintain your supply, put your extras in your checked bags.)

Before leaving on your trip, check the viewfinder of each camera. Photograph a grid (such as graph paper) and mark clearly on the page what you see in the corners of the viewing screen. When you get the slides back, compare the slide with the original marks. Some cameras give amazingly accurate results, others show more on the film than in the viewfinder, or vice versa. One camera body consistently gave me a crooked picture, with my horizon lines always slanting down to the right. Either get the camera corrected, or be aware of its bias when composing your pictures.

The lenses I found most useful for exotic landscapes were a 300mm, the extreme wide angles (18mm and 15mm), and a 1400–4200mm zoom. The 300mm was ideal for distant vistas and the 18mm was indispensible for those low-angle, wide-angle perspectives that give depth and scale to a photograph. But my two favorite toys were the two extremes of the focal length range. I carried a spotting scope with a camera adapter so powerful that at 4200mm I could get landscapes where the sun filled the entire sky, and double exposures combining a giant sun with a landscape taken with shorter lenses. My other pride and joy was an 8mm fish-eye lens that allowed me to photograph the sky with 360 degrees of horizon in the frame.

Cracking the zoom lens in China taught me a lesson. Although I replaced it with its twin from my main equipment arsenal left in Hong Kong, from now on I will always carry two 80–200mm zoom lenses because the focal length is ideal for both landscape and photojournalism. Lugging two sizeable camera cases full of equipment around the world was well worth the extra effort and expense for the variety of images I came home with.

A medium-weight tripod with tubular metal legs and ball-and-socket head went almost everywhere with me, while two extra ball-heads were stashed in my suitcase. On flights, the tripod travelled in its case as hand luggage. While hiking, I hoisted the whole unit over my shoulder, camera mounted on tripod and legs usually extended, making me just three seconds away from any picture. Only when I was trying for grab shots from a moving vehicle or boat did I dispense with the tripod.

The most important accessory is the cable release. An ideal companion to the tripod-mounted camera, it prevents camera shudder and fosters split-second timing. Cable releases are easy to lose or break, so buy sturdy ones that can withstand abuse, pack several extras, and tie a bright ribbon around each for easy recovery should it drop off the camera. A large assortment of filters accompanied me but the two most useful were the polarizer for reducing glare and giving punch to skyscapes, and the color-enhancer for adding warmth to blue-green landscapes. I also travelled with two flash units which were used for fill-in flash and night photography of megalithic stones such as at Stonehenge or Callanish. I also carried several extra camera eyepieces, which are almost impossible to find while travelling. An umbrella was indispensible; I used it in the rain as well as bright sun, and it travelled nicely in my tripod case. I found my photographer's vest indispensible for carrying cameras, extra lenses, film, filters, and lens tissue, not only when shooting but during travel; this way I did not have to check all my equipment and could be sure I would have some that would not be damaged or stolen. Major equipment was checked in a well-padded pelican case or carefully buried in a suitcase of film or clothing. On one previous trip my pelican case loaded with equipment was stolen during a flight, but I had no problem on this journey. I did, however, take the precaution of purchasing very expensive equipment insurance, which seemed sensible considering the cost of replacing any kind of photographic equipment.

I learned a lot about good and bad planning on this trip. I learned how to apportion film and equipment, but I also learned how to pace myself, and after months of almost daily photographing I feel much wiser about technique, and richer for the experience.

For a wealth of information about U.S. sites, write for your copy of the bimonthly *Photograph America Newsletter*, published by Pacific Image, 1333 Monte Maria Avenue, Novato CA 94947, or telephone Robert Hitchman at (415) 898-3736.

Selected Bibliography

Travel Guides

Australia Insight Guide. Hong Kong: APA Publications, 1987.

Automobile Association. *Camping and Caravanning in Europe.* Basingstoke, Hampshire, England, 1989.

Barber, Robin. *Greece Blue Guide.* London: A and C Black, 1988.

Bendure, Glenda, and Ned Friary. *Micronesia: A Travel Survival Kit.* Victoria, Australia: Lonely Planet Publications, 1988.

Bisignani, J. D. *Hawaii Handbook.* Chico, CA: Moon Publications, 1987.

Black, Star et al. *Bali Insight Guide.* Hong Kong: APA Publications, 1987.

Bloomgarden, Richard. *The Easy Guide to Palenque.* Mexico DF: Editur, SA, 1988.

Frazier, Charles. *Adventuring in the Andes.* San Francisco: Sierra Club Books, 1985.

Jackson, Bernard. *Places of Pilgrimage.* London: Geoffrey Chapman, 1989.

Kaplan, Fredric. *China 1989 Guidebook.* Teaneck, NJ: Eurasia Press, 1989.

Madsen, Ken and Graham Wilson. *Rivers of the Yukon, A Paddling Guide.* Whitehorse, Yukon: Primrose Publishing, 1989.

Marzuki, Yazir, and Toeti Herati. *Borobudur.* Indonesia, Djambatan: 1982, 1985, 1987.

Matlock, Gary, and Warren Scott. *Enemy Ancestors—The Anasazi World With a Guide to Sites.* Northland Press, 1988.

Michell, John. *The Traveller's Key to Sacred England.* London: Harrap Columbus, 1989.

Oey, Eric, ed. *Bali, The Emerald Isle.* Chicago, Illinois: NTC Publishing Group, Passport Books, 1990.

Parkes, Carl. *Southeast Asia Handbook.* Chico, CA: Moon Publications, 1990.

Peterson, Natasha. *Sacred Sites: A Traveller's Guide to North America's Most Powerful, Mystical Landmarks.* Chicago: Contemporary Books Inc., 1988.

Ponting, Margaret and Gerald. *New Light on the Stones of Callanish.* Callanish, Isle of Lewis: G. and M. Ponting, 1984.

Rachowiecki, Rob. *Peru: A Travel Survival Kit.* Berkeley, CA: Lonely Planet Publications, 1987.

Service, Alistair, and Jean Bradbery. *A Guide to the Megaliths of Europe.* London: Granada, 1981.

Showker, Kay. *Jordan and the Holy Land.* New York: Fodor's Travel Guides, 1984.

West, John Anthony. *Traveller's Key to Ancient Egypt.* London: Harrap Columbus, 1987.

History, Mythology, Mysticism, and Religion

Beckwith, Martha. *Hawaiian Mythology.* Honolulu: University of Hawaii Press, 1970.

Bernbaum, Edwin. *The Way to Shambhala.* New York: Anchor Press/Doubleday, 1980.

——. *Sacred Mountains of the World.* San Francisco, Sierra Club, 1990.

Bord, Janet and Colin. *Mysterious Britain: Ancient Secrets of the United Kingdom and Ireland.* London: Paladin, 1974.

——. *Sacred Waters: Holy Wells and Water Lore in Britain and Ireland.* Great Britain: Paladin/Collins, 1986.

Breedon, Stanley, and Belinda Wright. *Kakadu: Looking After the Country - The Gagadju Way.* Brookvale, Australia: Simon and Shuster, 1989.

Browning, Iain. *Petra.* rev. ed. London: Chatto and Windus, 1982.

Campbell, Joseph. *The Mythic Image.* Princeton: Princeton University Press, 1974.

Chatwin, Bruce. *The Songlines.* New York: Penguin, 1988.

Ellwood, Robert S., and Richard Pilgrim. *Japanese Religion.* Englewood Cliffs, NJ: Prentice-Hall, 1985.

Fox, Matthew. *The Coming of the Cosmic Christ.* San Francisco: Harper and Row, 1988.

Freeman, Michael, and Roger Wainer. *Angkor, The Hidden Glories.* Boston: Houghton Mifflin, 1990.

Groslier, Bernard, and Jacques Arthaud. *Angkor, Art and Civilization.* London: Thames and Hudson, 1957.

Hamilton, Edith. *Mythology: Timeless Tales of Gods and Heroes.* Meridian, 1940, 1969.

Heinberg, Richard. *Memories and Visions of Paradise: Exploring the Universal Myth of a Lost Golden Age.* Los Angeles, CA: Jeremy Tarcher, 1989.

Layton, Robert. *Uluru: An Aboriginal History of Ayers Rock.* Australia: University of Aboriginal Studies, 1986.

McNaughton, Trudie, comp. *Countless Signs: The New Zealand Landscape in Literature.* Auckland, New Zealand: Reed Methuen Publishers, 1986.

Mohen, Jean-Pierre. *The World of Megaliths.* New York: Facts on File, 1990.

Morris, Walter F., and Jeffrey J. Foxx. *Living Maya.* New York: Harry N. Abrams, 1987.

Mullikan, Mary Augusta, and Anna M. Hotchkis. *The Nine Sacred Mountains of China.* Hong Kong: Vetch and Lee, 1973.

Ono, Sokyo. *Shinto: The Kami Way.* Rutland, VI: Charles E. Tuttle, 1962.

Ruspoli, Mario. *The Cave of Lascaux: The Final Photographs.* New York: Harry N. Abrams, 1986.

Silverberg, Robert. *The Mound Builders.* Athens, Ohio: Ohio University Press, 1989.

Stuart, Gene S. *America's Ancient Cities.* Washington DC: National Geographic Society, 1988.

Sutton, Peter, ed. *Dreamings: The Art of Aboriginal Australia.* New York: George Brazillier Publishers & Asia Society Galleries of South Australia Museum, 1988.

Spiritual and New Age

Beck, Peggy et al. *The Sacred: Ways of Knowledge, Sources of Life*. Flagstaff, Arizona: Navajo Community College Press and Northland Publishing Co., 1990.

Benzinger, Charles. *Chaco Journey: Remembrance and Awakening*. Sante Fe, NM: Timewindow Publications, 1988.

Bryant, Page. *Terravision, A Traveller's Guide to the Living Planet Earth*. New York: Ballantyne Books, 1991.

Corbett, Cynthia. *Power Trips: Journeys to Sacred Sites as a Way of Transformation*. Sante Fe, NM: Timewindow Publications, 1988.

Fortune, Dion. *Glastonbury: Avalon of the Heart*. rev. ed. Wellingborough, England: Aquarian Press, 1986.

Khalsa, Parmatma Singh, ed. *A Pilgrim's Guide to Planet Earth*. CA: Spiritual Community Publications, 1981.

Munro, Eleanor. *On Glory Roads: A Pilgrim's Book About Pilgrimage*. New York: Thames and Hudson, 1988.

Sams, Jamie, and David Carson. *Medicine Cards: The Discovery of Power Through the Ways of Animals*. Sante Fe, NM: Bear and Co., 1988.

Sutphen, Dick. *Sedona: Psychic Energy Vortexes*. Malibu, CA: Valley of the Sun Printing Co., 1986.

Swan, James A. *Sacred Places: How the Living Earth Seeks Our Friendship*. Sante Fe, NM: Bear and Co., 1990.

Geomancy

Burl, Aubrey. *Prehistoric Astronomy and Ritual*. Aylesbury, England: Shire Publications, 1983.

Leonard, George. *The Silent Pulse*. New York: E. P. Dutton, 1986.

Lonegren, Sid. *Spiritual Dowsing*. Glastonbury, England: Gothic Image Publications, 1986.

Mann, Nicholas. *Sedona—Sacred Earth: A Guide to Geomantic Applications in the Red Rock Country*. Prescott, AZ: Zivah, 1989.

Merz, Blanche. *Points of Cosmic Energy*. Essex, England: C. W. Daniel Co. Ltd., 1987.

Michell, John. *The Earth Spirit: Its Ways, Shrines and Mysteries*. London: Thames and Hudson, 1975.

Pennick, Nigel. *Geomancy: The Ancient Science of Man in Harmony with the Earth*. London: Thames and Hudson, 1979.

———. *Earth Harmony*. London: Century, 1987.

Nature Philosophy and Environmental Ecology

Burger, Julian. *The Gaia Atlas of First Peoples: A Future for the Indigenous World*. New York: Anchor Books/Doubleday, 1990.

Card, Graeme. "Hymn to Wakantanka," from *Dorothea's Dream*. Toronto, Canada: Silver Bullet Productions, 1979.

Keswick, Maggie. *Chinese Gardens*. Great Britain: Academy Editions, 1978.

Lopez, Barry. *Crossing Open Ground.* London, England: Pan Books, 1989.

Nebon, Richard. *Island Within.* Vancouver, BC: Douglas and McIntyre, 1989.

Orbell, Margaret, and Geoff Moon. *Natural World of the Maori.* Auckland, New Zealand: Collins, 1985.

Trimble, Stephen, ed. *Words From the Land: Encounters with Natural History Writing.* Layton, UT: Gribbs M. Smith Inc., 1988.

Index

Numbers printed bold face indicate a photograph and photo tip on the site; photo tips also have a cross-reference to Courtney Milne's *The Sacred Earth,* for which this book may be used as a companion volume.